COLLECTED EPIPHANIES OF JAMES JOYCE

The Florida James Joyce Series

UNIVERSITY PRESS OF FLORIDA

Florida A&M University, Tallahassee
Florida Atlantic University, Boca Raton
Florida Gulf Coast University, Ft. Myers
Florida International University, Miami
Florida State University, Tallahassee
New College of Florida, Sarasota
University of Central Florida, Orlando
University of Florida, Gainesville
University of North Florida, Jacksonville
University of South Florida, Tampa
University of West Florida, Pensacola

Collected Epiphanies of James Joyce

A Critical Edition

EDITED BY

Sangam MacDuff, Angus McFadzean,
and Morris Beja

UNIVERSITY PRESS OF FLORIDA

Gainesville/Tallahassee/Tampa/Boca Raton
Pensacola/Orlando/Miami/Jacksonville/Ft. Myers/Sarasota

Published with the support of the Swiss National Science Foundation.

29 28 27 26 25 24   6 5 4 3 2 1

ISBN 978-0-8130-7067-4 (ePDF)
ISBN 978-0-8130-7342-2 (ePub)
DOI: http://doi.org/10.5744/9780813070674

Library of Congress Cataloging-in-Publication Data
Names: Joyce, James, 1882–1941, author. | MacDuff, Sangam, editor. |
    McFadzean, Angus, editor. | Beja, Morris, editor.
Title: Collected epiphanies of James Joyce : a critical edition / edited by
    Sangam MacDuff, Angus McFadzean, Morris Beja.
Other titles: Epiphanies | Florida James Joyce series.
Description: Gainesville : University Press of Florida, 2024. | Series: The
    Florida James Joyce series | Includes bibliographical references and
    index.
Identifiers: LCCN 2023028633 (print) | LCCN 2023028634 (ebook) | ISBN
    9780813069913 (hardback) | ISBN 9780813080710 (paperback) | ISBN 9780813073422 (ebook)
    | ISBN 9780813070674 (pdf)
Subjects: LCSH: Joyce, James, 1882–1941—Manuscripts—Criticism and
    interpretation. | Joyce, James, 1882–1941—Criticism and interpretation.
    | Authors, Irish—20th century—Criticism and interpretation. | BISAC:
    LITERARY CRITICISM / Modern / 20th Century | LITERARY CRITICISM /
    European / English, Irish, Scottish, Welsh
Classification: LCC PR6019.O9 E6 2024 (print) | LCC PR6019.O9 (ebook) |
    DDC 823/.912—dc23/eng/20231016
LC record available at https://lccn.loc.gov/2023028633
LC ebook record available at https://lccn.loc.gov/2023028634

The University Press of Florida is the scholarly publishing agency for the State University System of Florida, comprising Florida A&M University, Florida Atlantic University, Florida Gulf Coast University, Florida International University, Florida State University, New College of Florida, University of Central Florida, University of Florida, University of North Florida, University of South Florida, and University of West Florida.

University Press of Florida
2046 NE Waldo Road
Suite 2100
Gainesville, FL 32609
http://upress.ufl.edu

Contents

Figures

Foreword

In the "Proteus" episode of *Ulysses*, Stephen mildly mocks his youthful pretension of writing what he called his "epiphanies," "deeply deep, copies to be sent if you died to all the great libraries of the world, including Alexandria." This is a compositional practice Joyce shared, of writing down and collecting short texts that would each reveal some moment of significance occasioned through the closely observed precise representation of something seemingly quotidian. From 1901 to 1904, Joyce wrote as many as seventy-one epiphanies, of which only forty survive. While he never published these texts as such during his lifetime, some of them later provided source material for *Stephen Hero* and *A Portrait*, and a number of them are incorporated, with modifications, into *Ulysses*. The epiphanies—both as specific texts and as a compositional mode or practice—are thus arguably fundamental to Joyce's aesthetics, on both a practical and theoretical level. While the epiphanies as such have been known for a long time, their importance has been neglected or underestimated. In part this is because their publications to date have been, for various reasons, unsatisfactory. The present volume more than redresses this lamentable lacuna within Joyce studies and, indeed, within the Joyce canon. The volume begins with a masterful introduction that sets forth the importance of the epiphany for Joyce and its enduring relevance from beyond the time in which he was specifically composing them. That is, Joyce's own theory and practice of the epiphany evolved as he matured as an artist. Indeed, one can even trace out Joyce's maturation as an artist through the evolution of his use of the epiphanies. Because Joyce's understanding and use of the epiphanies evolved, their textual record is laden with inconsistencies and contradictions, which has been one more factor in their problematic reception. MacDuff, McFadzean, and Beja's introduction is remarkably lucid in untangling these contradictions and presenting a clear argument about the epiphanies.

The texts of the epiphanies are all newly transcribed and edited, and this work has helped eliminate some unfortunate errors. The epiphanies are also all annotated rigorously and thoroughly. The notes provide context for the epiphanies and also document their afterlives in Joyce's subsequent texts as Joyce reused and recycled and echoed various epiphanies across his works for the remainder of his life.

Sam Slote
Series Editor

Acknowledgments

Of course we owe a debt to the critics and scholars cited throughout this edition of Joyce's epiphanies. But we feel special gratitude to a number of Joyceans who have done a great deal to help and encourage us. Daniel Ferrer worked with us in shaping this project from an early stage. Sam Slote has also been helpful and encouraging throughout the process, as have been Ronan Crowley and Geert Lernout.

We are especially grateful to Seán Sweeney and Fionn Sweeney of the James Joyce Estate for permission to reproduce Joyce's epiphanies, and for their cooperation in producing this edition.

We owe a special debt to the Swiss National Science Foundation, whose generous funding helped make this edition possible.

The reviewers for the University Press of Florida were extremely supportive and helpful in their detailed commentaries, and Stephanye Hunter was extraordinarily involved and enthusiastic from the submission of our proposal.

The editors are, finally, fully aware of all they individually owe to Sabrina MacDuff, Rachel McPherson, and Ellen Carol Jones.

Abbreviations

CW   James Joyce. *The Critical Writings of James Joyce*. Edited by Ellsworth Mason and Richard Ellmann, Viking, 1959.

D   James Joyce. *Dubliners*. Penguin, 2000.

DD   Stanislaus Joyce. *The Dublin Diary of Stanislaus Joyce*. Edited by George Harris Healey, Faber and Faber, 1962.

E   James Joyce. *Exiles: A Play in Three Acts*. J. Cape, 1972.

FW   James Joyce. *Finnegans Wake*. Penguin, 1992.

JJA   James Joyce. *The James Joyce Archive*. Edited by Michael Groden, Hans Walter Gabler, David Hayman, A. Walton Litz, and Danis Rose, 63 vols., Garland, 1977–79.

JJII   Richard Ellmann. *James Joyce*. 1959. Oxford UP, 1982.

LI–LIII James Joyce. *Letters of James Joyce*. Edited by Stuart Gilbert and Richard Ellmann, 3 vols., Viking, 1957–66.

MBK   Stanislaus Joyce. *My Brother's Keeper: James Joyce's Early Years*. Edited by Richard Ellmann, 1958. Da Capo Press, 2003.

OCPW James Joyce. *Occasional, Critical, and Political Writing*. Edited by Kevin Parry, Oxford UP, 2000.

P   James Joyce. *A Portrait of the Artist as a Young Man: Authoritative Text, Backgrounds and Contexts, Criticism*. Edited by John Paul Riquelme, Hans Walter Gabler, and Walter Hettche, W. W. Norton, 2007.

PSW   James Joyce. *Poems and Shorter Writings*. Edited by Richard Ellmann, A. Walton Litz, and John Whittier-Ferguson, Faber and Faber, 1991.

SH   James Joyce. *Stephen Hero*. Edited by Theodore Spencer, revised ed. by John J. Slocum and Herbert Cahoon, New Directions, 1963.

SL   James Joyce. *Selected Letters of James Joyce*. Edited by Richard Ellmann, Viking, 1966.

U   James Joyce. *Ulysses: The Corrected Text*. Edited by Hans Walter Gabler, Penguin, 1986.

WD   Robert Scholes and Richard M. Kain, editors. *The Workshop of Daedalus: James Joyce and the Raw Materials for "A Portrait of the Artist as a Young Man."* Northwestern UP, 1965.

Note on the Text

The texts in this edition are based on transcriptions of the surviving manuscripts, preserving original spelling, punctuation, lineation, and typography in all features except underlining, which is replaced by italics. Where an epiphany survives in Joyce's hand, the holograph manuscript provides the source text: twenty-two are transcribed from Buffalo 1.A, and one from a draft in Cornell. The remaining seventeen epiphanies are transcribed from Stanislaus Joyce's "Selections in Prose from Various Authors," held at Cornell. The note to each epiphany lists the source text and any variants.

The epiphanies are presented in the order they appear in the source manuscripts, as follows: (1) the holograph epiphanies at Buffalo, sequenced according to their verso numbers; (2) "Is That for Gogarty?," a draft in Joyce's hand; and (3) the epiphanies preserved in "Selections in Prose from Various Authors," reproduced in the same order as in Stanislaus Joyce's notebook. This arrangement follows that in *The James Joyce Archive*, volume 7, except that Stanislaus's "Selections" are given precedence over the two copies he reused for his *Dublin Diary* (Cornell 15).

Introduction

A Book of Epiphanies

In *Stephen Hero*, an early version of the novel that was to become *A Portrait of the Artist as a Young Man*, the hero, Stephen Daedalus, overhears a snatch of conversation that makes him think of writing "a book of epiphanies":

> A young lady was standing on the steps of one of those brown brick houses which seem the very incarnation of Irish paralysis. A young gentleman was leaning on the rusty railings of the area. Stephen as he passed on his quest heard the following fragment of colloquy out of which he received an impression keen enough to afflict his sensitiveness very severely.
>
> The Young Lady—(drawling discreetly) . . . O, yes . . . I was . . . at the . . . cha . . . pel . . .
>
> The Young Gentleman—(inaudibly) . . . I . . . (again inaudibly) . . . I . . .
>
> The Young Lady—(softly) . . . O . . . but you're . . . ve . . . ry . . . wick . . . ed . . .
>
> This triviality made him think of collecting many such moments together in a book of epiphanies. By an epiphany he meant a sudden spiritual manifestation, whether in the vulgarity of speech or of gesture or in a memorable phase of the mind itself. He believed that it was for the man of letters to record these epiphanies with extreme care, seeing that they themselves are the most delicate and evanescent of moments.
>
> (*SH* 211)

Although Joyce never published the book Stephen envisages, between 1900 and 1904 he wrote at least forty short texts he called "epiphanies." Approximately half are snatches of dialogue, akin to the "fragment of colloquy" Stephen overhears; the rest are prose-poetic vignettes. These two types of epiphany seem to correspond to Stephen's definition, suggesting that the dramatic texts record the "vulgarity of speech or of gesture," while the lyrical pieces describe "memorable phase[s] of the mind." According to Stephen, both kinds record an everyday experience that occasions "a sudden spiritual manifestation." He proceeds to explain to his friend Cranly how even a "triviality," such as the Ballast Office clock they are passing, can awaken a "sudden" revelation when the "spiritual eye" of the beholder comes into focus with its object. The prospect that any event could occasion an epiphany is tantalizing, and the parallels between Stephen's account and Joyce's early texts make it tempting to read the epiphanies as attempts to record such "delicate and evanescent" moments. But if the experiences themselves are fleeting and difficult to capture, Joyce's epiphanies are equally evanescent, shimmering delicately between a sense of profound but ungraspable significance and inscrutable banality.

The publication of *Stephen Hero* in 1944 stimulated considerable interest in the concept of epiphany, with many critics regarding it as central to an understanding of Joyce. Critical interest continued to grow in the 1950s and 1960s when the epiphanies were published, first in a partial edition of twenty-two epiphanies at Buffalo in 1956, then in *The Workshop of Daedalus* (1965) as a complete set. A few critics, such as Morris Beja and A. Walton Litz, recognized Joyce's epiphanies as among his "earliest important literary compositions" (*PSW* 157) and thus as significant texts in their own right, but the majority of Joyceans focused on the account of epiphany in *Stephen Hero*. This emphasis on Joyce's discarded early novel meant that when literary scholars turned toward poststructuralism and other critical theories, the notion of epiphany seemed naive and outdated. From the 1970s to the early 2000s the epiphanies fell out of favor, as critics focused increasingly on *Ulysses* and *Finnegans Wake*, with a widespread assumption that Joyce had abandoned his epiphanies after *A Portrait of the Artist as a Young Man* (1916). This assumption is manifestly false—Joyce reused fifteen epiphanies in *Ulysses* and eight in *Finnegans Wake* (see the table of epiphanies)—but having been advanced in the first complete edition in *The Workshop of Daedalus*, it became the predominant view in Joyce studies for almost a half century, which is a major reason the epiphanies have not been published since *Poems and Shorter Writings* (1991).

The Workshop of Daedalus and *Poems and Shorter Writings* are valuable compendiums, but a new edition of Joyce's epiphanies is long overdue, as is a reassessment of these early works. This critical edition provides a corrected text, based on fresh transcriptions of the manuscripts, with a comprehensive list of textual variants, including those found in a typescript at Yale University in 2015 (MacDuff, "Yale"). The Yale typescript postdates 1927, providing further evidence that Joyce was drawing on his epiphanies when he composed *Finnegans Wake* (1923–39). It also raises questions about the order of the epiphanies, since the order in the typescript differs from that of the Buffalo manuscript it is copied from. Previous editions have presented the epiphanies in a numbered sequence, but there is not enough evidence to reconstruct that sequence with any certainty. Consequently, this edition reprints the epiphanies in their manuscript order, referring to individual epiphanies by the short titles Morris Beja has given them ("Epiphany" 712–13), on the basis that Joyce referred to his epiphanies by titles, not numbers. Each of these decisions is justified in the following sections, which also present an introduction to the historical, biographical, and literary contexts of the epiphanies, an overview of how Joyce reused them in his subsequent works, and a survey of their critical reception.

Before we turn to critical readings of the epiphanies, however, it may be useful to begin with their popular reception, because Joyce's early texts and the account in *Stephen Hero* have profoundly shaped our understanding of epiphany. The *Oxford English Dictionary* identifies two meanings of *epiphany*: the first, referring to the revelation of Christ to the Magi on January 6, the Feast of the Epiphany, is recorded in 1350; the second, in use since the late seventeenth century, refers to the "manifestation or appearance" of a divinity. Stephen's definition of epiphany as "a sudden spiritual manifestation" is clearly in keeping with these uses, though the "manifestation" he refers to is a "triviality," a "fragment of colloquy" overheard in the street, rather than a divine apparition. There is continuity here with classical and biblical theophanies, where deities appear in human or animal form (though they also come in the guise of angels, dreams, stars, and so on), but unlike their antecedents, Joyce's epiphanies are overwhelmingly secular (see Beja, *Epiphany* 14, 21, 24–27; MacDuff, *Panepiphanal* 23–30; Nichols 13–16). This shift in the use of epiphany was already underway in the nineteenth century—in 1838 Ralph Waldo Emerson called an epiphany "a fact . . . of God" (qtd. in Abrams, *Natural* 413), and in 1859 Thomas De Quincey referred to two "epiphanies of the Grecian intellect" (qtd. in *OED*)—but Joyce extends its secularization into everyday speech and gesture, or a "memorable phase of the mind." This transference pushes the word beyond its earlier senses, recorded in the *OED*, toward the dominant contemporary meaning of epiphany as "an illuminating discovery, realization, or disclosure" (*Merriam-Webster*, 3a). We are probably all familiar with such moments, however fleeting they may be, but they would rarely, if ever, have been called "epiphanies" before Joyce.

Joyce is also responsible for the use of *epiphany* as a literary term referring to "a revealing scene or moment" (*Merriam-Webster*, 3b). These definitions link the two senses, and the connection between epiphany as "a sudden manifestation or perception" (3a; Stephen's "sudden spiritual manifestation") and as "a revealing scene or moment" (3b; the dialogue that makes Stephen think of "a book of epiphanies") is brought out by Oliver St. John Gogarty, Joyce's contemporary, who speculated that "F[ather] Darlington had taught him, as an aside in his Latin class—for Joyce knew no Greek—that 'Epiphany' meant 'a showing forth.' So he recorded under 'Epiphany' any showing forth of the mind by which he considered one gave oneself away" (294–95). Gogarty, to his chagrin,[1] was the subject of an epiphany that exposes his own arrogance ("Is That for Gogarty?"), which may explain his aside on Joyce's lack of Greek. Joyce would surely have known the word *epiphany* from the liturgy, though, where the Epiphany season runs from Twelfth Night (January 6) to Candlemas (February 2, Joyce's birthday). Moreover, given Joyce's interest in etymology,[2] he might not have needed Father Darlington to tell him that the word is derived from the Greek prefix *epi* (to, upon, beside) and the verb *phainein*, to show. Regardless of where Joyce learned the word, Gogarty's recollection that Joyce "recorded under 'Epiphany' any showing forth of the mind by which he considered one gave oneself away" brings out the link between these inadvertent moments of revelation and the records of them, which Joyce titled "Epiphany."

Gogarty's singular, capitalized title, placed in quotation marks, offers an interesting comparison with Stephen Daedalus's idea of "collecting many such moments together in a book of epiphanies." The earliest reference to this projected work appears in a letter from Joyce to his brother Stanislaus, dated February 8, 1903, indicating that Joyce's work on "Epiphany" was well underway, for he had given a manuscript copy to George Russell, mentioning to Stanislaus that "my latest additions to 'Epiphany' might not be to his liking" (*LII* 28). This clearly implies a single, titled work that Joyce was composing in February 1903; just over a month later, Joyce informed his brother: "I have written fifteen epiphanies—of which twelve are insertions and three additions" (*LII* 35). Here, then, it seems that "Epiphany" was Joyce's working title for an ordered collection of "epiphanies," with new pieces intended as insertions or additions to the sequence. Joyce may even have considered publishing them in a slim "book of epiphanies," akin to *Chamber Music* (1907), the volume of poetry he was working on simultaneously, before deciding to reuse them in *Stephen Hero* and subsequent works.

In all, forty epiphanies survive. Twenty-three are in Joyce's hand, including a fair copy of twenty-two epiphanies at the University of Buffalo, and one draft ("Is That for Gogarty?"). Pencil numbering on the versos of the Buffalo manuscript suggests there were originally over seventy epiphanies, although it is not certain that the numbers are authorial. Stanislaus Joyce copied twenty-four epiphanies in his "Selections in Prose from Various Authors" (Cornell 4.10), seventeen of which are not in the Buffalo manuscript. He also copied three epiphanies ("Her Arm on My Knees," "Hoofs upon the Dublin Road," "She Comes at Night") twice, in the same order, on two sheets of foolscap, which he later recycled for his *Dublin Diary* (Cornell 4609 Bd Ms 3). Finally, a typescript of nineteen epiphanies was discovered in 2015 in the Eugène and Maria Jolas papers at Yale.

The twenty-two epiphanies in the Buffalo manuscript were first published in 1956, edited by Oscar A. Silverman, although—surprisingly—it was not until Peter Spielberg catalogued the collection in 1963 that the pencil numbers on the versos were discovered. As mentioned, Robert Scholes and Richard M. Kain published the first complete edition of the forty surviving epiphanies in *The Workshop of Daedalus* (1965), using the numbers on the Buffalo manuscript to place those epiphanies in order, and then assigning the remaining eighteen epiphanies at Cornell "to likely places in the ordered arrangement" (*WD* 6). It has become common practice to refer to the epiphanies by these numbers, especially since Richard Ellmann, A. Walton Litz, and John Whittier-Ferguson reprinted the epiphanies in the same order in *Poems and Shorter Writings* (1991), but in fact Scholes and Kain provide no justification for the order presented, only stating that it was "not hard" to "reconstruct with considerable certainty" the sequence (*WD* 4–6). In our view, it is not only difficult but impossible to reconstruct the original sequence with any certainty, first because there is not enough evidence, and second because Joyce may have experimented with different arrangements, as he did for *Chamber Music*.[3] Consequently, this edition reprints the epiphanies in their manuscript sequence. To avoid compounding errors from previous editions, each epiphany is transcribed directly from its source, following the original typography as closely as possible, with a comprehensive list of textual variants in the notes. The only substantive change is the addition of short titles, placed in brackets to emphasize that these titles are editorial, not authorial. They are not intended to be definitive, or to imply an evaluation or interpretation; their purpose is to facilitate ease of reference, which is why we have adopted the titles from Morris Beja's widely cited "Epiphany and the Epiphanies" (712–13). Ideally, Joyce's texts should be read alone, without editorial intervention, but given the need to identify individual epiphanies, we believe that brief titles drawn from the texts—such as those Joyce used in his notes and letters—are preferable to sequential numbers or cumbersome manuscript references.

The dates of Joyce's epiphanies is not known precisely, but they were likely written between 1900 and 1903, or possibly 1904,[4] the same period as *Chamber Music*. As early as 1903, Stanislaus drew attention to Joyce's two types of "'epiphanies'—his prose pieces . . . and his dialogues" (*DD* 14); as mentioned, the epiphanies are roughly divided between lyrical prose-poems and dramatic sketches, although a few of the former also incorporate dialogue. Never more than a page long, the dramatic sketches resemble the "fragment of colloquy" that precipitates Stephen's reflections in the passage quoted earlier, which may be based on a lost epiphany.[5] Its use of speech headings and parenthetical stage directions for the tone or manner of speaking resembles that of the dramatic epiphanies (elsewhere in *Stephen Hero*, dialogue is indicated by dashes, without parenthetical indications of tone); frequent ellipses, exclamations, false starts, and unfinished sentences give the impression that the speech has been transcribed directly, which is characteristic of Joyce's epiphanies; and the sense of something unspoken, mysterious, and highly charged is typical of the dramatic epiphanies, which often revolve around a resonant hiatus, as in "The Hole in Georgie's Stomach":

> [Dublin: in the house in
> Glengariff Parade: evening]
> Mrs Joyce — (*crimson, trembling, appears at the
> parlour door*) . . . Jim!
> Joyce — (*at the piano*) . . . Yes?
> Mrs Joyce — Do you know anything about the
> body? . . What ought I do? . . . There's
> some matter coming away from
> the hole in Georgie's stomach . . . .
> Did you ever hear of that happening?
> Joyce — (*surprised*) . . . I don't know . . . .
> Mrs Joyce — Ought I send for the doctor, do you
> think?

> Joyce   — I don't know . . . . . . What hole?
> Mrs Joyce — (*impatient*) . . . The hole we all have
>   . . . . . here (*points*)
> Joyce   — (*stands up*)

There is literally a "hole" in the text, repeated three times, and Mrs. Joyce's reluctance to name it causes confusion, even for Joyce, who asks, "What hole?" This uncertainty has a striking, almost visceral, impact because of its powerful bodily charge. Georgie's condition is obviously alarming—Mrs. Joyce appears "crimson, trembling" and wonders whether she need call a doctor—yet the final stage directions are almost comical, provoking a slapstick reaction in Joyce, which misleads some readers into thinking that his mother refers to the anus. At the same time, a certain vagueness surrounding "the hole we all have" invites metaphorical rather than physical interpretations. Thus, the text invites or incites a range of interpretations by evoking a hole that is both bodily and textual, physical and metaphorical, a matter of grave concern and a source of slapstick humor.

It might be argued that these interpretations are foreclosed by the biographical context of the epiphany, which points unequivocally to the navel. The scene is poignant because the real-life situation it is based on proved fatal for Joyce's younger brother Georgie, who died of peritonitis, complicated by a perforated intestine, at the age of fourteen, in March 1902. These facts are undeniable, yet the power of the epiphany as a literary text depends not just on its biographical context, but on the highly charged hiatus evoked by Mrs. Joyce's refusal to name the orifice, even in the face of a fatal illness, and the uncertainty this causes, even for the Joyce figure in the text. The entire epiphany revolves around this textual hole, offering an extreme example of a central feature of Joyce's dramatic epiphanies, which often hint toward something significant, but unspoken, through the uncertainty caused by ellipses, euphemisms, and broken or unfinished sentences. The stakes are not always as clear as in the pieces dealing with Georgie's death (cf. "I Was Sorry" and "Poor Little Fellow!"), but virtually all the dramatic epiphanies circle around a resonant hiatus, charged with hints and implications of mysterious significance, like the wickedly inaudible revelation that makes Stephen Daedalus think of collecting epiphanies.

This sense of something concealed that is hinted at but never openly stated tallies well with Stanislaus Joyce's recollection that the epiphanies "were in the beginning ironical observations of slips, and little errors and gestures—mere straws in the wind—by which people betrayed the very things they were most careful to conceal" (*MBK* 124). What is actually "be-trayed" in the epiphanies is far from obvious, even in the most striking ex-amples, like "The Hole in Georgie's Stomach," but the mention of verbal "slips" and "gestures" accords with Stephen's "vulgarity of speech or of ges-ture," as does their trivial nature—"mere straws in the wind." Stanislaus calls these early epiphanies "notes" or "brief sketches" that were "always very accurately observed," suggesting that they recorded revealing moments of real-life conversation (*MBK* 124), and there is good evidence that many, if not all, of the dramatic epiphanies were based on real-life incidents.

In *My Brother's Keeper*, Stanislaus says that as they developed, "the epiphanies became more frequently subjective and included dreams which he considered in some way revelatory" (*MBK* 125), leading several critics to conclude that Joyce progressed from dramatic to lyrical epiphanies, al-though this is by no means certain (see *JJA* 7:xxvii; MacDuff, *Panepiphanal* 55–57; McFadzean, *Epiphany* 44–45). *My Brother's Keeper* is a key source of information for the epiphanies, but it appeared in 1958, over fifty years after Joyce's vignettes, so its claims need careful weighing. There is little reason to doubt that the epiphanies included dreams, and Stanislaus may well have figured as "The Big Dog" in one of them, and as "An Arctic Beast" in another (*MBK* 135–36), but when Joyce adapted the latter epiphany for *Stephen Hero*, he presented it as a daytime incident by the beach at Fairview. "His Dancing," "She Comes at Night," and "The Two Sisters" probably re-cord dreams in which George Joyce, May Joyce, and Henrik Ibsen appear, but "His Dancing" draws heavily on literary representations of Salomé, and "The Two Sisters" is allegorical. If "the dreams are genuine," as Stanislaus says, "they have undergone literary treatment . . . to reproduce dream im-pressions" (*MBK* 127). He goes on to explain that "the revelation and impor-tance of the subconscious had caught [Joyce's] interest," and "he may have hoped [dreams] would reveal things our controlled thoughts unconsciously conceal" (*MBK* 126–27). In this sense, they are subjective counterparts to the dramatic epiphanies, for both seek to reveal "the significance of unre-flecting admissions and unregarded trifles" (*MBK* 127), whether through verbal slips or memorable phases of the mind.

Some of the prose epiphanies are based on real incidents rather than dreams (e.g., "I Lie along the Deck," "She Dances with Them in the Round," "Poor Little Fellow!"), but all are highly lyrical, creating memorable images and impressions through carefully wrought poetic language. Written at the same time as *Chamber Music*, they share many of the rhythmical and musical qualities of Joyce's lyrics, including alliteration, assonance, meter, and rhyme. For example, in "The Race,"

Bóokies are báwling out námes and príces;
Óne of them scréams with the vóice of a chíld—
Bónny Bóy! Bónny Bóy!

The first two lines have a marked dactylic rhythm, which contrasts nicely with the amphimacers in the horse's name. The alliteration at the beginning and end of the sentence also chimes as the long stressed vowels of "bookies" and "bawling" are shortened in "bonny" and wrenched up into the diphthong "boy." Without the marked stresses and line breaks, these effects are more subtle in the manuscript, but the musical quality of the bookmakers' cry plays a key role in turning prose into poetry, transforming a commonplace scene at the racetrack into a lyrical epiphany.

According to A. Walton Litz, these two kinds of epiphany represent "the twin poles of Joyce's art: dramatic irony and lyric sentiment" (*PSW* 158). The terms themselves are slightly misleading since there is little or no dramatic irony in the epiphanies, leading us to propose *ironic realism* and *lyrical symbolism* in their place. Nevertheless, Litz's recognition that the epiphanies are Joyce's "earliest important literary compositions" (*PSW* 157), and that the two types of epiphany represent "the twin poles of Joyce's art," is key to understanding their stylistic significance in Joyce's later work. The ironic realism of the dramatic epiphanies and the prose-poetic qualities of the lyrical epiphanies share many similarities with the elliptical dialogue and lyrical prose of Joyce's early fiction, from *Dubliners* to *Portrait* and the "initial style" of *Ulysses*, although there are also stylistic developments beyond this binary (see MacDuff, *Panepiphanal* 55–75).

Thus, Stephen's definition of *epiphany* provides a useful guide to Joyce's two types of epiphany, and it is clear that they play an important stylistic role in his oeuvre. However, there is continuing debate about Stephen's aesthetics in *Stephen Hero* and their bearing on Joyce's early texts. Discussion has often revolved around whether an epiphany is objective or subjective (e.g., Beja, *Epiphany* 77–81; Kenner 138; Noon 67–68; Zaniello), but Stephen's account is not clear and consistent enough to choose between these poles. When Stephen glances up at the Ballast Office clock and tells Cranly that it is "capable of an epiphany," he explains this as "the gropings of a spiritual eye that seeks to adjust its vision to an exact focus" ("Then all at once I see it and I know what it is: epiphany"). Here the epiphany is in the eye of the beholder, but at this very instant "the object is epiphanised" (*SH* 216–17). A similar blending of subject and object occurs at the culmination of Stephen's "esthetic theory":

> This is the moment which I call epiphany. First we recognise that the object is one integral thing, then we recognise that it is an organised composite structure, a thing in fact: finally, when the relation of the parts is exquisite, when the parts are adjusted to the special point, we recognise that it is that thing which it is. Its soul, its whatness, leaps to us from the vestment of its appearance. The soul of the commonest object, the structure of which is so adjusted, seems to us radiant. The object achieves its epiphany.
>
> (*SH* 213)

The object's "soul" or "whatness" seems "radiant" because Stephen equates Thomas Aquinas's term *claritas* with John Duns Scotus's *quidditas*, but it remains ambiguous whether the resulting epiphany is supposed to be subjective or objective ("seems to *us*," "*its* epiphany"). Both interpretations are plausible, and it is tempting to map them onto the two kinds of epiphany—the seemingly objective dramatic epiphanies, which "record" snatches of overheard dialogue, and the more subjective lyrical pieces, which evoke "a memorable phase of the mind." However, the ambiguity also points to an underlying confusion in Daedalus's understanding of epiphany, raising a larger question about the application of Stephen's aesthetics to Joyce's texts, for it is not entirely clear whether Joyce's epiphanies are supposed to be revelatory, and if so, whether this is through the objective "whatness" of the text or the apprehension of the reader.

Critics have noted many similarities between Joyce's epiphanies and their Romantic forebears, especially William Wordsworth's "spots of time," but the lack of obvious significance in Joyce is a major difference (see Abrams, *Natural* 418–19; Beja, *Epiphany* 33; Langbaum, *Poetry* 46–47; Nichols 5). Whereas Wordsworth's "spots of time" transform ordinary events into instances of the sublime, affording glimpses of infinitude in nature and/or the mind, Joyce's epiphanies remain resolutely banal. Put simply, Wordsworth reveals the extraordinariness of the ordinary, while Joyce shows us the ordinariness of the ordinary. We see the *quidditas*—the "whatness" of things—but not the *claritas*, the radiance. No matter how hard we look, it is difficult to find any clear revelation in Joyce's epiphanies. So are they failures, or do they point to a different understanding of epiphany? If they fail, is it because the moment of epiphany is too "delicate and evanescent" to capture, in Daedalus's terms, or does the absence of revelation in Joyce's texts discredit the concept in *Stephen Hero*? And if one thinks that there is, nonetheless, a hidden significance, does its opacity conceal an enigmatic insight, suggesting that every moment is an epiphany, if only one had the eyes to see it?

Some commentators have regarded the epiphanies as literary failures—trivial texts that belong with Joyce's juvenilia (e.g., Day; Scholes, "Joyce"; Scholes and Walzl). It has been argued that Joyce outgrew them, looking back on his early texts with irony, like Stephen Dedalus in "Proteus": "Remember your epiphanies written on green oval leaves, deeply deep, copies to be sent if you died to all the great libraries of the world, including Alexandria?" (*U* 3.141–43). There is no evidence that Joyce shared Dedalus's ironic attitude, however; on the contrary, Joyce's epiphanies were an important source for "Proteus," and Joyce continued to recycle them right through to *Finnegans Wake*. Of course, Joyce might have preserved the texts while rejecting the idea of epiphany in *Stephen Hero*, and even if he held by his epiphanies, there is nothing to stop readers from judging them failures. Nevertheless, the fact that Joyce continued to draw on the epiphanies up to thirty-five years after they were written, reusing a dozen or more in *Stephen Hero*, *Portrait*, and *Ulysses*, with eight in *Finnegans Wake*, suggests the significance his early compositions retained.

Even though Joyce chose not to publish these pieces in "a book of epiphanies," they contributed greatly to his developing fiction and aesthetics. In this edition, we indicate some of the ways they did so, returning to the literary, historical, and biographical contexts of the epiphanies to elucidate the enigmatic texts themselves, before examining how Joyce reused them in his literary works. The next two sections sketch the main outlines of these developments, while the notes and commentary that follow the epiphanies provide fuller discussion.

Contexts

Joyce's epiphanies, written around 1900 to 1903, are firmly rooted in the social, historical, and political contexts of turn-of-the-century Dublin, although the scenes focus primarily on Joyce's childhood and adolescent experiences, often in the company of family, friends, or acquaintances. Some of these figures, like Georgie Joyce and the Sheehys, are discussed below; others are identified in the notes, along with the settings and the cultural and political events alluded to. These references include many of Dublin's leading writers, because in the early 1900s Joyce moved beyond his immediate social circle, seeking out established authors like W. B. Yeats, George Moore, and Lady Gregory. While these authors are not represented directly, Yeats is evoked in a number of the lyrical pieces, alongside contemporaries like Ibsen and Gabriele D'Annunzio, who exemplified the prevailing trends of naturalism and symbolism. Whereas previous commentators have emphasized the influence of Wordsworth and the Romantic poets, Joyce's many allusions to late nineteenth- and early twentieth-century Irish and European authors suggest that the epiphanies respond primarily to their immediate literary contexts.

"Epiphany" is a good example: Joyce was familiar with the term from the liturgy, but his title also derives from D'Annunzio's *Il Fuoco* (*The Flame*, 1900), which Joyce considered "the highest achievement of the novel to date" (*MBK* 147).[6] Joyce read *Il Fuoco* in 1900, citing it in "The Day of the Rabblement" in October 1901 (*OCPW* 51), around the time he began writing epiphanies. The first section of D'Annunzio's novel, titled "L'Epifania del fuoco," reveals Giorgione's "secret of infusing a stream of luminous blood into the veins of the beings he creates"; through art, he represents the "Epiphany of the Flame" (*Flame* 66, 1).[7] The same phrase is used to describe the fireworks that erupt when the protagonist, Stelio, meets the object of his desire, Donatella Arvale, outside the Palace of the Doges in Venice. Where Giorgione transmutes his flaming epiphanies into paint, Stelio puts them into words: "He was gifted with an extraordinary facility of language that enabled him to instantly translate into words even his most complex modes of feeling with a precision so detached and vivid that they seemed at times to belong to him no longer, to have been made objective by the isolating power of style" (12). These verbal translations—precise, vivid, objective renderings of experience through "the isolating power of style"—sound almost like epiphanies.

Like Stelio, Walter Pater's Marius the Epicurean (of the eponymous 1885 novel) records epiphanic snapshots of his everyday "thoughts and humours,"[8] providing another fictional model for Joyce's epiphanies. Joyce also seems to have found examples in Paul Verlaine, Arthur Rimbaud, and Charles Baudelaire. Baudelaire's *Petits Poèmes en Prose* (1869), a collection of dialogues and lyrical vignettes with no fixed order, is perhaps the closest precursor to Joyce's epiphanies, and Joyce echoed two of Baudelaire's lyrics in "The Spell of Arms and Voices" and "They Pass in Twos and Threes." Many other literary sources also informed the epiphanies: "His Dancing" can be read as a response to Arthur Symons's "The Dance of the Daughters of Herodias" (1899); "The Lesson That She Reads" emulates Pater's *The Re-*

naissance (1873); "Her Arm on My Knees" draws on the Song of Songs; "She Comes at Night" echoes Cardinal John Henry Newman; and three epiphanies draw on Yeats ("Hoofs upon the Dublin Road," "Images of Fabulous Kings," "The Spell of Arms and Voices"). None are straightforward imitations; by transforming distinctive phrases and features from Yeats, Symons, Pater, Newman, and Baudelaire, Joyce created a style and voice of his own.

Despite this profusion of sources, the epiphanies are not literary inventions; in every case, they record real-life experiences, whether immediate, remembered, or dreamed. An early impulse was the recording of dreams. Stanislaus states that "An Arctic Beast" is a "note regarding a dream . . . one of the first of the collection, perhaps made before we left Royal Terrace" (*MBK* 126), implying that dreams were among the earliest subject matter of the epiphanies and that Joyce started writing them in Fairview, where they lived from May 1900 to late 1901 (Igoe, *James* 87). Dreams are a regular topos in the symbolist poetry Joyce admired, and his interest may also have been spurred by the English translation of Sigmund Freud's *The Interpretation of Dreams* (1900). In any case, five epiphanies apparently originated in dreams ("The Big Dog," "An Arctic Beast," "His Dancing," "She Comes at Night," and "The Two Sisters"). As noted previously, Stanislaus tells us "the dreams are genuine, though they have undergone literary treatment" (*MBK* 127), but it is not always clear where the dream ends and the literary treatment begins, because several of these epiphanies draw on literary sources or real-life events (e.g., "His Dancing," "The Two Sisters," "The Big Dog"). Scholes and Kain also note dreamlike elements in "Half Men, Half-Goats," "The Ship," "Images of Fabulous Kings," and "The Race" (*WD* 16, 38, 42), but Joyce's adaptation of "The Race" in "Nestor" implies that the scene was based on a real incident at the Leopardstown Racing Circuit in Dún Laoghaire, recast as Stephen's memory of a visit there with Cranly. Of course, waking experiences are frequently rehashed in dreams, and dreams can be recast in literary form, blurring the boundaries between immediate experience, dream, memory, and literary representation, which is precisely what happens in Joyce's dream-epiphanies. The category itself has fuzzy boundaries, with critics disagreeing as to whether epiphanies like "Half-Men, Half-Goats," "The Ship," and "Images of Fabulous Kings" actually record dreams. This very uncertainty raises an important point, because it indicates the stylistic similarity between all of Joyce's lyrical epiphanies, whether based on dreams or not. The seamless integration of these epiphanies into Joyce's narratives shows how their oneiric imagery and prose-poetic effects helped shape the lyrical symbolism of Joyce's fiction.

Dreams are not the only type of real experience Joyce records in the epiphanies. If Stanislaus is correct that Joyce started writing epiphanies in mid- to late 1900, then a number are based on memories of events and people from earlier in his life, such as his neighbors at Bray in 1891 ("Apologise") and a girl at a children's party at Harold's Cross circa 1893–94 ("The Last Tram"). Other "retrospective" epiphanies can be linked to Joyce's time at Belvedere College (1894–98): praying at the chapel ("Holy Queen, Mother of Mercy"), reading French novels ("A Story of Alsace"), and walking with Aunt Lillie through neighboring Mountjoy Square ("Forty Thousand Pounds"). It is not always clear why Joyce chose these memories in particular, but Joyce's adaptation of scenes like those in "Apologise" and "The Last Tram" in *Portrait* shows what a lasting and powerful impression they made.

Several other epiphanies may also be retrospective (e.g., "Is That Mary Ellen?"), but the majority are based on immediate personal experience. In some cases, they respond to major events, such as a death in the family, but just as often they record ephemeral moments, whose significance is not immediately clear. Stanislaus's description of verbal slips or revealing gestures, "mere straws in the wind" by which people betrayed themselves (*MBK* 125), is often apt. With a few notable exceptions, the majority of Joyce's early epiphanies, written between 1900 and 1902, are of this kind, recording snatches of dialogue in dramatic form. Two epiphanies—"There's Nothing like Marriage" and "The Lame Beggar"—are based on Joyce's visits to Mullingar in 1900 and 1901. "Fred Leslie's My Brother" was based on a visit to a brothel in Kennington during one of his visits to London between April 1900 and December 1902. The illness and death of Georgie Joyce at Glengariff Parade in March 1902 are recorded in three epiphanies: "The Hole in Georgie's Stomach," "Poor Little Fellow!," and "I Was Sorry." Several epiphanies belonging to Joyce's time at University College (1898–1902) seem surprisingly banal: a juxtaposition of convent girls and seminarists in "The Girls, the Boys," a glimpse of Gogarty in a chemist's ("Is That for Gogarty?"), a conversation in a pub about "The Priest That Writes Poetry." By contrast, "Upon Me from the Darkness," a lyrical epiphany based on a visit to a brothel, possibly in the company of Gogarty and John Eglinton, gives a rare glimpse of Joyce's transgressive sex life during this period.

The largest cluster centers on the Sheehys, who became family friends after Joyce enrolled at Belvedere College in 1893. Five epiphanies are located at the Sheehys' house at 2 Belvedere Place, where Joyce attended parties from 1894 until 1903, and three others feature at least one member of the family. Joyce knew the Sheehys through his classmate Richard Sheehy and his brother, Eugene, and he became friendly with their four sisters (Hanna, Margaret, Mary, and Kathleen), as well as their parents. These evenings continued during Joyce's university years (1898–1902), when he began writing epiphanies. The earliest datable epiphany (by a reference to Ibsen's age) occurs in 1900–1901. Another refers to Joyce's pamphlet "The Day of the Rabblement," published in October 1901. The latest, an account of Hanna's engagement to Francis Skeffington, must have occurred shortly before their marriage in July 1903. The rest refer to conversations and party games at the Sheehys' between 1894 and 1903. Stanislaus describes the regular Sunday evening gatherings at Belvedere Place, and Joyce provides a fuller depiction in *Stephen Hero*, where the Sheehys are named the Daniels. The evenings involved charades, skits, and homespun theater (Mary Sheehy wrote a play for them to perform in 1901), which Joyce simultaneously mocks and celebrates. In *Stephen Hero*, Stephen is acutely aware of the contrast between the warmth and atmosphere of the Daniels' happy bourgeois home and the strained circumstances of his own family life, as well as the banality of the Daniels' social interactions.

Such then are some of the personal experiences that Joyce commemorates in the epiphanies. But for a genre that depends so much on circumstantial encounters, it is striking what Joyce chose not to write about. Nothing on his father. Only one, "The Hole in Georgie's Stomach," where his mother appears directly. Nothing immediate on his mother's death, which is recalled so powerfully through Stephen's mourning in *Ulysses*. Instead, a dream of her ("She Comes at Night") and a boat journey back to Dublin ("I Lie along the Deck") stand in for scenic representation. No direct appearances by Stanislaus—only perhaps coded appearances in "An Arctic Beast" and "The Big Dog." Nothing from his many other siblings except Georgie, and even then not Georgie himself but his death. Little from his wider family—one of Aunt Lillie ("Forty Thousand Pounds") and another of a young cousin, Katsy ("The Lesson That She Reads"). Perhaps even more striking is the absence of his university friends J. F. Byrne and Vincent Cosgrave. Francis Sheehy Skeffington appears in three, but only in connection to the Sheehys' parties and the death of Georgie. Based on Gogarty's comments, we would expect to find him mentioned in several epiphanies, but he only features in one draft ("Is That for Gogarty?"). Otherwise, there is no record of Joyce's encounters with Yeats, George Moore, Eglinton, Lady Gregory, and J. M. Synge between 1901 and 1903. There are numerous epiphanies centered on the Sheehys, as we have seen, but with a notable absence. Accounts of Joyce's interest in the Sheehy parties often focus on his attraction for Mary and her contribution to Emma Clery in *Stephen Hero* and *A Portrait*, yet the epiphanies describe Hanna and Maggie (Margaret) Sheehy rather than Mary. Instead of the people most familiar to him, Joyce's epiphanies prioritize moments with passing acquaintances: Tobin in Mullingar ("There's Nothing like Marriage"), O'Mahoney in Dame Street ("The Priest That Writes Poetry"), Blake at the Sheehys' ("It's a Terrible Life"), and two prostitutes in London ("Fred Leslie's My Brother").

Despite this focus on passing acquaintances and seemingly trivial incidents, a number of common themes link the epiphanies to Joyce's later work, including sexuality and desire ("Is Mabie Your Sweetheart?," "They Pass in Twos and Threes," "Fred Leslie's My Brother," "Upon Me from the Darkness"); traumatic encounters ("Apologise," "An Arctic Beast," "Half-Men, Half-Goats," "The Lame Beggar"); death ("Poor Little Fellow!," "I Was Sorry," "Two Mourners," "She Comes at Night"); language and incomprehension ("An Arctic Beast," "The Ship," "Hoofs upon the Dublin Road"); and a young man who rejects the advice of his elders ("Forty Thousand Pounds," "There's Nothing like Marriage," "It's a Terrible Life"). Joyce's adaptations often seem thematically driven, with the later works returning to the epiphanies at moments when their central themes are most prominent. For instance, "Is Mabie Your Sweetheart?" typifies the intensity of youthful desire in both "Nausicaa" and the "Games" chapter of *Finnegans Wake*; "Apologise" becomes an archetypal scene of chastisement and rebellion in *Portrait*; "Two Mourners" provides a set piece in "Hades," and so on.

Joyce began to adapt his epiphanies in 1904, but his changing attitude toward them dates back to his graduation in October 1902. Until that point, Stanislaus was Joyce's primary reader, acting as a kind of sounding board during his early work on the epiphanies,[9] but in autumn 1902, Joyce sought a wider readership. In October or November he showed his epiphanies to Yeats,[10] who described them as "a beautiful though immature and eccentric harmony of little prose descriptions and meditations." Yeats recalls Joyce telling him "he had written a book of prose essays or poems. . . . He had thrown over metrical form, he said, that he might get a form so fluent that it would respond to the motions of the spirit" (qtd. in Ellmann, *Identity* 86). Assuming this is about the epiphanies, it is the only explicit record of Joyce's intentions for them. Stanislaus also mentions that Joyce "brought [Yeats] his poems and 'epiphanies'" (*MBK* 185) but suggests it was after Yeats returned from London: "He was about to start for London when my brother introduced himself; when he returned, my brother brought him his poems and epiphanies. Yeats read them carefully and then wrote him a long, four-page letter" (*MBK* 182).

Joyce also showed the epiphanies to other "men of letters," seemingly in concert with his poems. Stanislaus says he "lent the whole collection only to Gogarty, Yeats, [George] Russell, and one or two others," including George Moore, who received them from Russell (*MBK* 252). Gogarty clearly knew of the epiphanies and read them, describing the form they took and his annoyance at being a subject in one of them (293–95).[11] Joyce accosted Eglinton and likely showed him the epiphanies; in a later memoir, Eglinton suggests that Joyce found "a new method in literary art . . . in his Diary: a swift notation, at their point of origination, of feelings and perceptions" (qtd. in *WD* 204). Stanislaus interprets this comment as a reference to the epiphanies and castigates Eglinton for his error: "This collection [of epiphanies] was in no sense a diary. John Eglinton . . . mentions my brother's diary. . . . Jim never kept a diary" (*MBK* 125). Before leaving for Paris in December 1902, Joyce made a copy of his collection and gave it to Russell (*LII* 28).[12] Joyce spent a short time in Paris, before returning on January 23, 1903. A fortnight later, he informed Stanislaus that his collection of epiphanies was still with Russell: "I did well to leave my MSS with him for I had a motive. However I shall take them back as my latest additions to 'Epiphany' might not be to his liking" (February 8, 1903; *LII* 28). Joyce may have been concerned that some of the new epiphanies, such as "They Pass in Twos and Threes," would offend the prudish Russell; however, it is not clear what his "motive" was in leaving them with Æ (despite sharing the epiphanies with so many established writers, Joyce seems not to have raised the issue of publication), or whether he retrieved them.[13]

What is clear, though, is that Joyce was composing new epiphanies until at least 1903. On March 9, 1903, Joyce told Stanislaus he had written "fifteen new epiphanies—of which twelve are insertions and three additions" (*LII* 35). Having been in Paris for forty-five days, he had written, on average, one epiphany every three days—his most concentrated period of work on the collection. Curiously, however, only one epiphany is located there ("They Pass in Twos and Threes"). Another describes his journey back to Ireland after receiving news of his mother's illness ("I Lie along the Deck"), but fewer epiphanies survive from the time after his return from Paris in April 1903. Only two are known to have been written after his return: "She Dances with Them in the Round," based on Hanna Sheehy's engagement party in spring 1903, and "Two Mourners," based on a scene at Glasnevin Cemetery after May Joyce's death in August 1903. It is possible that "She Comes at Night" was also written after May Joyce's death, but none of the forty extant epiphanies can be dated securely after that autumn.

This fact suggests a change in Joyce's conception of the epiphanies in late 1903. In September of that year, Stanislaus began reusing paper Joyce had previously written on for a new diary, titled "My Crucible" (Cornell 4). Among the sheets Stanislaus recycled are two copies of three epiphanies. Early on in the diary, Stanislaus mentions Joyce's "'epiphanies'—his prose pieces (which I almost prefer to his lyrics) and his dialogues," which he considers "subtle": "He has put himself into these with singular courage, singular memory, and scientific minuteness; he has proved himself capable of taking very great pains to create a very little thing of prose or verse. . . . Whether he will ever build up anything broad—a drama, an esthetic treatise—I cannot say" (*DD* 14). Stanislaus's use of the present perfect ("has put," "has proved") rather than the simple present gives the sense of a finished action, as though Joyce is no longer composing epiphanies. There is nothing definite about the tense, of course, but it is interesting to note that in late 1903 Joyce was jotting down notes on aesthetics, and that by early 1904 he was recycling epiphanies for the first draft of "A Portrait of the Artist" (dated January 7, 1904, the Orthodox Epiphany). Joyce's lyrical, elliptical "Portrait" is one of his most epiphanic texts, providing a bridge from discrete epiphanies to extended prose narratives.[14] As though to reinforce this sense that Joyce had moved on from writing epiphanies and no longer considered publishing them, in October 1903 Stanislaus began a notebook titled "Selections in Prose from Various Authors" (Cornell 4.10), copying twenty-four of his brother's epiphanies alongside quotations from Leo Tolstoy, Johann Wolfgang von Goethe, Jean-Jacques Rousseau, and others. Given that Joyce had not yet written any of his major works, Stanislaus placed him in exalted company. Yet, in hindsight his judgment was vindicated, and we have Stanislaus to thank for preserving seventeen of the manuscript epiphanies, because just as he was copying them into his notebook, Joyce was beginning to expand and adapt them into his prose narratives.[15]

Echoes and Adaptations

Between 1904 and 1939 Joyce incorporated over thirty epiphanies into his subsequent works: fourteen are reused in *Stephen Hero*; thirteen are found in *A Portrait of the Artist as a Young Man*; fifteen are echoed or adapted in

Ulysses; and eight appear in *Finnegans Wake*. Joyce also recycled passages from the epiphanies in his 1904 sketch "A Portrait of the Artist," *Giacomo Joyce* (1915), and *Exiles* (1918). In *Stephen Hero* and *Portrait*, Joyce often inserted entire epiphanies, little changed, at key moments in the narrative. There is a fine irony when Daedalus thinks of collecting "a book of epiphanies" in *Stephen Hero* (211), since the manuscript itself could be described in similar terms; indeed, Robert Scholes asserts that the epiphanies form "the principal building blocks" of the novel (*WD* 6). His claim is difficult to judge, since half the manuscript has been lost, but it is striking how many key scenes in the surviving pages, such as the opening section, Isabel's death, and Stephen's aesthetic theory, center on epiphanies. In *Portrait*, the epiphanies' structural importance is even clearer, since Joyce reused three complete epiphanies at the beginning, middle, and end of the novel. These epiphany-based passages stand out as key moments in the narrative, whereas elsewhere, Joyce inserted his epiphanies so seamlessly that they can only be identified with reference to the original texts. This seamless quality of Joyce's adaptations raises an important point, for it suggests that the epiphanies served a stylistic, as well as a structural, purpose. *Dubliners* illustrates this well, for although it does not include any of the extant epiphanies— most likely because Joyce's short stories were written concurrently with *Stephen Hero*, and Joyce reserved the epiphanies for his autobiographical novel (see Walzl, "Dubliners" 168)—there are close stylistic similarities between the dialogue and narrative of *Dubliners* and Joyce's dramatic and lyrical epiphanies, respectively, indicating how the epiphanies helped shape Joyce's prose style, not just in *Dubliners* but also in *Portrait* and arguably *Ulysses*.

Nevertheless, the epiphanies are less structurally and stylistically noteworthy in the later works than they are in *Stephen Hero* and *A Portrait of the Artist as a Young Man*. In the later novels, Joyce's epiphanies are frequently reduced to fleeting echoes and phrases, yet these distilled references can still be highly significant because they incorporate central themes and motifs from the original epiphanies. And while there is a general trajectory from complete epiphanies, inserted with few changes, in Joyce's early prose, to fleeting echoes in the late works, there is also considerable variation in the way Joyce adapted his epiphanies, even when the same epiphany recurs within the same novel, which is why we provide a detailed account of Joyce's adaptations, both here and in the notes. Indeed, close analysis of Joyce's echoes and adaptations leaves little doubt that the epiphanies offer the most extensive example of textual recycling in Joyce's oeuvre, first, because he frequently inserted them as complete textual units, and second, because he adapted several of the epiphanies repeatedly, in multiple works, from "A Portrait" in 1904 through to *Finnegans Wake* in 1939.

It is impossible to know Joyce's original intentions for the epiphanies, but the clearest indication we have is a plan for chapters 8–11 of *Stephen Hero* (*JJA* 7:70–94), which includes the outline shown in figure 1.

August 1893 to December 1893

1) ~~Sensations coming home.—~~
2) Gradual irreligiousness ~~(Epiphany of Thornton)~~
3) Return to Belvedere: in second class: prefect
   at sodality: Fr MacNally.
4) Retreat before feast of S Francis Xavier.
   Six lectures

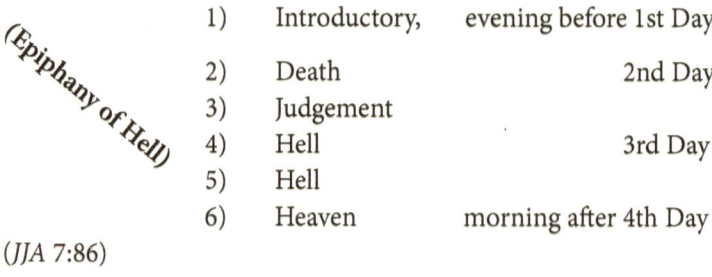

1)	Introductory,	evening before 1st Day
2)	Death	2nd Day
3)	Judgement	
4)	Hell	3rd Day
5)	Hell	
6)	Heaven	morning after 4th Day

(*JJA* 7:86)

The "Epiphany of Thornton" has been connected to Dick Thornton (see *MBK* 226–27), a friend of John Joyce, and the inspiration for Tom Kernan in "Grace" (*WD* 68n6).[16] Regrettably, this section of *Stephen Hero* does not survive, so little can be said about the role of these epiphanies in the retreat, but the titles suggest that they offered set pieces illustrating Stephen's "Gradual irreligiousness" and his "Epiphany of Hell."

Based on Joyce's adaptation in *Portrait*, the latter epiphany is usually identified with "Half-Men, Half-Goats." Written diagonally across the six lectures, Joyce's note might refer to the retreat as a whole, in the manner of D'Annunzio's "Epiphany of Love" and "Epiphany of Death," but an extended experience of this kind is inconsistent with the brevity of Joyce's manuscripts and the assertion in *Stephen Hero* that epiphanies record a "*sudden spiritual manifestation*" (216, emphasis added). Thus, it is more likely that the parentheses indicate that the epiphany was to be inserted as an exem-

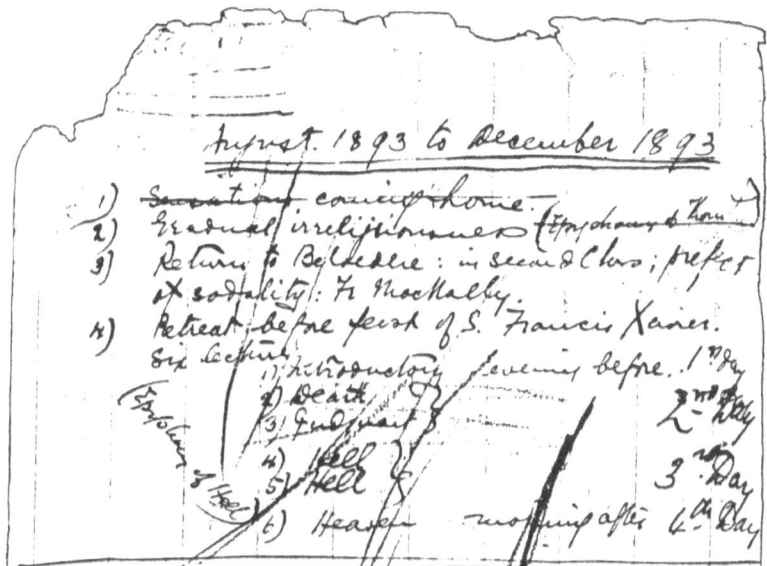

Figure 1. Notes for *Stephen Hero*. Buffalo 2.A.16 (*JJA* 7:86). Held by the Poetry Collection of the University Libraries, University at Buffalo, the State University of New York. Reprinted with the permission of the James Joyce Estate.

plum of "Hell," somewhere among the fourth and fifth sermons, in the same way that the "Epiphany of Thornton" presumably exemplifies "Gradual irreligiousness."

Joyce's notes for *Stephen Hero* also include a plan for chapter 9, which ends:

> Epiphany of Mr Tate.
> The Play at Whitsuntide: Emma again.
> (*JJA* 7:90)

Mr. Tate was based on George Dempsey, who taught Joyce English, history, and geography at Belvedere College (Bradley, 102–6). In *Portrait*, chapter 2, Stephen's English teacher has the same name, and on the night of the Whitsuntide play, Stephen recalls Mr. Tate accusing him of heresy (*P* 2.689–96). In view of these similarities, there is some likelihood that the scene includes or reworks the "Epiphany of Mr Tate," in which case it provides a rare glimpse of a "lost" epiphany. Based on the verso numbering on the Buffalo manuscript, there may originally have been over seventy epiphanies, but attempts to identify additional epiphanies in Joyce's works have generally floundered for lack of evidence.[17] This is one of the few cases where a plausible argument can be made, because Joyce titled the epiphany in his sister Mabel's copybook in January 1904.

Further references to lost epiphanies appear in Joyce's early commonplace book, dated November 1904:

> Epiphanies:
> ?Lola & Alice: The Boy in Dalkey: One servant
> ~~Dr Doherty and the Holy City~~
> Trained by Owner — Mr [or Mrs] Casey
> (National Library of Ireland MS 36,639/2/A)

If it were not for the heading, it would be virtually impossible to recognize these entries as referring to epiphanies. The phrases are difficult to read, let alone identify, but there is some indication that "Dr Doherty and the Holy City" refers to a conversation between Father Moran and Stephen involving "The Holy City" in chapter 17 of *Stephen Hero*. There, the "unsettled rage" Emma's admiration for Father Moran provokes in Stephen evokes other scenes based on epiphanies (see "The Last Tram" and "She Dances with Them in the Round"), as does Stephen's contempt for the priest's banal opinions, exemplified by Moran's admiration for "The Holy City" (*SH* 66). John Smurthwaite suggests that Doherty refers to Dr. William Doherty, curate at Dublin's pro-cathedral, who provided a model for Father Moran: "in real life [William Doherty] may have had a conversation with Joyce like the one Father Moran and Stephen have" (qtd. in Mamigonian and Turner 386). The evidence is inconclusive, but if Smurthwaite is correct, the note in the commonplace book must refer to a lost epiphany; the fact it has been crossed out probably indicates that by February 1905 Joyce had reused it in *Stephen Hero*.[18]

Unfortunately, chapters 1–15 of *Stephen Hero* were lost or destroyed, and none of the epiphanies mentioned in Joyce's notes survive (except, perhaps, the "Epiphany of Hell"), so we cannot tell how they were reused in *Stephen Hero*. Nevertheless, Joyce's notes alert us to an important difference in the way he adapted the epiphanies. In the copybook, Joyce identifies them by a single word or name ("Hell," "Tate," "Thornton"). If we assume that the "Epiphany of Hell" refers to "Half-Men, Half-Goats," it seems likely that the other titles recorded in January 1904 also refer to individual epiphanies. If this was a consistent naming convention, each noun phrase in the list of "Epiphanies" recorded in November 1904 would refer to a separate epiphany, but the conjunction and dash in lines 2 and 3 imply that each of these lines might refer to a single epiphany or a series of connected epiphanies. This difference between the two sets of notes suggests a change in the way Joyce planned to reuse his epiphanies—from discrete scenes, focused on a unifying theme or character, to a collection of fragments like "Lola & Alice: The Boy in Dalkey: One servant" that would provide material for *Stephen Hero*. We cannot know whether this was the case for the missing portion of *Stephen Hero*, but there is no doubt that within the surviving works there is a gradual shift in the way the epiphanies are adapted, from complete units of text based on individual epiphanies to fleeting echoes and phrases.[19]

This variation in the way Joyce adapted the epiphanies is adumbrated in *Stephen Hero*, and becomes increasingly pronounced in subsequent works. Intriguingly, the first surviving page of *Stephen Hero* begins in the middle of "The Spell of Arms and Voices," which is transposed to fit the third-person, past-tense narrative but is otherwise little changed. On the original manuscript, Joyce wrote "Departure for Paris" immediately after the epiphany. This is almost certainly a note for *A Portrait of the Artist as a Young Man*, since the same epiphany appears almost unchanged at the end of *Portrait*, as Stephen prepares to leave Dublin, whereas immediately after the epiphany in *Stephen Hero*, Daedalus travels to Mullingar. The following section, set in Mullingar, incorporates two further epiphanies ("The Lame Beggar" and "There's Nothing like Marriage"), which are also largely unchanged. The "Mullingar fragment" must have been composed in late 1904, since it precedes chapter 15, begun in December of that year (Mamigonian and Turner 351). Soon after, in January 1905, Joyce wrote Stanislaus, "when [Nora] saw me copy Epiphanies into my novel she asked would all that paper be wasted" (*LII* 78). Nora's thriftiness is comical, but Joyce did in fact copy a dozen epiphanies, with minor changes, directly into *Stephen Hero*. As well as the Mullingar pieces, these included three epiphanies originally set at the Sheehys' house in Belvedere Place, which Joyce transferred to the Daniels' house in Donnybrook (*SH* 42–47), where the narrative context helps elucidate enigmas like "Ibsen's Age" and "Your Favourite Poet." Joyce also reused four epiphanies for Isabel's illness and death (*SH* 169–74). Interestingly, three of these were originally written for Georgie, while "Two Mourners" describes a scene at May Joyce's funeral. Here again we see Joyce grouping epiphanies thematically and adapting them to the narrative, with some unexpected consequences, such as the anatomical possibility opened up by the switch from Georgie to Isabel when Mrs. Daedalus refers to "the hole *we* all have . . . here" (*SH* 163, emphasis added).

While the adaptation of this scene changes its significance, it is nevertheless striking that the epiphany is inserted as a complete textual unit; stage directions are incorporated into the narrative, with the dialogue substantially unchanged. There are, however, a few examples in *Stephen Hero* of epiphanies being echoed or adapted more freely, in the manner of Joyce's later works. For instance, a faint echo of "An Arctic Beast" may be heard in Stephen's "vision of the pleisiosauros emerging from his ocean of slime" (*SH* 33), and the last epiphany to feature in *Stephen Hero*, "The Girls, the Boys," picks up on an earlier scene at Clonliffe Seminary (*SH* 183–84, 74), creating a network of associations, from the seminarist life Stephen imagines to his complicated feelings for Emma Clery and his growing literary ambitions. In this case, the extended adaptation of the epiphany gives depth to the scene on the steps of the National Library, showing how Joyce was able to weave his epiphanies into the narrative rather than simply insert them as set pieces.

As with *Stephen Hero*, there can be little doubt that the epiphanies play a major structural role in *A Portrait of the Artist as a Young Man*. In all, thirteen are used at key points in the novel, including "Half-Men, Half-Goats" and "The Spell of Arms and Voices," at the middle and end of *A Portrait*, and Joyce's most famous epiphany, "Apologise," which provides such a memorable opening. While the first two have been adapted to fit their contexts (with Mr. Vance's role transferred to Dante, for example), Joyce was able to insert each of these epiphanies as a complete textual unit, epiphanizing key scenes in Stephen's growth from childhood to adolescence. As mentioned previously, "The Spell" is inserted virtually unchanged as Stephen's antepenultimate diary entry, and the journal as a whole reads almost like a series of epiphanies—as though Dedalus, at the end of the novel, has reached the point where he is able to record the epiphanies his fictional predecessor, Stephen Daedalus, thought of writing (*SH* 211). At least three entries are based directly on Joyce's manuscript epiphanies, and there may originally have been more. The "*25 March, morning*" entry is particularly interesting because it records "A night of troubled dreams," plural, beginning with a passage copied almost verbatim from "Images of Fabulous Kings," and following with a second paragraph whose style is indistinguishable from the first, though it is not based on any known epiphany (*P* 5.2672–768). Whether the second paragraph was drawn from a lost epiphany or not, its stylistic similarity, not just to "Images of Fabulous Kings" but to the diary as a whole, shows how finely Joyce's epiphanies are woven into the novel. This point is reinforced by three successive passages in chapter 2 beginning "He was sitting": two are based on epiphanies ("Is That Mary Ellen?," *P* 2.275–

302, and "The Last Tram," *P* 2.303–56), suggesting that the third ("The beautiful Mabel Hunter," *P* 2.252–74) may also be based on a lost epiphany. It is impossible to know, of course, but the very fact that we cannot tell shows how thoroughly Joyce integrated his epiphanies into the narrative and the extent to which the style of *A Portrait of the Artist as a Young Man* grows out of them.

The structural and stylistic significance of the epiphanies in *Portrait* comes partly from the key role they play in the genesis of the novel. Besides a few juvenile poems, Joyce's epiphanies are the earliest texts in *Portrait*'s genetic dossier, and it is striking that even in the final published version, Stephen's artistic growth stems from them. Immediately after the "He was sitting" sequence, Stephen attempts to write a poem, "To E— C—" (*P* 2.362), and it is precisely this memory, echoed in "The Last Tram," that Stephen returns to when he seeks inspiration for his villanelle (*P* 5.1762). If we recall that the "trivial incident" that set Stephen "composing some ardent verses which he entitled a 'Vilanelle [*sic*] of the Temptress'" in *Stephen Hero* was none other than the "fragment of colloquy" that made him think of collecting "a book of epiphanies" (*SH* 211), and that Dedalus's effusive villanelle in *Portrait* is merely the prelude to the epiphanic diary that epitomizes his development as a writer, it should become clear how deeply interwoven Joyce's epiphanies are in *A Portrait of the Artist as a Young Man*.

According to Frank Budgen, Joyce stressed the last four words of the title, drawing attention to Stephen's youth. Joyce's bildungsroman is commonly read as a satirical portrait of Stephen Dedalus, but the novel is not just satire,[20] and as Budgen realized, Joyce may have been emphasizing the fact that he began *Portrait* as a young man of twenty-two, not as the writer in his mid-thirties who was then working on *Ulysses*. The satirical view of Dedalus has led many critics to assume that Joyce distances himself from his early epiphanies in *Ulysses* when the twenty-two-year-old Stephen thinks, "Remember your epiphanies, deeply deep, copies to be sent if you died to all the great libraries of the world, including Alexandria?" (*U* 3.141–43). The passage is ironic, of course, but the deeper irony is that "Proteus" itself is shaped by the way Joyce remembers his epiphanies in the chapter, and Stephen's reflection ensures that we don't forget them. A partial early draft of "Proteus" in the National Library of Ireland is composed of sixteen fragments, each of which "could be construed as being analogous to Joyce's concept of the epiphany," with the last unit based directly on "They Pass in Twos and Threes" (Slote, "Epiphanic"). Several other epiphanies also seem to be echoed in the "Proteus" draft: the extended descriptions of Tatler, the cocklepickers' dog, nosing and circling the carcass of a dead dog near the beginning of the notebook recall the sorrowful howls of "The Big Dog" in Joyce's epiphany; the scene of misrecognition Stephen imagines were he to drop in on his Uncle Richie echoes "Is That Mary Ellen?"; and set alone, as a discrete fragment, Stephen's vision of stranded whales being butchered for their meat sounds almost like a lyrical epiphany:

> A school of turlehide whales stranded, spouting ~~and~~ flapping in the shallows: and from the cobbled starving city a horde of ^~~green~~^ jerkined dwarfs running, scaling, flaying with their knives, and hacking ~~the~~ [?^green^?] blubbery ^~~rancid~~^ flesh. Famine, plague, and slaughter. My people: their strange blood is in me, their thoughts,-- ~~in many~~ waves of my brain. A ^midnight^ multitude in the frozen Liffey among ~~resinous~~ hissing ~~torches bonfires~~ resin firs. My blood: my people.
>
> (National Library of Ireland MS 36,639/7/A)

Stylistically, this passage is reminiscent of the lyrical epiphanies (see, e.g., "An Arctic Beast"). Conceivably, it could be based on a lost epiphany; more likely, Joyce composed it in the same style, fashioning Stephen's interior monologue on June 16, 1904, in the image of his early epiphanies. That would make sense, because in 1904 Joyce began revising epiphanies into an expanding work of autobiographical fiction—first the "Portrait" sketch, and then *Stephen Hero*, where the concept of epiphany becomes central to Stephen's aesthetic theory (based on Joyce's own aesthetics, dated early 1904; see National Library of Ireland MS 36,639/2/A). In this context, it is not surprising that Stephen remembers the epiphanies in "Proteus," or that Joyce should draw on them so heavily in the chapter. In the process of revision, the text itself becomes protean, changing its form, sometimes radically, through successive drafts, so that it can almost seem as if the epiphanies in "Proteus" are "silted" over (Slote, "Epiphanic"). The most striking thing about the epiphanies reused in "Proteus," though, is the way Joyce transforms them from self-contained vignettes into fleeting echoes and fragments: five separate epiphanies can be traced through the published edition, but many of them have been transformed almost beyond recognition, like the faint traces of "The Ship" and "The Spell of Arms and Voices" that accompany the three-masted ship sailing silently into harbor at the end of the episode.

Fleeting as these echoes are, they play an important role in shaping Stephen's thoughts, memories, and perceptions. There *are* extended adaptations in *Ulysses*—the scene based on "Two Mourners" in "Hades" and the dialogue drawn from "Is Mabie Your Sweetheart?" in "Nausicaa," for example—but it is more common to find brief lines, phrases, or images that echo the epiphanies. While these verbal repetitions are less extensive, the process of reduction often increases the concentration, so that small fragments of the original text have a significant impact on the episode they are added to. For example, when May Dedalus's ghost appears to Stephen in "Circe," saying, "Who had pity for you when you were sad among the strangers? . . . Years and years I loved you, O, my son, my firstborn, when you lay in my womb" (*U* 15.4197, 15.4203–4), her words are drawn directly from "She Comes at Night," an epiphany in which Joyce's mother "had come to him in a dream" (*MBK* 229–30). The echo is brief—a mere three lines—but it constitutes the emotional climax of the scene, epitomizing the hold Stephen's mother still has on him. The lines resonate powerfully because, through a series of motifs like the prayer "*Liliata rutilantium*," they echo right back to "Telemachus," where "She Comes at Night" is subtly fused with another dream Joyce recorded in Trieste: "She came to me silently in a dream . . ." (*JJA* 7:141). On a first reading, the echo is slight, but associated motifs allow it to be recognized retrospectively as a prefiguration of the climax in "Circe," illustrating how Joyce creates dense networks of associations through subtle patterns of repetition. These variations are not limited to the epiphanies, of course, but Joyce's adaptation of the epiphanies is particularly instructive because the original texts are among Joyce's earliest mature literary compositions, and the use he made of them in subsequent works offers the most extensive example of textual recycling in his oeuvre: first, because Joyce inserted many epiphanies as complete textual units (unlike the fragments of other works he recycled); and second, because he adapted his epiphanies over and over again in multiple works, from "A Portrait of the Artist" in 1904 to *Finnegans Wake* in 1939.

Epiphanic echoes in the *Wake* can be as fleeting as "apullajibed" / "Apologise" (*FW* 317.26–30), but the fact that Joyce continued to reuse his epiphanies up to thirty-five years after they were written shows their enduring significance to him. Further evidence of Joyce's interest in the epiphanies during the years he was composing *Finnegans Wake* can be found in a typescript of nineteen epiphanies in the Eugène and Maria Jolas papers at Yale, almost certainly made by the Jolases or at their behest after 1927 (MacDuff, "Yale"). Another indication of the importance Joyce attributed to the epiphanies appears in "Shem the Penman," a highly autobiographical chapter that references *Chamber Music*, *Dubliners*, *Portrait*, *Exiles*, and *Ulysses*, before closing with an adaptation of "She Comes at Night" (*FW* 193.32–194.22). This self-reflexive return to the origins of Joyce's prose writing (excluding the shadowy "Silhouettes") draws attention to the remarkable fact that Joyce reused epiphanies in all his narrative works (with the possible exception of *Dubliners*), even writing extended meditations like "A Portrait of the Artist" and *Giacomo Joyce* in the style of epiphanies. In recent years, genetic scholars have begun to explore how this sustained rewriting of the epiphanies contributes to the complex palimpsests of Joyce's texts, but much remains to be discovered. In the notes and commentary to each epiphany, which include detailed accounts of Joyce's echoes and adaptations, we provide a starting point for this analysis in the hope that others will continue to revise and expand our understanding of the extraordinary role of the epiphanies in Joyce's oeuvre.

Critical Reception and Editorial History

Joyce's epiphanies have a complex history of reception. In D'Annunzio's *The Flame of Life*, Joyce found the term *epiphany* associated with a moment of revelation *and* with a genre of writing, yet critics of Joyce have often felt the need to prioritize one or the other of these aspects. From the 1940s, the sense of epiphany as revelation dominated, thanks to the aesthetic theory in *Stephen Hero* and *Portrait*. This provoked questions about how epiphany is related to the history of literary revelation and whether a typology of epiphanies could be created. Epiphany as revelation became established as a literary-critical *device* that was an integral part of Stephen and Joyce's aesthetics. Gradually, however, the forty extant sketches became more accessible to critics and foregrounded an understanding of epiphany as a literary *genre* that existed as freestanding prose poems of dialogue and narrative. Here, epiphany's combination of triviality and revelation and its dual status as sketch and insertion into the larger narrative sequences in the novels stood out. The relationship between the sketches and revelation remained unclear, but critics of epiphany often touched on both understandings of epiphany, while usually prioritizing one over the other.

Upon Joyce's death in 1941, the existence of the epiphanies was known to only a handful of Joyce's acquaintances. The main manuscript of the epiphanies must have passed at some point into the possession of Sylvia Beach; most likely, Joyce left his holograph manuscript of twenty-two epiphanies with her when he fled Paris in 1940. In 1949, Lucie Léon and Maria Jolas arranged for some of Beach's Joyce collection to be put on display at the Librairie La Hune, a new Left Bank bookshop. Information about the epiphanies was published in the catalogue of the exhibition, although, oddly, only nineteen were listed (Faucheux, Noël, and Friedlaender). Some items were sold to the Lockwood Library of the University of Buffalo, and in December 1958 the rest of Beach's Joyce collection was sold to the university as well (Fitch 412). Meanwhile, the twenty-four epiphanies transcribed by Stanislaus into his "Selections in Prose from Various Authors" were sold by Stanislaus's widow to Cornell University in 1957.

The first public acknowledgment of Joyce's sketches came a decade before the exhibition. In 1937, Oliver St. John Gogarty's memoir *As I Was Going Down Sackville Street* mentioned Joyce's habit of keeping a "secret record" of comments made by his associates. In 1941, in his *Definitive Biography* of Joyce, Herbert Gorman highlighted "a dozen or more plot-less sketches, flashes of life, manifestations of mood and place" that were inserted into *Portrait* (92). However, the identification of the epiphanies as sketches was not fully accepted. Harry Levin, in his *Critical Introduction* of 1944, ignored or was unaware of the sketches that Joyce tried to fuse into *Stephen Hero* (37). Instead, he identified epiphanies as moments of irony and sentiment that are found throughout Joyce's work, particularly in structurally significant positions like the ends of the chapters of *Portrait* (44, and see 31, 33, 86). Levin connected these moments to the ideas of impersonality, objectivity, and aesthetic distancing articulated by Stephen in *Stephen Hero* and *Portrait*.

The publication of Joyce's draft *Stephen Hero* in 1944, edited by Theodore Spencer, was the first opportunity for readers to encounter Stephen's full statement on epiphany as a concept within his aesthetic. Spencer's introduction understood epiphany as "moments" of intensity or climax within Joyce's texts, with a tension between moments and eternity that "emphasizes the radiance, the effulgence, of the thing itself revealed in a special moment, an unmoving moment, of time" (*SH* 17). He went on to develop this sense of tension into a literary-critical concept that could be used to understand Joyce's texts:

> This theory seems to me central to an understanding of Joyce as an artist, and we might describe his successive works as illustrations, intensifications and enlargements of it. *Dubliners* . . . is a series of epiphanies describing apparently trivial but actually crucial and revealing moments in the lives of different characters. The *Portrait* may be seen as a kind of epiphany—a showing forth—of Joyce himself as a young

man; *Ulysses*, by taking one day in the life of the average man ... is the epiphany of Leopold Bloom, just as, years earlier, the trivial conversation overheard on a misty evening in Eccles Street (where, incidentally, Mr. Bloom lived) was the epiphany of those two people's lives, shown forth in a moment. And *Finnegans Wake* may be seen as a vast enlargement, of course unconceived by Joyce as a young man, of the same view.

(*SH* 16–17)

As Joyce's texts are all "enlargements" of this concept (see also Mamigonian and Turner; Melchior; Spencer), epiphany is also a form of text that Joyce specializes in, not a short prose sketch as such but a narrative in which the moments of revelation of the text foreshadow the reader's experience of finishing Joyce's text and realizing its whole vision. This expanded notion of epiphany set the stage for the reception of epiphany as revelation but neglected Joyce's sketches, some of which had been inserted into the manuscript of *Stephen Hero* (Spencer does not connect the term *epiphany* to these inserted sketches).[21]

Irene Hendry Chayes's foundational essay of 1946, "Joyce's Epiphanies," consolidated this idea of epiphany as revelation rather than sketch.[22] Chayes speculated about the existence of sketches but, following Spencer, perpetuated an expanded sense of epiphany as a moment of revelation, articulated by Stephen's terminology of *integritas*, *claritas*, and *quidditas*. She reviewed various moments of revelation and showed how epiphany provides Joyce's writing with nuances, gestures, and details ("local colour") that flesh out his scenes (40–46). Chayes also aligned with Spencer in categorizing epiphany as an experience offered at different scales within Joyce's writing: Joyce's work is "a tissue of epiphanies, great and small, from fleeting images to whole books, from the briefest revelation in his lyrics to the epiphany that occupies one gigantic, enduring 'moment' in *Finnegans Wake*" (40). A scholar of William Blake and the Romantics, Chayes initiated a succession of Romantic scholars engaging with the notion of epiphany as revelation.

The 1950s were the key decade in reasserting the connection between the Joycean epiphany and the extant prose sketches. Having brought Sylvia Beach's Joyce collection to Buffalo, Oscar A. Silverman published twenty-two sketches in 1956 with brief notes on each. Soon after, the publication of Stanislaus Joyce's *My Brother's Keeper* (1958) and *Dublin Diary* (1962, but written in 1903–5) further emphasized the significance of the sketches as an "experimental form" of "manifestations or revelations" (*MBK* 134–35; see *DD* 14).[23] Stanislaus's definition of epiphanies as "little errors and gestures . . . by which people betrayed the very things they were most careful to conceal" (*MBK* 134) echoed Gogarty's earlier comment about Joyce's covert scribblings being "any showing forth of the mind by which he considered one gave oneself away" (293–95).[24] Both comments, from people who knew Joyce well, supported the identification of Joyce's prose sketches with the term *epiphany* and simultaneously affirmed their connection to forms of revelatory disclosure.

At the same time, early critics such as Hugh Kenner, William T. Noon, and Richard Ellmann took contrasting approaches to Joyce's epiphany.[25] In his 1955 study *Dublin's Joyce*, Kenner ignored the sketches and read epiphany as part of Stephen's theory of aesthetic apprehension and as a process of "epiphanizing" (144–54). His contribution lay in proposing that "it is *things* which achieve epiphany under the artist's alchemical power, and not his own soul which he manifests" (141, original emphasis). Language is among the "things" that can epiphanize: "He saw clearly that for his almost anthropological purposes a word *is* a 'thing'" (151, original emphasis). Kenner thereby implied a *linguistic* epiphany, by which a prose configuration provokes a revelation in the reader. This emphasis on language anticipated later assertions of the textuality of Joyce's epiphanies.[26]

In his 1957 study *Joyce and Aquinas*, Noon attempted to ground the theory of epiphany in the theological and philosophical aspects of Stephen's aesthetics. By linking epiphany to *claritas,* he contextualized Stephen's definition of epiphany in *Stephen Hero* against Aristotelian philosophy and Thomist theology, ultimately suggesting that Joyce's aesthetics are quite different from what can be derived from Thomist aesthetics (61, 67).[27] Noon also sought out Joyce's sketches at the University of Buffalo, but didn't integrate them into his reading. Rather, he developed the idea that ultimately epiphany became synonymous with "symbol" and was abandoned by Joyce for being too subjective (35).

In contrast to Noon, Ellmann, in his 1959 biography of Joyce, prioritized the sketches over the theory of epiphany, while maintaining an emphasis on revelation. Ellmann characterized the sketches as "prose poems" that convey "moments of fullness and of passion," "the accession of a sudden joy," or a "call to the soul."[28] He asserted that Joyce considered "forming them into a small book" and "only later, in 1904, . . . saw he could insert them instead in *Stephen Hero*" (*JJII* 83–85). He also recognized the sketches' role in developing the style of Joyce's later writings: "just as the lyrical epiphanies had led Joyce towards *Portrait of the Artist*, so the bald, underplayed epiphanies led him toward the first story in *Dubliners*" (*JJII* 163).

These scholars of the 1950s wrote without the prose sketches being easily available in a published volume. This was finally remedied by Robert Scholes and Richard M. Kain's *The Workshop of Daedalus* in 1965. For the first time, a complete set of forty sketches was available to Joyce scholars, and the accompanying introduction and notes came to define the early reception of the epiphanies. Scholes and Kain distinguished between "narrative" and "dramatic" epiphanies, identifying the first with "memorable phases" of the mind, and the second with "vulgarity of speech or of gesture" (Stanislaus recognized a similar division between lyric and dramatic in his own account). They also foregrounded the compositional role of the epiphanies in Joyce's writing ("Epiphanies became the principal building blocks for the novel [*Stephen Hero*]" [*WD* 4–6]) and claimed that the presence of some epiphanies in *A Portrait of the Artist as a Young Man* indicated that they still had a role in Joyce's mature works. More controversially, they contended that the epiphanies were ordered into a "meaningful progression" (4) that could be partially recovered via the verso numbering of the manuscripts. This numbering (the upper number is 71) also permitted the idea that there were at least thirty-one lost epiphanies, some of which might be hiding in plain sight in Joyce's published texts.

Both Scholes and Kain wrote about epiphanies in other contexts, and Scholes in particular established himself as an authority on Joyce's epiphanies.[29] The arguments of *The Workshop* were preceded by Scholes's 1964 essay "Joyce and the Epiphany: The Key to the Labyrinth?," where he considered Joyce's description of epiphanies in chapter 25 of *Stephen Hero*, Stephen's aesthetic theory in *Portrait*, and the adaptation of the sketches into Joyce's novels. Scholes's intervention is most notable for his resistance to the extension of the term away from Joyce's original intention. He protested against epiphany becoming "a term to be used in the criticism of Joyce's art itself" and insisted that the significance of epiphany was limited to the early period of Joyce's writing career; after *Stephen Hero*, Joyce "probably lost interest in it." Scholes asserted that in the process of adaptation epiphanies cease to be epiphanies and become "incident[s]": "a piece of prose . . . functioning dramatically in an artistic context, revealing character, attitude, and emotion." Although he would write in *The Workshop* that the epiphanies were Joyce's "principal building blocks," here he denied the epiphany as "a principle of structure in fiction" and debunked the idea that the epiphanies could function as the "key to the labyrinth" of Joyce's writings (70–76).

In 1965, Florence L. Walzl connected Joyce's notion of epiphany to the liturgical epiphanies in the Epiphany season rites, and subsequently to the *Dubliners* stories, reasserting the expanded interpretation of epiphany as a literary device linked to revelation ("Liturgy"). In doing so, she drew Scholes's ire. In a critical comment in *PMLA* (published alongside a defense from Walzl), Scholes restated his opposition to the extension of the term beyond its references to the sketches: "'Epiphany' designated a prose genre in which [Joyce] worked," not an "artistic device," and critics were in his opinion misguidedly using Joyce's "word to refer to an aspect of his work other than the one he intended by it" (Scholes and Walzl 152). Despite having raised awareness of epiphany in *The Workshop of Daedalus*, Scholes lamented its transformation into "a cliché . . . in Joyce criticism" and suggested that "we put this particular formula aside" (154). Walzl, in response to Scholes, observed that epiphany had "two distinct meanings in Joyce criticism." The first referred to the sketches, the second to "*revelation* or *illumination* in certain literary and technical senses" (152, original emphasis). Although they have often been separated, these two meanings are both important to understanding the Joycean epiphany. The tension between them—between epiphany as a literary *device* of revelation and epiphany as a literary *genre* of prose sketches (which often seemed inadequately revelatory)—would go on to shape the reception of Joyce's epiphany, as it was picked up by Romanticists, genetic critics, and other writers.

Epiphany in the Mid-Twentieth Century

The reception of epiphany was dominated by this expanded sense of epiphany as revelation. As early as 1945, Joseph Frank's three-part essay "Spatial Form in Modern Literature" argued that the literature of T. S. Eliot, Ezra Pound, Marcel Proust, and James Joyce was meant to be apprehended "spatially, in a moment of time, rather than as a sequence" (*Sewanee* 225).[30] Although Frank did not use the word *epiphany*, he described how Joyce presented his narrative in "fragments" and said that "the reader is forced to read *Ulysses* . . . continually fitting fragments together and keeping allusions in mind until, by reflexive reference, he can link them to their complements" (234–35). His description corresponds to the sense of epiphany as it became popularized among critics; epiphanies were "fragments," and the perception of these fragments in the light of the whole of the text would create "a unified spatial apprehension of his work" that would be tantamount to an epiphanic revelation (235). Frank connected revelation to large-scale narratives, not short prose-poems. Epiphany, then, was a literary-critical term that named a literary device, and through the 1950s it was taken up by other non-Joyceans who linked it to a history of revelation, to other writers of his period, to a typology of epiphanies, and to the synecdochical relationship between "fragment" and whole.

Frank's characterization was developed implicitly and sometimes explicitly in three works of Romantic criticism published in 1957: Northrop Frye's *The Anatomy of Criticism*, Frank Kermode's *Romantic Image*, and Robert Langbaum's *The Poetry of Experience*. Frye does not engage with Joyce's prose sketches or even with his definition of epiphany in *Stephen Hero*. Instead he writes as if he is inventing the term himself and applying it for the first time to biblical and Romantic literature. Frye's epiphanies are essentially synonymous with the sublime in Romantic literature: he offers as examples "mountain-top epiphanies in the Bible" as well as "sexual fulfilment" (*Anatomy* 204–5), and he asserts that the Bible's structure can be seen as a "sequence of epiphanies, a discontinuous but rightly ordered series of significant moments of apprehension of vision" (326). Frye traces the "point of epiphany" to writings of the post-Romantic period (223), in which "the central episodic theme is the theme of the pure but transient vision, the aesthetic or timeless moment," experienced by the artist as "a dedicated spirit, a saint or anchorite of poetry" (61). However, in more recent literature, the point of epiphany "is often ironically reversed, or brought to terms with greater demands for credibility" (206), and Frye goes on to mention examples from Ibsen, Yeats, Eliot, and Virginia Woolf. This literary tradition of revelation (in both its Romantic and modernist variants) is aligned with the anagogical approach to literature ("the poem appears as a microcosm of all literature, an individual manifestation of the total order of words" [121]), and Frye explicitly relates this to Joyce: "It is this conception which Joyce expresses, in terms of subject-matter, as 'epiphany'" (121). The Joycean epiphany, then, is the narrative of literary revelation as well as being a moment of sublime revelation within the work.[31]

Frye's emphasis on revelation is continued in Kermode's *Romantic Image*, which opens by identifying the "main topic" as "that 'esthetic image' explained in Thomist language by Stephen Dedalus in *Portrait of the Artist as a Young Man*," "that 'epiphany' which is the Joycean equivalent of Pater's 'vision'" (4). No mention is made of Joyce's prose sketches, nor does he develop his opening remarks on Joyce. Instead, Kermode unfolds a history whereby the artist, estranged from society by industrialization, forges in solitude a vision of joy, an "image," "a radiant truth out of space and time" (5), and he traces this vision through the Romantics, symbolists, and modernists. Although Kermode's study focuses on Yeats's version of the image, Stephen's theory of aesthetics—with its terms of beauty, integrity, consonance, clarity, *quidditas*, and stasis—is the culminating instance of this tradition.[32] The third study of 1957, Langbaum's *The Poetry of Experience*, argues that epiphany is "a manifestation in and through the visible world of an invisible life" (46). Langbaum shares Frye's sense that epiphany can be true or trustworthy or potentially false and deceptive. But because his focus is on Romantic poetry, he doesn't develop the role of epiphany in Joyce's writing; he simply accepts that it means revelation and associates it with "the short stories of Joyce or Chekhov" (46).

The work of Frye, Kermode, and Langbaum in the 1950s consolidated *epiphany* as a term of literary criticism that refers to a literary device—a moment of revelation—and also as a narrative that prioritizes revelation. The consequences of this expansion of the term for Joyce studies were addressed by Morris Beja in his 1963 doctoral thesis, revised and published in 1971 as *Epiphany in the Modern Novel*. Beja went further than his predecessors by relating revelation to Joyce's sketches and reviewing some representative examples of their adaptation in *Portrait* (the triad of epiphanies in *Portrait* beginning "He was sitting," alongside the epiphanies "Apologise," "The Ship," "The Spell of Arms and Voices," and "She Comes at Night"). Yet while Beja appreciated Scholes's work on the prose sketches, he contested Scholes's delimitation of the epiphany to Joyce's prose sketches and his idea of the unimportance of epiphany to Joyce (*Epiphany* 84). Indeed, in the wake of this wave of Romantic criticism, Beja was generally sympathetic to an expanded meaning of *epiphany* as a literary term denoting a scene of revelation, and so he accepted the legitimacy of talking about the epiphanies of *Dubliners* (see Beja, "One Good") and the bird-girl scene in *Portrait*. His contribution was that, for the first time, the characteristics of the Romantic moment of revelation were distinguished from modernist epiphany's "suddenness," its spiritual and "fleeting" nature, and the trivial matter that prompts it (what Beja calls the criteria of "incongruity" and "insignificance"). For Beja, epiphanies "are produced much less frequently by concrete objects than by events, people, snatches of talk, gestures, dreams, phases of the mind" (81), and he refuses Kenner's emphasis that the *object* epiphanizes, in favor of the perceiver. That said, Beja's use of *epiphany* is not extended indefinitely: he rejects its use as a term for extended narratives, because such a use would not fit the "suddenness" of Joyce's definition (74). Sudden revelation is critical for Beja, and he examines how other modernists (Woolf, Thomas Wolfe, William Faulkner) and postmodernists (Samuel Beckett, Lawrence Durrell, Alain Robbe-Grillet) have developed forms of epiphany (both as sketches and revelations) in their own writings.[33]

Beja's thesis went on to influence M. H. Abrams's account of Romantic revelation, *Natural Supernaturalism*, also published in 1971. Expanding on Frye's history of the "point of epiphany," Abrams traces a particularly Christian history of such moments from Saint Augustine's *Confessions* through the writings of various Christian mystics and the more secular and empirical vision in Rousseau's *Reveries of a Solitary Walker*. Friedrich Wilhelm Joseph Schelling, Friedrich Hölderlin, Goethe, and Novalis all experience versions of what Abrams calls a "Moment," in which "an instant of consciousness, or else an ordinary object or event, suddenly blazes into revelation" (*Natural* 385). From them, it is imported into the works of English Romantics such as William Blake, William Wordsworth, and Percy Bysshe Shelley, later symbolists like Walter Pater, and from thence into "James Joyce . . . , who by deliberately transferring the theological term into a naturalistic aesthetic, affixed to the Moment what seems destined to become its standard name" (421). Abrams's extended history is extremely valuable, but he sees epiphany simply as "a principle of literary organization . . . precipitating the narrative resolution" (418)—that is, as a literary device—and doesn't explore its relationship with large-scale narratives or fragmentary prose-poems.

Through the combined force of Frye, Kermode, Langbaum, and Abrams, then, this historical interpretation of epiphany came to dominate the reception of the Joycean epiphany.[34] Epiphany was imported into Romantic criticism to facilitate the connection between forms of Romantic revelation and modernist revelation. The Romantic history of aesthetics from Immanuel Kant and Edmund Burke in the nineteenth century, which focused on the sublime, entered literature through Wordsworth, Samuel Taylor Coleridge, and other Romantics, modulated into the "religion of art" of the late nineteenth century, and emerged in modernism as a new secularized spiritual revelation.[35] Joyce's epiphany became the clearest expression of this reformulation of Romantic revelation, a moment distinct from theophany, conversion experiences, and mystical revelation (other ways of conceptualizing epiphany have included transformation, transcendence, ecstasy, and catharsis, but revelation gives epiphany the appropriate religious or "spiritual" flavor). The roots of Joyce's epiphany in Romanticism had been obscured because of Joyce's aversion to claiming his Romantic inheritance, and his use of neo-Thomist Aristotelianism as the aesthetic support of epiphany. But the theory of aesthetic perception in chapter 25 of *Stephen Hero*, and the description of epiphany as a "sudden spiritual manifestation" (*SH* 211), confirmed epiphany's connection to a legacy of Romantic revelation.[36] The idea that Joyce's epiphany was primarily a literary device within a narrative—and only secondarily a genre of prose sketch and the various material contained in such sketches—became dominant and spread beyond these Romantic critics into modern criticism generally (see, e.g., Harrison; Marcus).

Perhaps unsurprisingly, further debate over this extension of the term arose among Joyce scholars in the early 1970s. Continuing the disagreement between Scholes and Walzl, Sidney Feshbach sided with Walzl and supported the extension of Joyce's term away from the specifics of Joyce's meaning, into a literary concept referring to revelation. His main interest lay with Stephen's *theory* and the "epiphanization" of objects, and he was untroubled by broader applications of the term, supporting the idea of extending it to whole works, such that Joyce himself "constructed a fiction employing . . . the structure of epiphanization" (304). However, his intervention also returned focus to the prose sketches. He challenged Scholes's method for reconstructing the sequencing of the epiphanies and questioned whether any sequence could be confidently posited, or whether the verso numbering could tell us there were seventy-one epiphanies. He also challenged Scholes's idea that the epiphanies were "building blocks" for *Stephen Hero* and *Portrait* and criticized Scholes's "fundamentalist" approach to the use of the term (304–6). Scholes did not reply, unfortunately, but Beja did, agreeing with Feshbach's sense of the general significance of the epiphany, although he had reservations about the specifics ("Mau-Mauing").

By the end of the 1970s, then, there was a sense that the Joycean epiphany had been exhaustively considered. The Romantic understanding of epiphany was used to describe scenes of revelation in Joyce's fiction (*Portrait*'s bird-girl scene, Molly Bloom's monologue in *Ulysses*) and structural configurations (the episodes of "Wandering Rocks," the fragments of *Giacomo Joyce*). The remaining issue of debate involved the typology of epiphanies: was *epiphany* singular or plural, noun or verb, event or process? This was often expressed in the question of how to characterize the division between positive and negative epiphanies, "real" and "false" epiphanies, sincere and ironic ones. Frye mentioned a "demonic epiphany" (*Anatomy* 223), and Langbaum a "negative" epiphany ("Epiphanic" 340). Beja wrote of "the 'retrospective' epiphany" and "'the past recaptured'" (*Epiphany* 15), Feshbach of an "Epiphany" and "epiphany-process" (305), Thomas Zaniello of the "epiphanic moment" (286).[37] Zack Bowen distinguished between "revelations of truth or character" and revelations which are only true for "the consciousness which experiences them" ("Circe" 11). David Hayman talked of "lyrical (+) epiphanies" and "ironized (−) anti-epiphanies" ("Joycean" 141), and Kevin J. H. Dettmar distinguished between "epiphany" and "epiphony," the deflationary ending common to the *Dubliners* short stories and parts of *Portrait* (76–105). These were understandable attempts to negotiate between objective and subjective aspects of epiphany, yet they introduced conceptual divisions that were never part of Joyce's formulation.[38] And beyond this debate remained intractable questions about the prose sketches. Scholars were uncertain how many epiphanies there were, whether there were epiphanies hiding in Joyce's fictions, whether they were ever sequenced, and what their role was in Joyce's compositional procedures.

In the 1980s, Joyce scholars moved on to new areas of investigation, and interest in the epiphany waned. For example, a wave of feminist-inspired Joycean criticism developed powerful new readings of Stephen's theory and its relationship to Joyce's aesthetics, but touched on epiphany only in passing; writers in this camp include Bonnie Kime Scott, Suzette Henke, Christine van Boheemen, Kimberly J. Devlin, Marilyn French, Christine Froula, Jeri Johnson, and Margot Norris. Developments in the epiphanies were limited to a series of interventions made by Bowen, Langbaum, Beja, and Ashton Nichols.[39] In the 1981–82 essay "Joyce and the Epiphany-Concept," Bowen queried whether artists and ordinary people have different experiences of epiphany and whether epiphanies are always reliably true (106; see also Bowen, "Circe," "Epiphanies"). Langbaum's 1983 essay "The Epiphanic Mode in Wordsworth and Modern Literature" addressed the Joycean epiphany more directly than his 1957 study had done. However, his exploration of "the *structure* of epiphany" and the way different kinds of epiphany are created in the reader is ultimately more pertinent to Wordsworth than to Joyce and promotes a number of confusions, such as associating epiphany with *epicleti*, a word Joyce uses in relation to *Dubliners* ("Epiphanic" 336, original emphasis; see Steppe; MacDuff, *Panepiphanal World* 76, 244n2). Beja's 1984 essay "Epiphany and the Epiphanies" reiterated his position regarding the use of the term while also attempting to return focus to the prose sketches. He provided an amended count of the use of epiphanies in *Stephen Hero*, *Portrait*, *Ulysses*, and *Finnegans Wake* and reviewed the adaptation of "Half-Men, Half-Goats," "Ibsen's Age," and "The Stars on Joyce's Nose."

Nichols's 1987 study *The Poetics of Epiphany* was the first book-length treatment of epiphany since Beja's *Epiphany in the Modern Novel* sixteen years earlier and addressed the relationship of the epiphany to Victorian and modernist poets. Joyce's epiphany is cited at the start, and Nichols acknowledges its dual significance as "the moment of revelation, in which an object (often a person) or an experience reveals itself" and "the verbal strategy by which numerous details in a poem or story are coalesced into a sudden disclosure of meaning" (10). Nichols raises Kenner's question of the "linguistic" epiphany: the idea that epiphany could be a configuration of language that would provoke a sudden realization of meaning in the reader. However, Nichols does not pursue this idea.[40] Rather, he creates a typology of epiphany, distinguishing modern literary epiphanies from theophanies, and "proleptic" (transforming the past) epiphanies from "adelonic" (present-focused). In this, he perpetuates the emphasis on epiphany as revelation, at the cost of Joyce's prose sketches.

Finally, in the midcentury period the French literary scene also received Joyce's epiphany and reflected the dominance of the theory of epiphany over the prose sketches.[41] Following the French translation of *Ulysses* in 1929, French literary critics began to engage seriously with Joyce's writing, but it was not until long after the translation of *Stephen Hero* in 1948 that they engaged with the question of epiphany. Their readings largely depended on applying the theory of epiphany in *Stephen Hero* across Joyce's texts, neglecting the prose sketches until Jacques Aubert published a French translation of them in 1982.[42] Before that, Hélène Cixous published her doctoral thesis on Joyce in 1968, translated four years later as *The Exile of James Joyce*, a volume that at times reads almost like a study on epiphany itself.[43] Jacques Lacan presented at the International James Joyce Symposium in Paris in 1975, commenting on the description of epiphany in *Stephen Hero* (149–65). Jacques Aubert supplemented William T. Noon's study of Joyce and Aquinas, writing a Lacanian- and Hegelian-inspired study of Joyce's aesthetics in 1973 (translated into English in 1992), which distinguished "epiphany as revelation" from "epiphany as verbal strategy" (*Aesthetics* 23). This was followed by a paper on Joyce's epiphanies in 1978 ("L'Épiphanie") and his translation of the epiphanies in 1982 (Joyce, *Épiphanies*).[44] And Catherine Millot considered epiphany from a Lacanian perspective in the late 1980s, likening Joyce's epiphanies to the burned-out cinders of illumination, a residue of the inexpressible Real ("Épiphanies"; "On Epiphanies"). Despite the variety and suggestiveness of these readings, the idea of epiphany as revelation remained the dominant understanding throughout the period of structuralist and poststructuralist criticism.

Epiphany in the Late Twentieth Century: The Rise of Genetic Criticism

New ways of understanding epiphany through the prose sketches opened up with the turn to genetic criticism in the 1970s. Scholes and Kain's *The Workshop of Daedalus* in 1965 was part of a wave of scholarship in the early 1960s from Fred H. Higginson (Joyce, *Anna*), A. Walton Litz, Thomas E. Connolly (*James Joyce's*), Clive Hart, David Hayman (Joyce, *First-Draft*), and others that focused on Joyce's manuscripts and compositional procedures. These studies accepted that epiphany represented a form of revelation and performed a functional element throughout his novels, regardless of whether a particular instance derived from the prose sketches. Litz largely avoided the term *epiphany* and instead drew on Richard Wagner's concept of the leitmotif and Ezra Pound's "doctrine of the 'Image,' an aesthetic concept which illuminates Joyce's mature methods," but in doing so, he rehearsed a number of ideas concerning epiphany's temporal and spatial character (53, and see 53–71). Hart suggested a comparable shift from epiphany to *leitmotiv*, claiming that "the best of the motifs in *Finnegans Wake* serve much the same type of function as do the epiphanies of the early books" (168). Michael Groden's 1977 volume *"Ulysses" in Progress* underscores the growing rearticulation of epiphany's place within the larger genetic corpus. Epiphanies are still moments of revelation (deriving from prose sketches or not), but they "now served as specific manifestations of the larger historical pattern" deriving from the "Homeric parallels" (36). Notwithstanding Beja's resistance to collapsing epiphany into images and leitmotifs, such terms allowed these scholars to develop a more accurate vocabulary to describe recurring structural features or climaxes in Joyce's writing, while gradually *restricting* the idea of epiphany to the original prose sketches.

In the late 1970s, Joycean critics began to turn to genetic criticism in greater numbers. Between 1977 and 1979, *The James Joyce Archive* was published by Garland. Volume 7 included a black-and-white facsimile of Joyce's holograph manuscripts at Buffalo, and of Stanislaus's copies at Cornell (*JJA* 7:1–69), along with a preface by Hans Walter Gabler (*JJA* 7:xxiii–xxvii). This allowed the manuscript sketches to reach a wider scholarly audience and permitted further genetic work to take place. Under the editorship of Claude Jacquet, numerous publications began to fill in the genetic landscape of Joyce's manuscripts, notesheets, typescripts, placards, proof pages, and other drafts and notes, leading to a boom in articles and publications, particularly on *Ulysses* and *Finnegans Wake* (see her *Genèse de Babel, Ge-*

nèse et metamorphoses, and *Scribble 1*; see also Jacquet and Topia, *Scribble 2*; Jacquet and Rabaté, *Scribble 3*). Within this, some genetic investigation of the sketches and their adaptations was undertaken: Jacquet worked on the use of epiphanies in *Portrait* ("James Joyce: Les 'Épiphanies'"; "James Joyce: Quelques"), and Jean C. Noel wrote on the Cornell 17 manuscript. But the sketches have otherwise not received the attention they deserve, probably because only four manuscripts and one typescript of the epiphanies survive (with relatively few variations between them), in contrast to the wealth of prepublication material available for the later chapters of *Ulysses* and the *Wake*.

Following his first article on the epiphanies in 1964 ("*Portrait*"), David Hayman commented on the prose sketches and their adaptations in a number of interventions over four decades (see, e.g., "Joycean"). His notes on the epiphanies were published with a Spanish translation of the sketches in 1996 (Joyce, *Epifanías*, trans. Galdámez). His most significant essay, "The Purpose and Permanence of the Joycean Epiphany," from 1998, explored the way that epiphanies had been fragmented through adaptation into *Stephen Hero*, *Portrait*, and the early episodes of *Ulysses*: "A mood, a pattern of sounds, a repetition or memorable image, a cluster of words—any or all of these can combine to recycle the epiphany within a fresh context" (645). Hayman was interested in the passages that suggested themselves as "lost" epiphanies, ones that could still be traced through their insertions into Joyce's manuscripts. He suggested that Joyce's impulse to write epiphanies persisted in his practice of jotting down notes from personal or overheard experience throughout his career, and invented the term *epiphanoid* to refer to such notes. Although he insisted that "there are relatively few epiphanoids in relation to the mass of notes" ("Epiphanoiding" 27), the notion of epiphanoids has not been taken up by genetic scholars, and Beja has disagreed about the utility of the term when discussing the notebooks for *Finnegans Wake* (see "James Joyce").

Through the early 2000s, genetic and textual critics such as Luca Crispi, Daniel Ferrer, Dirk Van Hulle, Mikio Fuse, Jed Deppman, Finn Fordham, and Vincent Deane have continued to reveal details of the genesis of Joyce's texts, and articles on epiphany that draw on genetic criticism have proliferated. In particular, Ilaria Natali has investigated the use of the prose sketches in *Stephen Hero* and *A Portrait of the Artist as a Young Man* (see, e.g., "Portrait"; "Questioning"; "This Diverting"). She offers an extended reading of how the sketches were adapted into these novels, characterizing Joyce's compositional procedures as subtraction ("decremento") and expansion ("incremento"), with amplifications and additions ("sia amplificazioni, sia aggiunte") (*Ur-Portrait* 44–45, 147–48). She also asserts that both the sketches and *Stephen Hero* comprise sources for the epiphanies in *Portrait* (48). However, Natali limits her analysis to ten or so representative epiphanies, rather than all forty. Other genetic work has explored further corners of Joyce's oeuvre. Michel Delville ("At the Center"; "Epiphanies") and John McCourt investigated the epiphanic form of *Giacomo Joyce*. Sam Slote explored how the "Proteus" manuscripts have been fused together, describing the epiphanic character of the early "Proteus" drafts ("Epiphanic"; "Protean"). And in 2017, Sangam MacDuff found a new typescript of nineteen epiphanies in the Jolas papers at Yale, which draws some long-held assumptions about the number, order, and status of the prose sketches into question ("Yale").

Epiphany in the Twenty-First Century

Through the twentieth century, Joyce's *epiphany* traveled out of academia to become a word of common parlance, deployed in everyday life to mean a eureka moment of realization or revelation. This contemporary usage derives from Joyce but is now so different from his use that few would connect it back to Joyce's epiphanies. This sense of epiphany is not quite the literary device identified in Joyce's writing by Spencer and other critics. Rather, it constitutes a modernization of traditional Aristotelian recognition (anagnorisis), which has been deployed throughout modern fiction to create moments of climax, where rational realization follows logically as the effect of a cause. Beja insists on the separation of classical recognition or anagnorisis from Joycean epiphany, where revelation is out of proportion to the trivial experience that inspires it, and is spiritual rather than rational (*Epiphany* 15–16). But in practice these two senses of epiphany as revelation are often conflated. *Dubliners* influenced subsequent fiction writers partly through its modernization and ironization of traditional climax, and the association of Joyce with epiphany encouraged the idea that the ambiguous climaxes of *Dubliners* could be called "epiphanies." The examples of Joyce (and of Anton Chekov, to a degree) were most prominently taken up by Ernest Hemingway in the 1920s and Raymond Carver in the 1960s and 1970s to exemplify the "epiphanic" short story, one that combines realistic Aristotelian recognition with the Joycean tradition of "ironized" spiritual epiphanies.[45] Epiphany in this sense is now a standard device in the craft of fiction and the "minimalist" short story (see Hallett; McGurl).

Meanwhile, novelists of the mid- and late twentieth century developed their own moments of revelation that seem to imply an aesthetic philosophy and can be referred to as epiphanies. Jean-Paul Sartre developed his idea of secular revelation with respect to phenomenology and an emergent existentialism in the 1938 novel *La Nausée (Nausea)*. Vladimir Nabokov's belated form of Russian modernism involves scenes of transcendent perception of transient phenomena, encapsulated by his notion of the "otherworld" (see Alexandrov 27–28).[46] Beja pursues the use of the epiphany into Nathalie Sarraute's *Tropismes* (Tropisms, 1939) and Alain Robbe-Grillet's *Instantanés* (Snapshots, 1962), reading them as preliminary sketches to the style of these authors' later novels. Beja also cites Beckett, Durrell, and John Barth as practitioners of epiphany (*Epiphany* 211–33). Arthur M. Saltzman has investigated epiphanies in Robert Coover, Gilbert Sorrentino, and others, and Paul Maltby has traced epiphanies through the writings of Flannery O'Connor, Jack Kerouac, Saul Bellow, Alice Walker, and Don DeLillo. Epiphany has taken its place as one literary device among many in modern Anglophone literature and beyond. Yet since there is no way of marking whether the term is being used as a general literary device or as Joyce's specific formulation, there is much scope for confusion.

Among scholars, by the 1980s at least, there was a feeling that Joyce's epiphany had been heavily worked over since it first came to attention in 1944 and was exhausted of possible interest or fresh interpretations. Even when the prose sketches were foregrounded, their genetic interest was slight compared to the corpus of manuscripts and notebooks for *Ulysses* and *Finnegans Wake*. As for any missing epiphanies, Scholes's warning about the dangers of "epiphany-hunting" had been well taken ("Joyce" 66). Joyce's epiphanies remained a popular topic for undergraduate essays and master's theses, but this also suggested that interest in the epiphanies was a juvenile infatuation that Joyce scholars were wise to move on from.

Nevertheless, many scholars have continued to explore Stephen Daedalus's aesthetic theory and the idea of epiphany as revelation, often with a greater acknowledgment of the prose sketches. In the past thirty years, four scholars have written full-length studies focused on Joyce's epiphanies and their presence in the novels. Vivian Heller's 1995 monograph *Joyce, Decadence, and Emancipation* surveyed moments of revelation across Joyce's texts and offered a complex typology of epiphanies ("In *Dubliners*, epiphany is analytical; in *Portrait*, it is relativistic; in *Ulysses*, it is structural" [8]) within an overarching dialectic of decadence and emancipation. Her interest was in how these moments related to the larger "symbolic structures" of the text (16), but she ignored the prose sketches and their insertion into Joyce's texts. Tomasz Gornat's 2006 study *"A Chemistry of Stars": Epiphany, Openness and Ambiguity in the Works of James Joyce* argued that Joyce's "epiphanic technique" led to the open-ended stories of *Dubliners* and provided the "operative structure" of *Portrait*, becoming increasingly open, comical, and equivocal in *Ulysses* (231). Angus McFadzean's *Epiphany and Transgression: From Aesthetics to Narrative in the Novels of James Joyce*, a doctoral thesis of 2012, read Joyce's adaptations of the epiphanies into his novels as instances of transgression rather than revelation. And in 2020, Sangam MacDuff published the first monograph solely on Joyce's epiphanies (*Panepiphanal World: James Joyce's Epiphanies*).

Most monographs published in the past thirty years have considered Joyce's epiphanies in relation to the epiphanies of other nineteenth- or twentieth-century writers. Martin Bidney's 1997 monograph *Patterns of Epiphany: From Wordsworth to Tolstoy, Pater, and Barrett Browning* explored the Romantic epiphany through Gaston Bachelard and phenomenology, though he stopped before Joyce. In 1999, Wim Tigges edited a collection of essays, *Moments of Moment: Aspects of the Literary Epiphany*, that featured an essay on epiphanies in *Portrait* by Christine van Boheemen-Saaf, articles covering Romantic and modernist writers, and articles on authors like Elizabeth Bowen, James Agee, Thomas Pynchon, and Seamus Heaney (see esp. Tigges's own essay, "The Significance of Trivial Things"). Monographs by Paul Maltby, Hugues Azérad, Birgit Neuhold, Gerald Gillespie, Sharon Kim, Tudor Balinisteanu, and Brian Gingrich (*Pace of Fiction*) have continued a comparative or historical approach to epiphany, situating Joyce as one exemplary instance of a long-standing literary tradition.[47]

Although this work typically redeploys the established interpretation of epiphany as revelation, it also makes new connections that challenge our sense of epiphany's relationship to narrative, history, and philosophy. For example, Neuhold's study *Measuring the Sadness* reiterates the history of "European epiphany" constructed by Romantic critics (with special emphasis on Pater and Friedrich Nietzsche) in a comparative study of epiphanies in Joseph Conrad, Joyce, and Woolf. But she also analyses the prose sketches and their insertion into Joyce's texts, identifying an alternation of epiphanic scenes and diegetic summary in his narratives (178–84). This turn to narratology was subsequently pursued by Gingrich, who sees the Joycean epiphany as negating the usual "scene-and-summary pace" of nineteenth-century fiction and establishing a "paused" scene that expresses "the pace of epiphanic modernism" ("Pace" 373).

Furthermore, Kim's 2012 study *Literary Epiphany in the Novel, 1850–1950* incorporates Joyce into an alternate history of epiphany that is notably feminine and Protestant. Beginning with Susan Warner's 1850 novel *The Wide, Wide World* and continuing with George Eliot and Edith Wharton, among others, Kim suggests that "the adaptation of Puritan spiritual autobiography . . . led to modern epiphany" (27). This study offers the prospect of a history of literary epiphany that emphasizes other forms of revelation and different typologies, recontextualizing the emergence of Joyce's Catholic-derived epiphany and its exclusively masculine history. Kim's use of Martin Heidegger and Emmanuel Levinas also indicates a further trend in recent criticism, anticipated by Bidney's use of Georges Poulet and Gaston Bachelard: a phenomenological epiphany. Jūratė Levina's 2017 article "The Aesthetics of Phenomena" draws on Maurice Merleau-Ponty and Mikel Dufrenne to explore Joyce's "phenomenology of aesthetic experience," which positions epiphany "at the epicenter of this vision" (185). Stephen's experience of epiphany is essentially "a phenomenal appearance of a thing" (194), rather than the manifestation of a Kantian noumenon that lies behind appearance. Sara Crangle also positions Stephen's theory of epiphany as an attempt to know the otherwise unknowable Kantian noumenon (41–43). For her, Stephen follows Arthur Schopenhauer in his desire for certain knowledge, but this is tempered by his Levinasian acceptance of the uncertainty of the unknown in *Ulysses* (28–70). These studies indicate the possibility of exciting revisions to our sense of epiphany, its history, its aesthetics, and its place within extended narrative structures.

This avalanche of scholarship over the past four decades suggests that despite being over a hundred years old, Joyce's epiphanies and his concept of epiphany have lost none of their power to fascinate (see, e.g., Bazargan; Bénéjam; Ebury; Fordham; Gingrich, "Pace"; Hong; Kearney; Kurnick 158–66; MacDuff, "Death"; Mahaffey; McFadzean, "Aesthetic"; Norris; Sayeau 189–249). As long as *epiphany* remains a word describing an everyday experience of revelation, writers will represent such experiences in fiction, and in turn scholars will have recourse to the literary idea of epiphany and its origin in Stephen's theory and Joyce's prose sketches. Further work on the epiphanies can be expected from scholars interested in phenomenology, aesthetics, theology, narratology, genetic criticism, modernist studies, Romanticism, and many other fields of inquiry,[48] both in English studies and in other literary traditions. By the end of the twentieth century, the epiphanies had been translated into German (1968), French (1982), Italian (1982), Danish (1991), Greek (1994; see also Marangopoulos), and Spanish

(1996), and in the past decade there have been new French, Italian, Polish, and Portuguese translations. However, the epiphanies have not been published in English since 1991, so we are grateful to the James Joyce Estate for granting us permission to reprint them in this critical edition, which we hope will prove a valuable scholarly resource, stimulating new research into Joyce's epiphanies.

Notes

1 Gogarty complained that "to be an unwilling contributor to one of [Joyce's] 'Epiphanies' is irritating" (295).

2 In *Stephen Hero*, Daedalus reads Walter Skeat's *Etymological Dictionary* "by the hour" (*SH* 32).

3 Stanislaus claims responsibility for the final arrangement of poems in *Chamber Music* (*PSW* 8).

4 Ellmann and Scholes suggest 1900–1903 (*JJII* 83; *WD* 5); Litz proposes 1901/2 to 1904 (*PSW* 157).

5 Angus McFadzean argues that in addition to sharing formal similarities, the "fragment of colloquy" in *Stephen Hero* is linked to Joyce's epiphanies through a "discourse of transgression" (*Epiphany* 10ff.; and see "Aesthetic").

6 Joyce read about D'Annunzio in Arthur Symons's *The Symbolist Movement in Literature* (1900). C.P. Curran makes the connection between epiphany and D'Annunzio in *James Joyce Remembered* (9, 110). Many passages in *Il Fuoco* (published in translation as *The Flame of Life* in 1900) and *Le Vergini delle Rocce* (The Virgins of the Rocks, 1895) are reminiscent of Joyce's prose style in *Portrait*, particularly Stephen's moments of exultation (Curran, 53, 105–15). See also *MBK* 166–67; *WD* 269–79; Eco, "Joyce" 1968; Lucente; Ricca.

7 An earlier novel, *Il trionfo della morte* (1894, published in translation as *The Triumph of Death* in 1898), also includes references to the "Epiphany of Love" and "Epiphany of Death."

8 "It was become a habit with Marius—one of his modernisms—developed by his assistance at the Emperor's 'conversations with himself,' to keep a register of the movements of his own private thoughts and humours; not continuously indeed, yet sometimes for lengthy intervals, during which it was no idle self-indulgence, but a necessity of his intellectual life, to 'confess himself,' with an intimacy, seemingly rare among the ancients" (173). See also Moliterno; Perlis.

9 As well as transcribing and preserving them, Stanislaus played a role in several epiphanies, such as "The Big Dog," and Joyce seems to have regarded Stanislaus's Dublin diaries as material for his early fiction. Stanislaus's first diary, kept from 1901 to 1903, was "a journal of [James Joyce's] life with detailed conversations with him and between him and Irish men of letters, poets, etc., covering often 3 and 4 pages of close-written foolscap" (*DD* 25). Unfortunately, this diary was burned by Stanislaus; Joyce "said he was very sorry I burnt it, as it would have been of great use to him in writing his novel, and if it would have been of use, I am sorry too" (*DD* 104).

10 Ellmann suggests October 1902; Roy Foster suggests November. See Crowley 35n5.

11 Gogarty calls the epiphanies Joyce's "secret record" and says that "secrecy of any kind corrupts sincere relations," although Stanislaus recollects of his brother that "Jim always had a contempt for secrecy" (*MBK* 124).

12 It is possible that Russell had seen some of Joyce's epiphanies before Yeats. Joyce visited Russell in July–August 1902 and showed him his work, prompting Russell to write to Yeats: Joyce "writes amazingly well in prose though I believe he also writes verse" (qtd. in *WD* 166). It is unlikely these were prose essays or the abandoned "Silhouettes," suggesting that Joyce may have shown Russell a few epiphanies in summer 1902, before passing on a more extended collection that December.

13 Hans Walter Gabler suggests there must have been "originals and copies retained by Stanislaus and James Joyce themselves" (*JJA* 7:xxiv).

14 After the magazine *Dana* rejected Joyce's "Portrait" sketch (circa March 1904), he decided to elaborate it into a novel (*DD* 25).

15 The compositional arc of Joyce's epiphanies bears comparison with that of *Chamber Music*: "By late 1902 Joyce has a substantial collection of poems in hand"; he "continued to write and revise poems through the emotionally charged years 1903–1904," but "after the autumn of 1904 Joyce was concerned only with the arrangement of the volume" (*PSW* 248).

16 If Joyce reused this epiphany in "Grace," it would be the only attributable epiphany in *Dubliners*. Tom Kernan also appears in "Hades," "Wandering Rocks," and "Sirens."

17 David Hayman proposes several "lost epiphanies" ("Purpose" 647). See also Heller; McFadzean, *Epiphany*.

18 The other references are obscure. Joyce's eldest sister was called Margaret Alice (or "Poppie" by the family), and an Alice is mentioned in Bella Cohen's brothel in *Ulysses* (15.2980), but the links are tenuous. "Trained by Owner" is used twice in *Ulysses* (11.415, 15.3088), though not in connection with Mr. Casey. In *Stephen Hero*, Daedalus's Irish teacher is called Mr. Casey. Another Casey, probably based on the Fenian Joseph Casey, plays a significant role in the Christmas dinner scene in *Portrait*, which could plausibly include an epiphany. See Mamigonian and Turner 406; Simpson, "They Simply."

19 This shift raises an interesting question about the relationship between Joyce's epiphanies, which seem to have served as notes or sketches for his autobiographical fiction, and the extensive notes he took for his later works. David Hayman has proposed that hundreds of Joyce's notes for *Finnegans Wake* should be described as "epiphanoids" ("Epiphanoiding").

20 Budgen observed that there was "only one kind of critic" Joyce resented: "The kind that affects to believe that I am writing with my tongue in my cheek" (108).

21 *Stephen Hero* was translated into French (by Ludmila Savitsky, 1948), Spanish (Roberto Bixio, 1960), and German (Klaus Reichert, 1968) before the epiphanies themselves were translated.

22 Also in 1946, Luigi Berti presented the theory of the epiphany in Italian (Joyce, "La teoria"). See also Prescott.

23 However, the authenticity of this diary as a day-to-day account of the period has been questioned by Laura Pelaschiar ("Of Brother"; "Stanislaus").

24 Some of Stanislaus's expressions echoed Gogarty's account, suggesting that he might have been implicitly responding to it.

25 Other critics writing on the epiphanies in the 1950s include William York Tindall, Dorothy Van Ghent, Geddes MacGregor (who compares the Joycean epiphany to the Crocean "moment of expression"), and Shiv K. Kumar.

26 Kenner's idea of a linguistic epiphany has been alluded to more often than investigated. For example, Robert Scholes referred to a Joyce-inspired "structuralist epiphany" in his 1974 *Structuralism in Literature* (192), and J. Hillis Miller addressed the "linguistic moment" in his 1985 collection of essays, exploring how moments of revelation in Romantic and modernist poetry trouble language (xiv). For a sustained reading of Joyce's epiphanies as linguistic events, see MacDuff, *Panepiphanal World*.

27 Other critics who connect the epiphany to aesthetics in this period include William York Tindall (*Reader's* 11), Maurice Beebe, and S. L. Goldberg (*Classical* 41–64, 78, 214–15, 269–70). See also Goldberg, *Joyce* 8–11; Connolly, "Joyce's."

28 Ellmann would make no reference to Joyce's epiphanies in his later volumes *Ulysses on the Liffey* and *The Consciousness of Joyce*.

29 Kain's 1976 article "Epiphanies of Dublin" grounds its reading of *Portrait* in Joyce's insertion of epiphanies into that text, particularly the various adaptations of "The Last Tram," but also looks at moments of specific and suggestive local detail.

30 Frank's essay was split over three issues of the *Sewanee Review* in 1945; a revised version was published in 1963, Frank's "Answer to Critics" in 1977, and his response to developments in theory and structuralism in 1978.

31 Frye concludes that "in *Finnegans Wake* the whole of history itself is presented as a single gigantic anti-epiphany" because the main theme of such an encyclopedic novel is "the comparison of such instants with the vast panorama unrolled by history" (61). Frye also wrote about *Finnegans Wake* and William Blake in his 1955 paper "Quest and Cycle in *Finnegans Wake*."

32 Writing in *The Sense of an Ending* a decade after *Romantic Image*, Kermode was critical of Joseph Frank's formulation of "spatial form" (*Sense* 176–80). Frank responded to Kermode in 1977 ("Spatial Form: An Answer to Critics"), and Kermode replied the following year ("A Reply to Joseph Frank"). Their dispute, about the boundaries between Kermode's "romantic image" and Frank's modernist "spatial form," touches on the relationship between modernist epiphanies and Romanticism. See also Frank, *Sense* 47; Beja, *Epiphany* 71–111.

33 Beja's argument finds a companion in Peter K. Garrett's 1969 study that treats Joyce's epiphany in the context of his use of symbolism and compares it to late nineteenth-century precursors, such as Henry James.

34 Abrams compares his approach to Kermode's *Romantic Image*, where "the premises of the modern movement" are traced back to the Romantics: "the concept of the self-sufficient image or symbol; the concept of the poem as an object which, insulated from the world and from ordinary human concerns, exists only for its own perfection; and the related concept of the alienated and anguished artist whose

priestly vocation entails the renunciation of this life and of this contemptible world in favor of that other world which is the work of his art" (Abrams, *Natural* 427). Abrams also includes epiphany as an entry in his *A Glossary of Literary Terms*, indicating its acceptance as a literary device, a "description . . . of the sudden flare into revelation of an ordinary object or scene" (81).

35 This reading of epiphany as revelation continued among American Romanticists. See, for example, Bloom 10, 158, 172; see also Weiskel.

36 Despite Joyce's emphasis on Aristotle and Aquinas, Scholes and Marlena G. Corcoran described Stephen's aesthetic as "German to the core, deriving from the tradition that includes . . . Kant, Schelling, and Hegel" (692–93).

37 Zaniello's "The Epiphany and the Object-Image Distinction" suggests that Joyce revised the ideas of epiphany after reading Benedetto Croce's *Estetica* in 1913, during the final stages of writing *Portrait* (286).

38 Other critics who commented on the epiphany in this period include Marilyn French and C. H. Peake.

39 In passing, we can note critics considering the links between Joyce's epiphanies and Walter Pater: see Scotto; Perlis; Iser. Jay Brian Losey completed a doctoral thesis, "Modern Epiphany from Wordsworth to Joyce," in 1986, publishing two articles on Pater and epiphany.

40 C. G. Săndulescu traced a shift from visual epiphanies to "linguistic epiphanized entities" in a 1968 article in Romanian.

41 For the epiphany's early reception in Germany, see Bohrer; Höllerer; Müller; Neuhold; Weninger; Ziolkowski.

42 Interestingly the term *epiphany* already had currency among French avant-garde writers. The French poet Henri Pichette took the word as the title of a theatrical performance at the Théâtre des Noctambules in December 1947, subsequently published as the volume *Les Epiphanies* in 1948.

43 Cixous also wrote about the "Apologise" epiphany in the 1987 article "Reaching the Point of Wheat."

44 In 2003, Aubert sketched out a possible history of epiphany, in which Joyce initially used epiphany as a form of Romantic inspiration and later reinterpreted it as a textually based "play of letters": epiphany "was [Joyce's] central invention: it was, at one and the same time, a *name* of his own creation, and *the act itself of naming*, a specific type of enunciation, equivalents of which are only to be found in theology" ("Joyce's" 21, original emphasis).

45 According to Günter Leypoldt, Carver "allows the 'sudden illumination' to converge with rational recognition. . . . The Wordsworthian 'moment' . . . slides into a more positivist sense of revelation—where one also suddenly understands the mechanics of a complex external world" (533). Leypoldt built up a typology of Carver's epiphanies—arrested epiphany, ironized epiphany, comic epiphany—while acknowledging Carver's versatile approach.

46 Nabokov refers to "what present-day critics would call an epiphany" in a lecture on Proust delivered between 1941 and 1958 and reproduced in his *Lectures on Literature* (222).

47 A number of articles from the 1990s and 2000s also take a comparative approach to epiphany, especially Jacobs; McGowan; Weir, "Epiphanoumenon."

48 For example, Sophie Grace Chappell, writing in 2022, ascribes the invention of the contemporary usage of epiphany to Joyce and develops her own moral philosophy of it as a realization of value, drawing on Bernard Williams and phenomenology. See also Gumbrecht 91–132.

Table of Epiphanies

Page	Epiphany	Commentary	WD no.	Stephen Hero	Portrait	Ulysses	Finnegans Wake
57	Apologise	99	1		1.29–40		317.26–30
58	Forty Thousand Pounds	102	4				
59	There's Nothing like Marriage	104	9	251			
60	The Priest That Writes Poetry	106	10				
61	Ibsen's Age	107	11	45–46			
62	Your Favourite Poet	110	12	43			
63	It's a Terrible Life	112	13				
64	Order, Order!	114	14	44–45			
65	The Lame Beggar	116	15	244–45		10.239–56	15.29–16.09
66	An Arctic Beast	118	16	33–34		3.300–309	17.26–28
67	The Day of the Rabblement	121	17				
68	The Stars on Joyce's Nose	124	18			9.939–44, 17.1256–58	
69	The Hole in Georgie's Stomach	126	19	162–63			323.05–6
70	Two Mourners	129	21	167		6.517–20	
71	I Was Sorry	131	22	169			
72	The Race	133	32			2.307–12, 15.3964–85	

Page	Epiphany	Commentary	WD no.	Stephen Hero	Portrait	Ulysses	Finnegans Wake
73	She Comes at Night	136	34			1.102–5, 1.270–79, 2.139–47, 15.4191–204	193.32–194.22, 548.10–12
74	Fred Leslie's My Brother	142	35			15.4795–97	8.16–10.21
75	The Two Sisters	144	36				
76	I Lie along the Deck	146	37				
77	Is Mabie Your Sweetheart?	147	38		2.595–945	13.64–74	233.21–26
78	The Lesson That She Reads	150	39			13.107–27	
79	Is That for Gogarty?	153	40			5.472–518, 10.314–23	
80	The Spell of Arms and Voices	157	30	237	5.2778–84	3.503–5	
81	Her Arm on My Knees	160	24		4.183–88		
82	The Big Dog	162	8	38			
83	Hoofs upon the Dublin Road	164	27		5.2728–36		
84	The Last Tram	167	3	67–68	2.303–56		
85	She Dances with Them in the Round	172	26		5.1613–27		
86	Poor Little Fellow!	174	20	165			
87	Holy Queen, Mother of Mercy	176	7				
88	A Story of Alsace	178	2				
89	His Dancing	180	23				
90	They Pass in Twos and Threes	182	33			3.209–15, 7.720–24	

Page	Epiphany	Commentary	WD no.	Stephen Hero	Portrait	Ulysses	Finnegans Wake
91	Upon Me from the Darkness	185	31		2.1392–413		
92	Is That Mary Ellen?	187	5		2.275–302	3.70–75, 17.139–41	
93	Images of Fabulous Kings	191	29		5.2674–83	2.155–72	
94	The Ship	193	28		1.695–715	3.503–5	
95	Half-Men, Half-Goats	195	6		3.1216–83		352.37–353.05
96	The Girls, the Boys	199	25	74, 183–84	5.1485–522		

EPIPHANIES

[Apologise]

[Bray: in the parlour of the house
in Martello Terrace]

Mr Vance — (*comes in with a stick*) . . . O, you know,
He'll have to apologise, Mrs Joyce.

Mrs Joyce — O yes . . . Do you hear that, Jim?

Mr Vance — Or else—if he doesn't—the eagles'll
come and pull out his eyes.

Mrs Joyce — O, but I'm sure he will apologise.

Joyce — (*under the table, to himself*)

— Pull out his eyes,
Apologise,
Apologise,
Pull out his eyes.

Apologise,
Pull out his eyes,
Pull out his eyes,
Apologise.

Notes and commentary on page 99

[Forty Thousand Pounds]

[Dublin: on Mountjoy Square]

Joyce   — (*concludes*) . . . . That'll be forty thousand pounds.

Aunt Lillie — (*titters*) — O, laus! . . . . I was like that too . . . . . .
    . . . When I was a girl I was *sure* I'd marry a
    lord . . . or something . . .

Joyce   — (*thinks*) — Is it possible she's comparing
    herself with me?

Notes and commentary on page 102

[There's Nothing like Marriage]

[Mullingar: a Sunday in July:
noon]

Tobin — (walking noisily with thick boots and
tapping the road with his stick) . . . . O
there's nothing like marriage for
making a fellow steady. Before I came
here to the *Examiner* I used knock about
with fellows and boose . . . . Now I've a
good house and . . . . . I go home in the
evening and if I want a drink . . . . . .
well, I can have it . . . . My advice to
every young fellow that can afford it
is: marry young.

Notes and commentary on page 104

[The Priest That Writes Poetry]

[Dublin: in the Stag's Head,
Dame Lane]

O'Mahony — Haven't you that little priest that
writes poetry over there — Fr Russell?

Joyce — O, yes . . . I hear he has written verses.

O'Mahony — (*smiling adroitly*) . . . Verses, yes . . . that's
the proper name for them . . . .

Notes and commentary on page 106

[Ibsen's Age]

[Dublin: at Sheehy's, Belvedere Place]

Joyce — I knew you meant him. But you're wrong
     about his age.

Maggie Sheehy — (*leans forward to speak seriously*) Why,
   how old is he?

Joyce — Seventy-two.

Maggie Sheehy — Is he?

Notes and commentary on page 107

[Your Favourite Poet]

                          [Dublin: at Sheehy's, Belvedere
                          Place]
O'Reilly   —   (with developing seriousness) . . . . Now
                        It's my turn, I suppose . . . . . (quite
                        seriously) . . . . Who is your favourite
                        poet?
                              (a pause)
Hanna Sheehy — . . . . German?
   O'Reilly   — . . . . . . Yes.
                              (a hush)
Hanna Sheehy — . . I think . . . . . Goethe . . . . .

Notes and commentary on page 110

[It's a Terrible Life]

[Dublin: at Sheehy's, Belvedere
Place]

Fallon — (*as he passes*) — I was told to congratulate
you especially on your performance.

Joyce — Thank you.

Blake — (*after a pause*) . . I'd never advise anyone
to . . . O, it's a terrible life! . . . .

Joyce — Ha.

Blake — (*between puffs of smoke*) — Of course . . . it
looks all right from the outside . . . to
those who don't know . . . . But if
you knew . . . . it's really terrible. A
bit of a candle, no . . . dinner, squalid
. . . . poverty. You've no idea simply . . . .

Notes and commentary on page 112

[Order, Order!]

[Dublin: at Sheehy's, Belvedere
Place]

Dick Sheehy — What's a lie? Mr Speaker, I must ask.
Mr Sheehy   — Order, order!
Fallon   — You know it's a lie!
Mr Sheehy   — You must withdraw, sir.
Dick Sheehy — As I was saying . . . .
Fallon   — No, I won't.
Mr Sheehy   — I call on the honourable member
                for Denbigh . . . . Order, order! . . .

Notes and commentary on page 114

[The Lame Beggar]

[In Mullingar: an evening
in autumn]

The Lame Beggar — (*gripping his stick*) . . . . . It was
you called out after me yesterday.

The Two Children — (*gazing at him*) . . . No, sir.

The Lame Beggar — O, yes it was, though . . . . (*moving
his stick up and down*) . . . . But
mind what I'm telling you . . . .
D'ye see that stick?

The Two Children — Yes, sir.

The Lame Beggar — Well, if ye call out after me
any more I'll cut ye open with
that stick. I'll cut the livers
out o' ye . . . . (*explains himself*)
. . . D'ye hear me? I'll cut ye
open. I'll cut the livers and
the lights out o' ye.

Notes and commentary on page 116

[An Arctic Beast]

A white mist is falling in slow flakes. The
path leads me down to an obscure pool.
Something is moving in the pool; it is an
arctic beast with a rough yellow coat. I
thrust in my stick and as he rises out of
the water I see that his back slopes towards
the croup and that he is very sluggish. I
am not afraid but, thrusting at him often
with my stick drive him before me. He
moves his paws heavily and mutters words
of some language which I do not understand.

Notes and commentary on page 118

[The Day of the Rabblement]

[Dublin: at Sheehy's, Belvedere
Place]

Hanna Sheehy — O, there are sure to be great crowds.
  Skeffington   — In fact it'll be, as our friend
                Jocax would say, the day of the
                rabblement.
Maggie Sheehy — (*declaims*) — Even now the
                rabblement may be standing
                by the door!

Notes and commentary on page 121

[The Stars on Joyce's Nose]

[Dublin, on the North Circular
Road: Christmas]

Miss O'Callaghan — (*lisps*) — I told you the name,
The Escaped Nun.

Dick Sheehy — (*loudly*) — O, I wouldn't read
a book like that . . . I must
ask Joyce. I say, Joyce, did
you ever read *The Escaped
Nun?*

Joyce — I observe that a certain
phenomenon happens about
this hour.

Dick Sheehy — What phenomenon?

Joyce — O . . . the stars come out.

Dick Sheehy — (*to Miss O'Callaghan*) . . Did you
ever observe how . . . the
stars come out on the end
of Joyce's nose about this
hour? . . . (*she smiles*) . . Because
I observe that phenomenon

Notes and commentary on page 124

[The Hole in Georgie's Stomach]

[Dublin: in the house in
Glengariff Parade: evening]

Mrs Joyce — (*crimson, trembling, appears at the
parlour door*) . . . Jim!

Joyce — (*at the piano*) . . . Yes?

Mrs Joyce — Do you know anything about the
body? . . What ought I do? . . . There's
some matter coming away from
the hole in Georgie's stomach . . . .
Did you ever hear of that happening?

Joyce — (*surprised*) . . . I don't know . . . .

Mrs Joyce — Ought I send for the doctor, do you
think?

Joyce — I don't know . . . . . . What hole?

Mrs Joyce — (*impatient*) . . . The hole we all have
. . . . . here (*points*)

Joyce — (*stands up*)

Notes and commentary on page 126

[Two Mourners]

Two mourners push on through the crowd. The
girl, one hand catching the woman's skirt,
runs in advance. The girl's face is the face
of a fish, discoloured and oblique-eyed; the
woman's face is small and square, the face
of a bargainer. The girl, her mouth distorted,
looks up at the woman to see if it is time
to cry; the woman, settling a flat bonnet,
hurries on towards the mortuary chapel.

Notes and commentary on page 129

[I Was Sorry]

[Dublin: in the National Library]

Skeffington — I was sorry to hear of the death of
     your brother . . . . sorry we didn't
     know in time . . . . . to have been at
     the funeral . . . . .
 Joyce — O, he was very young . . . . a boy . . . .
Skeffington — Still . . . . . it hurts . . . .

Notes and commentary on page 131

[The Race]

The human crowd swarms in the enclosure,
moving through the slush. A fat woman passes,
her dress lifted boldly, her face nozzling in
an orange. A pale young man with a Cockney
accent does tricks in his shirtsleeves and
drinks out of a bottle. A little old man has
mice on an umbrella; a policeman in
heavy boots charges down and seizes the
umbrella: the little old man disappears.
Bookies are bawling out names and prices;
one of them screams with the voice of a
child — "Bonny Boy!" "Bonny Boy!" . . . Human
creatures are swarming in the enclosure,
moving backwards and forwards through
the thick ooze. Some ask if the race is going
on; they are answered "Yes" and "No." A
band begins to play . . . . . . A beautiful brown
horse, with a yellow rider upon him, flashes
far away in the sunlight.

Notes and commentary on page 133

[She Comes at Night]

She comes at night when the city is still;
invisible, inaudible, all unsummoned. She
comes from her ancient seat to visit the
least of her children, mother most venerable,
as though he had never been alien to her.
She knows the inmost heart; therefore
she is gentle, nothing exacting; saying,
I am susceptible of change, an imaginative
influence in the hearts of my children.
Who has pity for you when you are sad
among the strangers? Years and years I
loved you when you lay in my womb.

Notes and commentary on page 136

[Fred Leslie's My Brother]

[London: in a house at
Kennington]
Eva Leslie —Yes, Maudie Leslie's my sister an'
Fred Leslie's my brother — yev
'eard of Fred Leslie? . . . (*musing*) . . .
O, 'e's a whoite-arsed bugger . . . 'E's
awoy at present . . . .
(*later*)
I told you someun went with me
ten toimes one noight . . . . That's
Fred — my own brother Fred . . . .
(*musing*) . . . 'E is 'andsome . . . O I
do love Fred . . . .

Notes and commentary on page 142

[The Two Sisters]

Yes, they are the two sisters. She who is
churning with stout arms (their butter is
famous) looks dark and unhappy: the
other is happy because she had her way.
Her name is R . . . . Rina. I know the verb
'to be' in their language.

       — Are you Rina? —

I knew she was.
But here he is himself in a coat with tails
and an old-fashioned high hat. He
ignores them: he walks along with tiny
steps, jutting out the tails of his coat . . . .
My goodness! how small he is! He must
be very old and vain . . . . . Maybe he isn't
what I . . . It's funny that those two big
women fell out over this little man . . . .
But then he's the greatest man in the
world . . . .

Notes and commentary on page 144

[I Lie along the Deck]

I lie along the deck, against the engine-house,
from which the smell of lukewarm grease
exhales. Gigantic mists are marching under
the French cliffs, enveloping the co[ast]
from headland to headland. The sea
moves with the sound of many scales . . . .
Beyond the misty walls, in the dark cathedral
church of Our Lady, I hear the bright,
even voices of boys singing before the
altar there.

Notes and commentary on page 146

[Is Mabie Your Sweetheart?]

[Dublin: at the corner of
Connaught St, Phibsborough]
The Little Male Child — (*at the garden gate*) . . Na . . o.
The First Young Lady — (*half kneeling, takes his
hand*) — Well, is Mabie
your sweetheart?
The Little Male Child — Na . . . o.
The Second Young Lady — (*bending over him, looks
up*) — *Who* is your
sweetheart?

Notes and commentary on page 147

[The Lesson That She Reads]

She stands, her book held lightly at her breast,
reading the lesson. Against the dark stuff
of her dress her face, mild-featured with
downcast eyes, rises softly outlined in light;
and from a folded cap, set carelessly forward,
a tassel falls along her brown ringletted
hair . . .
       What is the lesson that she reads — of apes,
of strange inventions, or the legends of
martyrs? Who knows how deeply meditative,
how reminiscent is this comeliness of
Raffaello?

Notes and commentary on page 150

[Is That for Gogarty?]

in O'Connell St:
[Dublin : ∧in Hamilton, Long's,
the chemist's,]

Gogarty — Is that for Gogarty?

The Assistant — (<u>looks</u>) — Yes, sir . . . Will you ~~take~~ ∧pay∧
~~it with you?~~ for it now?

Gogarty — No, ~~send it~~ put it in the
account; send it on. You know
the address.
(<u>takes a pen</u>)

The Assistant — ~~Yes.~~ Ye . . es.

Gogarty — 5 Rutland Square.

While

The Assistant — (<u>half to himself ~~as~~ he writes</u>)
. . 5 . . . <u>Rutland</u> . . . Square.

Notes and commentary on page 153

[The Spell of Arms and Voices]

The spell of arms and voices — the white arms
of roads, their promise of close embraces, and the
black arms of tall ships that stand against
the moon, their tale of distant nations. They
are held out to say: We are alone, — come. And
the voices say with them, We are your people.
And the air is thick with their company as they
call to me their kinsman, making ready to go,
shaking the wings of their exultant and terrible
youth.

Notes and commentary on page 157

[Her Arm on My Knees]

Her arm is laid for a moment on my knees
and then withdrawn and her eyes have revealed
her — secret, vigilant, an enclosed garden — in
a moment. I remember a harmony of red and
white that was made for one like her, telling her
names and glories, bidding her arise, as for
espousal, and come away, bidding her look
forth, a spouse, from Amana and from the
mountains of the leopards. And I remember
that response whereto the perfect tenderness
of the body and the soul with all its mystery
have gone: Inter ubera mea commorabitur.

Notes and commentary on page 160

[The Big Dog]

       Dull clouds have covered the sky. Where
three roads meet and before a swampy beach
a big dog is recumbent. From time to time he
lifts his muzzle in the air and utters a prolonged
sorrowful howl. People stop to look at him and
pass on; some remain, arrested, it may be, by
that lamentation in which they seem to hear
the utterance of their own sorrow that had once
its voice but is now voice less, a servant of
laborious days. Rain begins to fall.

Notes and commentary on page 162

[Hoofs upon the Dublin Road]

Faintly, under the heavy summer night,
through the silence of the town which has turned
from dreams to dreamless sleep as a weary lover whom
no carresses move, the sound of hoofs upon
the Dublin road. Not so faintly now as they
come near the bridge; and in a moment as
they pass the dark windows the silence is cloven
by alarm as by an arrow. They are heard now
far away — hoofs that shine amid the heavy
night as diamonds, hurrying beyond the grey,
still marshes to what journey's end — what
heart — bearing what tidings?

Notes and commentary on page 164

[The Last Tram]

       The children who have stayed latest
are getting on their things to go home for
the party is over. This is the last tram. The
lank brown horses know it and shake
their bells to the clear night, in admonition.
The conductor talks with the driver; both
nod often in the green light of the lamp.
^There is nobody near.^
We seem to listen, I on the upper step and
she on the lower. She comes up to my step
many times and goes down again, between
our phrases, and once or twice remains
beside me, forgetting to go down, and
then goes down . . . . . . Let be; let be . . . . . And
now she does not urge her vanities, — her fine
dress and sash and long black stockings,
for now (wisdom of children) we seem to
know that this end will please us better
than any end we have laboured for.

Notes and commentary on page 167

[She Dances with Them in the Round]

She is engaged. She dances with
them in the round — a white dress lightly
lifted as she dances, a white spray in her
hair; eyes a little averted, a faint glow on
her cheek. Her hand is in mine for a moment,
softest of merchandise.

       — You very seldom come here now. —
       — Yes I am becoming something of a recluse. —
       — I saw your brother the other day . . . . . .
       He is very like you. —
       — Really? —

She dances with them in the round —
evenly, discreetly, giving herself to no one.
The white spray is ruffled as she dances,
and when she is in shadow the glow is
deeper on her cheek.

Notes and commentary on page 172

[Poor Little Fellow!]

They are all asleep. I will go up now . . . . . He
lies on my bed where I lay last night: they
have covered him with a sheet and closed
his eyes with pennies . . . . . Poor little fellow!
We have often laughed together — he bore his
body very lightly . . . . I am very sorry he died.
I cannot pray for him as the others do . . . . .
Poor little fellow! Everything else is so uncertain!

Notes and commentary on page 174

[Holy Queen, Mother of Mercy]

It is time to go away now — breakfast is
ready. I'll say another prayer . . . . . I am hungry;
yet I would like to stay here in this quiet
chapel where the mass has come and gone
so quietly . . . . . Hail, holy Queen, Mother of
Mercy, our life, our sweetness and our hope!
Tomorrow and every day after I hope I shall
bring you some virtue as an offering for I
know you will be pleased with me if I do. Now,
goodbye for the present . . . . . O, the beautiful
sunlight in the avenue and O, the sunlight
in my heart!

Notes and commentary on page 176

[A Story of Alsace]

No school tomorrow: it is Saturday night
in winter: I sit by the fire. Soon they will
be returning with provisions, meat and vegetables,
tea and bread and butter, and
white pudding that makes a noise on the
pan . . . . I sit reading a story of Alsace, turning
over the yellow pages, watching the men
and women in their strange dresses. It pleases
me to read of their ways; through them I seem
to touch the life of a land beyond them to enter
into communion with the German people.
Dearest illusion, friend of my youth! . . . . In him
I have imaged myself. Our lives are still sacred
in their intimate sympathies. I am with him
at night when he reads the books of the philosophers
or some tale of ancient times. I am with him
when he wanders alone or with one whom he has
never seen, that young girl who puts around
him arms that have no malice in them, offering
her simple, abundant love, hearing and answering
his soul he knows not how.

Notes and commentary on page 178

[His Dancing]

That is no dancing. Go down before the
people, young boy, and dance for them . . . . He
runs out darkly-clad, lithe and serious to
dance before the multitude. There is no music
for him. He begins to dance far below in the
amphitheatre with a slow and supple movement
of the limbs, passing from movement
to movement, in all the grace of youth and
distance, until he seems to be a whirling
body, a Spider wheeling amid space, a
star. I desire to shout to him words of praise,
to shout arrogantly over the heads of the
multitude "See! See!" . . . . . His dancing is not the
dancing of harlots, the dance of the daughters
of Herodias. It goes up from the midst of the
people, sudden and young and male, and
falls again to earth in tremulous sobbing to
die upon its triumph.

Notes and commentary on page 180

[They Pass in Twos and Threes]

They pass in twos and threes amid the life
of the boulevard, walking like people who have
leisure in a place lit up for them. They are in
the pastry cook's, chattering, crushing little
fabrics of pastry, or seated silently at tables
by the café door, or descending from carriages
with a busy stir of garments soft as the voice
of the adulterer. They pass in an air of
perfumes: under the perfumes their bodies
have a warm humid smell . . . . . No man
has loved them and they have not loved
themselves: they have given nothing for all
that has been given them.

Notes and commentary on page 182

[Upon Me from the Darkness]

Here are we come together, wayfarers; here are
we housed, amid intricate streets, by night and silence
closely covered. In amity we rest together, well content,
no more remembering the deviousness of the ways that
we have come. What moves upon me from the darkness
subtle and murmurous as a flood, passionate
and fierce with an indecent movement of the loins?
What leaps, crying in answer, out of me, as eagle to eagle
in mid air, crying to overcome, crying for an iniquitous
abandonment?

Notes and commentary on page 185

[Is That Mary Ellen?]

High up in the old, dark-windowed house: firelight
in the narrow room: dusk outside. An old woman
bustles about, making tea; she tells of the changes, her
odd ways, and what the priest and the doctor said . . . . .
I hear her words in the distance. I wander among the
coals, among the ways of adventure . . . . . . Christ! What
is in the doorway? . . . . . A skull — a monkey; a creature
drawn hither to the fire, to the voices: a silly creature.

    — Is that Mary Ellen? —

    — No, Eliza, it's Jim —

    — O . . . . . . O, goodnight, Jim —

    — D'ye want anything, Eliza? —

    — I thought it was Mary Ellen . . . . . I thought you
were Mary Ellen, Jim —

Notes and commentary on page 187

[Images of Fabulous Kings]

A long curving gallery: from the floor arise pillars
of dark vapours. It is peopled by the images of fabulous kings,
set in stone. Their hands are folded upon their knees, in token
of weariness, and their eyes are darkened for the errors of men
go up before them for ever as dark vapours.

Notes and commentary on page 191

[The Ship]

A moonless night under which the waves gleam feebly. The ship is entering a harbour where there are some lights. The sea is uneasy, charged with dull anger like the eyes of an animal which is about to spring, the prey of its own pitiless hunger. The land is flat and thinly wooded. Many people are gathered on the shore to see what ship it is that is entering their harbour.

Notes and commentary on page 193

[Half-Men, Half-Goats]

A small field of stiff weeds and thistles alive with confused
forms, half-men, half-goats. Dragging their great
tails they move hither and thither, aggressively. Their
faces are lightly bearded, pointed and grey as india-rubber.
A secret personal sin directs them, holding them
now, as in reaction, to constant malevolence. One is clasping
about his body a torn flannel jacket; another complains
monotonously as his beard catches in the stiff
weeds. They move about me, enclosing me, that old sin
sharpening their eyes to cruelty, swishing through the
fields in slow circles, thrusting upwards their terrific
faces. Help!

Notes and commentary on page 195

[The Girls, the Boys]

The quick light shower is over but tarries, a cluster of diamonds, among the shrubs of the quadrangle where an exhalation arises from the black earth. In the colonnade are the girls, an April company. They are leaving shelter, with many a doubting glance, with the prattle of trim boots and the pretty rescue of petticoats, under umbrellas, a light armoury, upheld at cunning angles. They are returning to the convent — demure corridors and simple dormitories, a white rosary of hours — having heard the fair promises of Spring, that well-graced ambassador . . . .

Amid a flat rain-swept country stands a high plain building, with windows that filter the obscure daylight. Three hundred boys, noisy and hungry, sit at long tables eating beef fringed with green fat and vegetables that are still rank of the earth.

Notes and commentary on page 199

NOTES AND COMMENTARY

[Apologise]

The Joyces lived at 1 Martello Terrace in Bray, a popular seaside resort about twenty kilometers (twelve miles) south of Dublin, from May 1887 until January or February 1892, when Joyce was between five and ten. The Vances, who occupied 4 Martello Terrace, were family friends: James Vance and John Joyce sang come-all-ye's together, and "the two fathers often spoke half-seriously of uniting" their eldest children, James and Eileen (*JJII* 26). However, May Joyce was a devout Catholic, while the Vances were Protestant: sectarian tensions underlie the epiphany. Mr. Vance's faith is evident in his biblical threats, alluding to Proverbs 30:17 ("The eye that mocketh at his father, and that despiseth the labour of his mother in bearing him, let the ravens of the brooks pick it out, and the young eagles eat it" [KJV]) via Isaac Watts's *Divine and Moral Songs for Children* (1715):

> What heavy guilt upon him lies!
>   How cursed is his
> name! The ravens
> shall pick out his eyes,
> And eagles eat the
> same.
>   (Watts 46)

In the epiphany, Mr. Vance's "stick" continues the suggestion of physical punishment.

Echoes and Adaptations

A Portrait of the Artist as a Young Man

The epiphany is used in the opening scene of *A Portrait of the Artist as a Young Man*:

> When they were grown up he was going to marry Eileen.
>   [Stephen] hid under the table. His mother said:
> —O, Stephen will apologise.

Dante said:
—O, if not, the eagles will come and pull out his eyes.

Pull out his eyes,
Apologise,
Apologise,
Pull out his eyes.

Apologise,
Pull out his eyes,
Pull out his eyes,
Apologise.

(*P* 1.29–40)

Replacing Mr. Vance with Mrs. O'Riordan, a fervent Catholic whom the family called Dante, accentuates the sectarian tensions in the epiphany, shifting the threat of punishment from a Protestant outside the family to a Catholic within. Like Eileen Vance, the Eileen Stephen thinks of is Protestant (*P* 1.1000), and in the absence of any other explanation, the idea that they will marry becomes vaguely associated with the threat, although it could be a non sequitur. Joyce's substitution of Dante for Vance also affects the portrayal of gender and authority: the opening thirty lines move rapidly from Mr. Dedalus's storytelling to Mrs. Dedalus's insistence that Stephen apologize and Dante's threats of punishment, indicating a broader shift toward female figures of authority, while the switch from Vance to Dante indicates that the center of religious and political power in *Portrait* is not the patriarchal Anglo-Irish Ascendancy, but Mother Church and Mother Ireland. These hints of sexual attraction and religious tension give a background charge to the scene, but Stephen's transgression, if there is one, is never specified. The biblical threats are left hanging in the air, evoking a general atmosphere of fear and oppression, until Stephen transforms them into his chiastic verse, prophetically turning the threat of punishment into a miniature work of art.

The stage directions and punctuation of the epiphany indicate that Joyce says the lines to himself, but in the novel this is less clear. The final holograph manuscript and the serialized version published in the *Egoist* (February 2, 1914) preserve his original punctuation, with a dash after "Dante said . . . eyes——" (*JJA* 9:8–9, 7:293), confirming that she is not the speaker. Most published editions set the verse in italics, which leaves them floating freely, with no sign that they are spoken. However, Joyce's drafts have them in roman, like the epiphany, strengthening the possibility that Stephen says them to himself—an early example of interior monologue.

Finnegans Wake

Another fleeting reference to the epiphany appears in book 2, chapter 3, of *Finnegans Wake*:

> —A ninth for a ninth. Take my worth from it. And no mistaenk, they thricetold the taler [. . .]. Place the scaurs wore on your groot big bailey bill, he apullajibed, the O'Colonel Power . . .
>
> (*FW* 317.26–30)

In the first draft (1935), Joyce wrote "apullagibed" (*JJA* 54:21), which is closer to "apologised"; all subsequent versions, from the first typescript through to publication, print "apullajibed" (*JJA* 54:67, 111, 160, 202, 228, 265). Both *gibe* and *jibe* (variant spellings) suggest that the tailor is mocking HCE's humpback, while apologizing for the ill-fitting suit he has made; Joyce may have preferred *jibe* because the tailor is also a sailor (the Norwegian captain), suggesting that he pulls and jibes the cloth like a sail over HCE's back. A paragraph break and dash before "Place the scaurs" in the first and second typescripts (*JJA* 54:67, 111) make it clear that it is the tailor speaking and "apullajib[ing]," partly in response to "A ninth for a ninth" (*FW* 317.27), or an "eye for an eye" (Matthew 5:38). This allusion to the Sermon on the Mount recalls another verse: "if thy right eye offend thee, pluck it out" (Matthew 5:29), linking back to the original epiphany, which helps bring out the religious and political significance of the scene (alluding, among other things, to Daniel O'Connell, who campaigned for Catholic emancipation and the repeal of the Acts of Union that placed Ireland under British rule).

Source: Buffalo 1.A.1 (*JJA* 7:1–2). Marked with a cross in the upper left corner. Numbered 1 on the verso.

Variants: The Yale typescript has "Mr." and "Mrs."; also a line break after "Pull out his eyes" (line 10). The cross is copied in blue pencil or crayon (Yale GEN MSS 108 XV.64.1503.7).

[Forty Thousand Pounds]

Mountjoy Square, the setting for "Forty Thousand Pounds," is close to Belvedere College in North Central Dublin. The Joyces lived in the vicinity of Mountjoy Square from 1894 to 1898, when Joyce was a student at Belvedere.

Aunt Lillie Murray (born Elizabeth Harris) was married to Joyce's maternal uncle, John "Red" Murray. John Murray worked in the accounts department of the *Freeman's Journal*. According to Stanislaus Joyce, he was a "reformed drunkard and atheist" (*MBK* 234) who had occasional lapses. They married in 1891, after Lillie became pregnant with their first daughter. They lived on Drumcondra Road, north of Mountjoy Square. Aunt Lillie's marriage with him was unhappy, and Joyce's father often mocked them. Here, Aunt Lillie appears to be ruing her marriage and indirectly admitting its inadequacies. She does not appear in Joyce's work directly, but he drew on John and his brother William Murray to create the brothers Joe and Alphy in "Clay," and Murray appears as Red Murray in *Ulysses*.

The manuscript of this epiphany, like the other epiphanies at Buffalo, is an autograph fair copy, but unlike any of the others, "Forty Thousand Pounds" has a note or fragment penciled beneath the epiphany in Joyce's hand:

> *Kinahan*
> Civilising work of the Jesuit in
> Paraguay, Mexico and Peru and in the
> Seyshelle Islands, described as an
> earthly paradise the nomad races into
> reductions, war dance.
>   (*JJA* 7:3)

Luca Crispi is probably right that the Kinahan fragment is unrelated to the epiphany ("Epiphanies I"), but considering how carefully Joyce copied the manuscript and seemingly kept it with him through all his peregrinations until the winter of 1940, it seems unlikely that he would use it as scrap paper to scribble down an odd note.

As Ilaria Natali points out, the Kinahan fragment may be a note for *Stephen Hero*, although she states that Kinahan was the model for McCann:

he was in fact the model for Moynihan (*Ur-Portrait* 42). Two brief notes in Joyce's commonplace book of 1903–4 make this connection clear, as Robert Scholes and Richard M. Kain have shown (*WD* 149–50). They point out that Robert Kinahan, who matriculated with Joyce in the summer of 1899 (Davison 394), was "auditor," or president, of the University College Dublin Literary and Historical Society from 1901 to 1902 (*WD* 153–54), a position Joyce may have aspired to. In *Stephen Hero*, Moynihan's inaugural paper, along with those of all the speakers who follow, "praise[s] the work done by the Jesuits" (*SH* 177).

This tentative connection between the note and *Stephen Hero* may imply an analogous connection between the epiphany and the novel, but if Joyce adapted "Forty Thousand Pounds" for *Stephen Hero*, those pages are now lost, and even if both note and epiphany were intended to provide material for *Stephen Hero*, the relationship between them is cryptic. One possibility is that Aunt Lillie's gentle mockery of Joyce's artistic pretensions in the epiphany is implicitly compared, via Kinahan, to the Literary and Historical Society students' mockery of Joyce's Mangan paper, in which he first expressed his faith in literature as "the continuous affirmation of the human spirit" (*CW* 83; and see *JJII* 96). By analogy, Kinahan, who was then president of the society, becomes the focal point for Joyce's ire, explaining the ungenerous description of Moynihan as a "comic Irishman" (*P* 5.703) and "an ugly young man" who "was going to be a solicitor" (*SH* 149); Kinahan did in fact become "an eminent K.C." (Mamigonian and Turner, 438).

Source: Buffalo 1.A.5 (*JJA* 7:3–4). This epiphany has a cross in the upper left corner and is numbered 5 on the verso.

Variants: The Yale typescript shows minor variations in lineation (lines 4 and 6) and punctuation: "concludes" is not underlined (line 2); no full stop after "pounds" (line 2); four dots after "too" (line 3), two dots before "When" (line 4). The Kinahan fragment is copied with no changes except lineation (lines 1–3) (Yale GEN MSS 108 XV.64.1503.11).

[There's Nothing like Marriage]

"There's Nothing like Marriage" and "The Lame Beggar" are set in Mullingar, a town in County Westmeath about eighty kilometers (fifty miles) from Dublin, which Joyce visited with his father in late June or early July 1900, and again in summer 1901. The two Mullingar epiphanies suggest that by mid-1901 Joyce was composing epiphanies regularly. Assuming the scene took place during one of Joyce's Mullingar holidays, the reference to "a Sunday in July: / noon" narrows the date to July 8, 15, 22, or 29, 1900, or July 7, 14, 21, or 28, 1901.

As Richard Ellmann notes, "Some of the places [Joyce] noticed" in Mullingar, "such as Phil Shaw's photographic shop, stayed with him, and he put Milly Bloom to work there in *Ulysses*." Ellmann also asserts that while in Mullingar Joyce wrote *A Brilliant Career* (*JJII* 78).

Mr. Tobin is Michael Tobin, a "well-known reporter of strong nationalist feeling" who wrote for *Westmeath Examiner* and reported on the Land League (Daly 48).

Echoes and Adaptations

In the Mullingar fragment of *Stephen Hero*, Nash introduces Stephen to Mr. Garvey, who works for the *Examiner*. After meeting at the Greville Arms Hotel, they set out for a walk, during which Mr. Garvey delivers some "sound advice":

> Mr Garvey whistled the terrier out of the office and they set out for a walk. Mr Garvey wore heavy boots and he plodded along sturdily in them, tapping the road with his stick. The road and the actual sultry day had made him sensible and he gave the younger men some sound advice.
>
> —After all, there's nothing like marriage for making a fellow steady. Before I got this sit on the *Examiner* here I used knock about with the lads and boose [a] bit . . . You know, he said to Nash—Nash nodded.
>
> —Now I've a good house, said Mr Garvey, and . . . I go home in the evening and if I want a drink . . . well, I can have it. My advice to every young fellow that can afford it is: marry young.

—There's something in that, said Nash, when you've had your fling, that is.

—O, yes, said Mr Garvey. By the bye, I hope you'll come and see me some evening and bring your friend. You'll come, Mr Daedalus? The missus'll be glad to see you: she plays a bit, you know.

Stephen mumbled his thanks and decided that he would endure severe bodily pain rather than visit Mr Garvey.

(*SH* 251–52)

The original stage directions are incorporated into the narrative here, and Garvey's advice is drawn directly from the epiphany, with minor changes to the dialogue ("O" becomes "After all"; "before I came here to the *Examiner*" becomes "Before I got this sit on the *Examiner*," etc.). The fact that Joyce preserves "I used knock about" from the epiphany indicates that it was not a mistake, as the editors of *Stephen Hero* supposed, but an authentic expression of Tobin's. Besides substituting Garvey for Tobin, the only significant change is that Joyce has adjusted the time to fit the narrative: where the epiphany took place at noon, Nash and Stephen arrange to meet at two o'clock (*SH* 246).

Source: Buffalo 1.A.12 (*JJA* 7:5–6). Lead pencil cross, upper left corner. Numbered 12 on the verso.

Variants: The Yale typescript has a line break after "noon" (line 2), three dots before "O" (line 4), four dots after "and" (line 9), five dots after "drink" (line 10). Changes to lineation in lines 5–13 (Yale GEN MSS 108 XV.64.1503.4).

[The Priest That Writes Poetry]

The Stag's Head, where the epiphany is set, is a long-standing pub on the corner of Dame Court and Dame Street in Temple Bar. Stanislaus Joyce relates that after his mother's death, when Joyce was drinking heavily, he used to obtain sack from a bodega on Dame Street (*MBK* 246).

O'Mahony probably refers to the lawyer, journalist, and Dublin "character" John O'Mahony (1870–1904), who was educated at Queen's College, Cork, and worked as a journalist on the *Cork Daily Herald* before moving to Dublin, where he reported for the *Dublin Evening Herald*. He later studied for the bar, establishing a reputation as a brilliant lawyer, though he was equally well known for his literary interests, his nationalist sympathies, and his pub going. In "Aeolus" he appears as J. J. O'Molloy: "Cleverest fellow at the junior bar he used to be. Decline, poor chap. That hectic flush spells finis for a man" (*U* 7.292). According to O'Mahony's sister-in-law Katharine Tynan, "For some two years before his death he suffered greatly, but put his sufferings out of sight" (17). Since there is no indication that O'Mahony is unwell in the epiphany, the scene is likely to have occurred well before his death in November 1904.

Father Russell is a reference to Matthew Russell, SJ (1834–1912), editor of the *Irish Monthly*, which published many of the major figures of the Irish Literary Revival (O'Keefe). With his ironic use of the term *verse*, Joyce may be hinting at Russell's *Erin: Verses Irish and Catholic* (1881). Harald Beck writes that Russell "had encouraged Katherine [*sic*] Tynan to contribute to his journal and would have been familiar to and familiar with John O'Mahony."

Source: Buffalo 1.A.13 (*JJA* 7:7–8). Numbered 13 on the verso.

Variants: The Yale typescript has a space in "Ve rses" (line 5) and line breaks after "Lane" (line 2), "Fr." (line 4), and the ellipsis in line 6 (Yale GEN MSS 108 XV.64.1503.7).

[Ibsen's Age]

The stage directions place this epiphany at the Sheehys' house at 2 Belvedere Place. In 1893, at the age of eleven, Joyce enrolled at Belvedere College, where he met Richard and Eugene Sheehy. Through them he attended social parties organized by David Sheehy, MP, on Sunday evenings at their home. These parties may have begun as early as 1893, and continued until 1904, when Joyce left Dublin. Since he began recording epiphanies around 1900 or 1901, some of the dialogue pieces based at the Sheehys' must have been written long after the event, as "retrospective" epiphanies (Beja, *Epiphany* 15).

The Sheehys had four daughters, Hanna, Margaret (Maggie), Mary, and Kathleen. Of the epiphanies related to the Sheehy soirees, "Ibsen's Age" includes Maggie; "Your Favourite Poet" involves Hanna; "Order, Order!" features Richard and David Sheehy; and "The Stars on Joyce's Nose" involves Richard. Surprisingly, none of them include Mary Sheehy, who caught Joyce's eye and became the muse of his *Chamber Music* cycle. Mrs. Sheehy doesn't appear in the epiphanies but appears in *Ulysses*, where she encounters Father John Conmee in Mountjoy Square (*U* 10.12–29).

Joyce's use of this epiphany in *Stephen Hero* helps clarify the context. A guessing game is being played, and Joyce has been asking questions to guess the name of Henrik Ibsen. Ibsen turned seventy-two in March 1900, dating the scene to that year. Joyce's admiration for Ibsen was well known because he had published a review of Ibsen's *When We Dead Awaken* in the *Fortnightly Review* in April 1900. Ibsen thanked Joyce for his review via William Archer (*JJII* 74). Joyce subsequently wrote a personal letter to Ibsen in March 1901, which went unanswered (*JJII* 86–87).

Stanislaus Joyce recalls another guessing game featuring Maggie in his "Crucible" (*DD* 55; see also *MBK* 72–73).

Echoes and Adaptations

Stephen Hero features an extended scene of a party at the Daniels' house in Donnybrook (*SH* 42–47) that brings together a series of epiphanies based on the Sheehy gatherings at Belvedere Place, specifically "Your Favourite Poet" (*SH* 43), "Order, Order!" (*SH* 45), and "Ibsen's Age" (*SH* 46). The party provides the context for the guessing game epiphanized in "Ibsen's Age":

> Another favourite was "Who's Who." A person goes out of the room and the rest of the company choose the name of someone who is supposed to have special attractions for the absent player. This latter, when he returns to the company, has to ask questions all around and try to guess the name. [. . .] The players were unable to answer [Stephen's] questions when he returned to the room: such questions as: "Where does the person live?" "Is the person married or single?" "What age is the person?" could not be answered by the circle until McCann had been consulted in a swift undertone. The answer "Norway" gave Stephen the clue at once and so the game ended and the company proceeded to divert themselves as before this serious interruption. Stephen sat down beside one of the daughters and, while admiring the rural comeliness of her features, waited quietly for her first word which, he knew, would destroy his satisfaction. Her large handsome eyes looked at him for a while as if they were about to trust him and then she said:
> —How did you guess it so quickly?
> —I knew you meant him. But you're wrong about his age.
> Others had heard this: but she was impressed by a possible vastness of the unknown, complimented to confer with one who conferred directly with the exceptional. She leaned forward to speak with soft seriousness.
> —Why, how old is he?
> —Over seventy.
> —Is he?
> (*SH* 45–46)

The dialogue is similar to the epiphany, although Ibsen's age has been generalized to avoid dating the scene. His name is still unspoken, but there is now a hint of romance between Stephen and his unnamed interlocutor: he is attracted to the "rural comeliness of her features" and "her large handsome eyes," while she is impressed by Stephen's learning, though the narrator gives a more ironical view of Stephen as "one who conferred directly with the exceptional."

Source: Buffalo 1.A.14 (*JJA* 7:9–10). Lead pencil cross, upper left corner. Numbered 14 in ink on the verso.

Variants: The Yale typescript has a line break after the header (line 2), no full stop after "age" (line 4), no comma after "Why" (line 5), no full stop after "Seventy-two" (line 5), change of lineation (line 3) (Yale GEN MSS 108 XV.64.1503.17).

[Your Favourite Poet]

Like "Ibsen's Age," this epiphany is set at the Sheehys' in Belvedere Place, where they are playing a guessing game.

O'Reilly has not been identified, although Eugene Sheehy recalls Joyce asking about an O'Reilly in 1928: "he became quite impatient that I could not call to mind at once one Jack O'Reilly, who had faded from the Dublin scene for many years" (O'Connor 37).

Hanna Sheehy (born 1877) was the eldest of the four Sheehy girls. According to Robert Scholes and Richard M. Kain, "Along with her younger sister Mary, she contributed something to the Emma Clery of *Stephen Hero* and *A Portrait*" (*WD* 36), although Hanna Sheehy was a radical feminist, republican, and suffragette (see Ward, *Fearless*; Ward, *Hanna*). She married Joyce's university friend Francis Skeffington in 1903 (see "The Day of the Rabblement" for notes on Skeffington).

Echoes and Adaptations

"Your Favourite Poet" features in *Stephen Hero*, along with "Order, Order!" (*SH* 45) and "Ibsen's Age" (*SH* 46):

> The young men and the daughters amused themselves tolerably under Mr Daniel's eye but whenever there was an approach to artistic matters during the process of their games Stephen with egoistic humour imagined his presence acting as a propriety. He could see seriousness developing on the shrewd features of a young man who had to put a certain question to one of the daughters:
> —I suppose it's my turn now . . . Well . . . let me see . . . [. . .] Who is your favourite poet, Annie?
> Annie thought for a few moments: there was a pause. Annie and the young man were 'doing' the same course.
> — . . . German?
> — . . . Yes.
> Annie thought for another few moments while the table waited to be edified.

—I think . . . Goethe.
(*SH* 43)

The scene follows the epiphany closely, with minor adjustments to the dialogue, and with stage directions elaborated in the narrative (e.g., "*quite / seriously*" is expanded into "and here he became as serious as a young man [. . .] can become" [*SH* 43]).

In Joyce's novel, Hanna Sheehy becomes Annie Daniel, while the young man is unnamed. The latter change may be motivated by Sheehy's marriage to Skeffington, who shares her feminist principles: in the novel, Annie and the young man are following the same course, which would have been unusual given the prevalence of single-sex education at the time.

The scene and epiphany are echoed in *Portrait* when Stephen asserts that Byron is "the greatest poet" (*P* 2.741), refusing to "admit that Byron was no good" (*P* 2.782).

Source: Buffalo 1.A.16 (*JJA* 7:11–12). Lead pencil cross, upper left corner. Numbered 16 on the verso.

Variants: The Yale typescript has a line break after the header (line 2), four dots after "suppose" (line 4), five dots in lines 8 and 9, three dots before "I think" (line 11) (Yale GEN MSS 108 XV.64.1503.1).

[It's a Terrible Life]

"It's a Terrible Life" is another epiphany centered on the Sheehy family and their residence on Belvedere Place. See "Ibsen's Age" for notes on the Sheehy household.

The Sheehy soirees included songs, burlesques, and charades (*JJII* 51–54), suggesting that Joyce's performance in the epiphany was musical or theatrical (although Fallon's secondhand congratulations may refer to an earlier performance). In *Stephen Hero*, singing and piano recitals feature regularly at the Daniels' parties, where Stephen is encouraged to sing professionally (*SH* 42–43), just as Joyce was in his early twenties. After coming in fourth at the Feis Ceoil contest for solo tenor in April 1904, Joyce took lessons with Benedetto Palmieri, one of Dublin's leading teachers: "Palmieri is now training Jim's voice for nothing and advises Jim to take to concert singing as a profession" (*DD* 37).

Thus, the "terrible" profession mentioned in the epiphany may relate to the life of a professional musician, but Joyce also performed onstage, famously parodying Father Henry at Belvedere (Sullivan 88–89), giving rise to the parody of Father Conmee in *Portrait* (*P* 2.556–64). Joyce also performed in a number of family plays at the Sheehys', including T. W. Robertson's *Caste*, as well as *Hamlet*, in which Joyce played a melodramatic Gertrude wailing over a comic Ophelia (William Fallon in drag), like "a woman 'keening' at an Irish wake" (Bowker, *James* 62). This cross-dressing W. G. Fallon, a handsome student of Belvedere and University College who was "much sought after by female students at the university" (O'Connor 39), was the model for Fallon in the epiphany. He is mentioned in passing in *Portrait*: "A boy named Fallon, in Belvedere, had often asked him with a silly laugh why they moved [house] so often" (*P* 4.577–78).

The model for Blake has not been identified. One possibility is the real-life writer of "Phil Blake's Pat and Bull story" (*U* 7.84), "a well-known figure in Dublin in artistic, theatrical Blake's and musical circles" (Igoe, *Real* 30). Alternatively, the dismal view of the young artist's prospects in the epiphany chimes rather ironically (if fancifully) with Joyce's depiction of William Blake languishing in "a poor London room" that smelled of "eggs fried in lard" (*CW* 218).

Source: Buffalo 1.A.19 (*JJA* 7:13–14). Lead pencil cross, upper left corner. Numbered 19 on the verso.

Variants: The Yale typescript has a line break after the header (line 2); no full stop after "performance" (line 4); "of" for "Of" (line 9); one dot after "pause" (line 6); three dots after "know," "squalid," and "simply" (lines 11 and 14); five dots in lines 8 and 9; three dots before "I think" (line 11); lineation not preserved (lines 6, 9–11) (Yale GEN MSS 108 XV.64.1503.16).

[Order, Order!]

"Order, Order!" describes another parlor game at the Sheehys' house at 2 Belvedere Place, this time parodying the language of the House of Commons.

Mr. Sheehy refers to David Sheehy, MP. In his youth, Sheehy belonged to the Irish Republican Brotherhood and was active in the Land League; he was imprisoned on six occasions for his part in the Land War. At the 1885 general election he was elected unopposed as MP for South Galway, keeping his seat in 1886. In the 1892 general election, when the Irish Party split over the leadership of Charles Stewart Parnell, Sheehy joined the anti-Parnellite majority, retaining his seat until the 1900 general election. However, he chose not to stand that year and was out of Parliament for the next three years, when Joyce was writing his epiphanies.

Mr. Sheehy's son Richard "Dick" Sheehy was a friend of Joyce's from Belvedere. Stanislaus Joyce calls him a "big, stalwart, good-natured fellow" (*MBK* 112). See "Ibsen's Age" for further notes on the Sheehy family.

Fallon is William G. Fallon, a friend of Joyce's from Belvedere and University College (see "It's a Terrible Life"). When David Sheehy calls on the "honourable member / for Denbigh," this is perhaps a reference to the fact that Fallon lived in Denbigh, an area in Rathdown Park, Terenure.

The epiphany likely records a charade, but David Sheehy's checkered political career, and the fact that they are imitating the British Parliament, seen by many nationalists as the illegitimate imposition of a colonizing power, politicizes the scene.

Echoes and Adaptations

As with the other "Sheehy" epiphanies reused in *Stephen Hero*, Joyce adapted "Order, Order!" for the party at the Daniels' house in Donnybrook.

A parliamentary charade was frequent. Mr Daniel had sat for his county some years before and for this reason he was chosen to impersonate the Speaker of the House. McCann always represented a member of the Opposition and he spoke point-blank. Then a member would protest and there would be a make-believe of parliamentary manners.

   —Mr Speaker, I must ask . . .

   —Order! Order!

   —You know it's a lie!

   —You must withdraw, Sir.

   —As I was saying before the honourable gentleman interrupted we must . . .

   —I won't withdraw.

   —I must ask honourable members to preserve order in the House.

   —I won't withdraw.

   —Order! Order!

   (*SH* 44–45)

While speech prefixes have been removed to fit the narrative conventions of *Stephen Hero*, the dialogue is largely in keeping with the epiphany. It may be significant that Sheehy's counterpart, Mr. Daniel, has been "chosen to impersonate the Speaker." Like David Sheehy, Mr. Daniel, the Speaker in the epiphany, is a former MP, but in Joyce's novel, he has also been "manager of a theatre in Wexford" (*SH* 44). This change brings out the implication, already present in the epiphany, that the humor of the charade is meant to unmask the absurdity and theatricality of parliamentary debate. Joyce shows a farcical attempt to maintain order crumbling in the face of accusations, falsehoods, and stubbornness.

Source: Buffalo 1.A.21 (*JJA* 7:15–16). Lead pencil cross, upper left corner. Numbered 21 on the verso.

Variants: The Yale typescript has a line break after the header (line 2), "Mr. Sheehy" (lines 4, 6, 9), no full stops after "ask" (line 3) or "won't" (line 9), three dots after "saying" (line 7) and "Denbigh" (line 10), lineation changed in line 9 (Yale GEN MSS 108 XV.64.1503.15).

[The Lame Beggar]

This is another epiphany set in Mullingar (see "There's Nothing like Marriage"). Joyce visited Mullingar (County Westmeath) in late June or early July 1900 and again in summer 1901. However, the opening stage direction sets the scene in autumn, which may indicate that there was a later trip, or that the epiphany has been fictionalized (see Daly 33–35).

The latter possibility is interesting in light of Stephen Daedalus's emphasis on *recording* epiphanies with extreme care in *Stephen Hero*. "The Lame Beggar" most likely derives from a real experience, but, like "Apologise," it evokes the myth of Prometheus. In "Apologise," Stephen is threatened with blinding; here the threat of cutting "the livers / out o' ye" recalls Prometheus's punishment for stealing fire from the gods: after he was chained to a rock, an eagle was sent to cut out Prometheus's liver and eat it, repeating the disembowelment each time his liver regrew.

Echoes and Adaptations

The encounter with the lame beggar is elaborated in *Stephen Hero*. During Stephen's trip to Mullingar, he and Dan, the servant of Mr. Fulham, visit a chemist:

> One day Dan was sent into the town to buy some medicine at the druggist's and Stephen went in with him. The trap stopped in the main street before the druggist's and Dan handed down the order to a ragged boy telling him to take it into the shop. The ragged boy first showed the paper to an equally ragged friend and then went into the shop. When they came out they stood at the door of the shop gazing alternately from Stephen to the horse's tail and back again. While they were thus gazing they were confronted by a lame beggar who advanced towards them gripping his stick:
> —It was yous called out names after me yestherday. The two children huddling in the doorway, gazed at him and answered:
> —No, sir.
> —O yes it was, though.

The beggar thrust his malign face down at their faces and began moving his stick up down.

—But mind what I'm tellin' you. D'ye see that stick?

—Yes, sir.

—Well, if ye call out after me the next time I'll cut yez [yous] open with that stick. I'll cut the livers out of ye.

He proceeded to explain himself to the frightened children.

—D'ye hear me now? I'll cut yez open with that stick. I'll cut the livers and the lights out of ye.

This incident was stolidly admired by a few bystanders who made way for the beggar as he limped along the footpath. Dan, who had watched the scene from the trap, now descended to the ground and asking Stephen to look to the horse went into a very dirty public-house. Stephen sat alone in the car thinking of the beggar's face. He had never before seen such evil expressed in a face. He had sometimes watched the faces of prefects as they "pandied" boys with a broad leather bat but those faces had seemed to him less malicious than stupid, dutifully inflamed faces. The recollection of the beggar's sharp eyes struck a fine chord of terror in the youth [. . .].

(*SH* 244–45)

Where the epiphany is set in an evening in autumn, this scene takes place on a summer's day. The dialogue is little changed, save for plurals and contractions, but the removal of ellipses from the epiphany accelerates the exchange and gives it a stronger sense of continuity. The descriptive details Joyce adds about the "ragged" pair of boys and the beggar, whose "evil" face and "sharp eyes" frighten Stephen, make the scene more vivid.

Echoes of the epiphany may also be heard in the frightening encounter between the two boys and the "queer old josser" in "An Encounter" (*D* 18), the "redrimmed horny eyes" of the old man in *Portrait* (*P* 5.2754), the "onelegged sailor" who begs for money watched by "Two barefoot urchins" in "Wandering Rocks" (*U* 10.239–56), and the lame-footed Jute in *Finnegans Wake* (15.29–16.09), although none of these is a clear adaptation.

Source: Buffalo 1.A.22 (*JJA* 7:17–18). Lead pencil cross, upper left corner. Numbered 22 on the verso.

Variants: The Yale typescript has a line break after the header (line 2); three dots instead of four in lines 3, 6, 7, and 14; "o'ye" for "o' ye" (line 17); lineation altered in lines 3, 7, and 11–17 (Yale GEN MSS 108 XV.64.1503.5).

[An Arctic Beast]

Stanislaus Joyce says this epiphany is "one of the first of the collection, perhaps made before we left Royal Terrace" (*MBK* 126). This comment suggests that Joyce began recording epiphanies between May 1900, when the family moved into 8 Royal Terrace in Fairview, and late 1901, when they moved to Glengariff Parade (see Igoe, *James* 83–87).

Stanislaus calls it an account of a "dream," "Which interpreted signified that I was the sluggish 'arctic beast'" (*MBK* 126). In his *Dublin Diary*, Stanislaus is more specific: Joyce "has written an epiphany of a sluggish polar bear on me" (*DD* 26). As well as an arctic beast and a polar bear, Joyce apparently regarded his younger brother as something reptilian: "He used to say that I reminded him of a sluggish saurian, whose scaly hide occasionally reflected glints of light" (*MBK* 149).

The sense of failed communication in "An Arctic Beast" recurs in "The Big Dog," and is implied in other epiphanies such as "Forty Thousand Pounds," "The Hole in Georgie's Stomach," and "I Was Sorry."

Echoes and Adaptations

Stephen Hero

There are no clear adaptations of this epiphany, but "An Arctic Beast" is echoed in Stephen's attempts to glimpse the origin of art in *Stephen Hero*:

> He doubled backwards into the past of humanity and caught glimpses of emergent art as one might have a vision of the pleisiosauros emerging from his ocean of slime. He seemed almost to hear the simple cries of fear and joy and wonder which are antecedent to all song, the savage rhythms of men pulling at the oar.
> (*SH* 33–34)

This "pleisiosauros" (or plesiosaurus, an extinct genus of large marine reptiles; Greek *plesios* [near to] + *sauros* [lizard or reptile]) "emerging from his ocean of slime" may recall the image of Stanislaus as a "sluggish saurian." The link is strengthened when Stephen looks "contemptuously at the laughing faces" of his ignorant classmates and thinks "of a self-submersive reptile" (*SH* 34). The link between Stanislaus and the classmates who approve of *Othello* as a masterpiece seems to be their complacent conventionality, something Joyce mocks in "Your Favourite Poet."

Ulysses

There may also be a subtle link between Daedalus imaginatively doubling back into the past of humanity to hear "the simple cries of fear and joy and wonder . . . the savage rhythms of men pulling at the oar" and Stephen's vision of his Viking ancestors butchering a school of beached whales in "Proteus":

> Galleys of the Lochlanns ran here to beach, in quest of prey, their bloodbeaked prows riding low on a molten pewter surf. Dane vikings, torcs of tomahawks aglitter on their breasts when Malachi wore the collar of gold. A school of turlehide whales stranded in hot noon, spouting, hobbling in the shallows. Then from the starving cagework city a horde of jerkined dwarfs, my people, with flayers' knives, running, scaling, hacking in green blubbery whalemeat. Famine, plague and slaughters. Their blood is in me, their lust my waves. I moved among them on the frozen Liffey, that I, a changeling, among the spluttering resin fires. I spoke to no-one: none to me.
>
> (*U* 3.300–309)

The differences are greater than the similarities, but there seems to be an echo, nonetheless, between the arctic beast rising from the water to be prodded and driven by the speaker in the epiphany and the violent attack on the whales Stephen imagines.

Finnegans Wake

A further echo of "An Arctic Beast" flitters into *Finnegans Wake*, book 1, chapter 1. As Mutt talks to Jute about the contents of a refuse tip or grave where versions of HCE and ALP's encounter have collected, the "slow flakes" of the epiphany become "flowflakes" and the "obscure pool" is whirlpooled into "whirlworlds" on the white "plage" (beach, page) of Joyce's earlier adaptations:

> Countlessness of livestories have netherfallen by this plage, flick as flowflakes, litters from aloft, like a waast wizzard all of whirlworlds.
>
> (*FW* 17.26–28)

Source: Buffalo 1.A.26 (*JJA* 7:19–20). Numbered 26 on the verso.

Variants: Cornell 17.48, Stanislaus Joyce's copy, has changes to the lineation and also omits "often / with my stick drive him" (lines 8–9) and the comma after "but" in line 8. The epiphany is ticked in blue ink in Stanislaus's "Selections" (*JJA* 7:58). The epiphany is also copied in the Yale typescript, which agrees with Joyce's holograph in all respects except lineation (Yale GEN MSS 108 XV.64.1503.18).

[The Day of the Rabblement]

This is another epiphany set at the Sheehys' house in 2 Belvedere Place. See "Ibsen's Age" and "Your Favourite Poet" for more on the location, Maggie Sheehy, and Hanna Sheehy.

Skeffington is Francis Sheehy Skeffington, "considered one of the brilliant students of University College and something of a character, because he was a teetotaller, mainly a vegetarian, a feminist, and a pacifist" (*MBK* 110). Skeffington married Hanna Sheehy in 1903 (their engagement is alluded to in "She Dances with Them in the Round"). Despite the fact that he was a committed pacifist, Skeffington was arrested as a supposed Sinn Feiner during the Easter Rising and murdered by an English soldier on April 26, 1916. Joyce fictionalized Skeffington as McCann in *Stephen Hero* and MacCann in *Portrait*.

In October 1901, Joyce wrote an article titled "The Day of the Rabblement" condemning the parochialism of the Irish national theater (*OCPW* 50–52, 295), which he submitted to the student literary magazine *St Stephen's*. It was rejected because of a reference to Gabriele D'Annunzio's *Il Fuoco* (1900), which was on the Vatican Index of Prohibited Books. Skeffington's article "A Forgotten Aspect of the University Question," which advocated equal status for women as students of the university, was also rejected by the magazine. In response, Joyce and Skeffington had the two articles printed privately in a pamphlet and distributed it themselves (figure 2).

Maggie's line "Even now the / rabblement may be standing / by the door!" parodies the conclusion of Joyce's essay:

> Elsewhere there are men who are worthy to carry on the tradition of the old master who is dying in Christiania. He has already found his successor in the writer of *Michael Kramer*, and the third minister will not be wanting when his hour comes. Even now that hour may be standing by the door.
>
> (*OCPW* 52)

The "old master" is Henrik Ibsen, and Joyce's last line is an allusion to act 1 of Ibsen's play *The Master Builder*: "I tell you the younger generation will

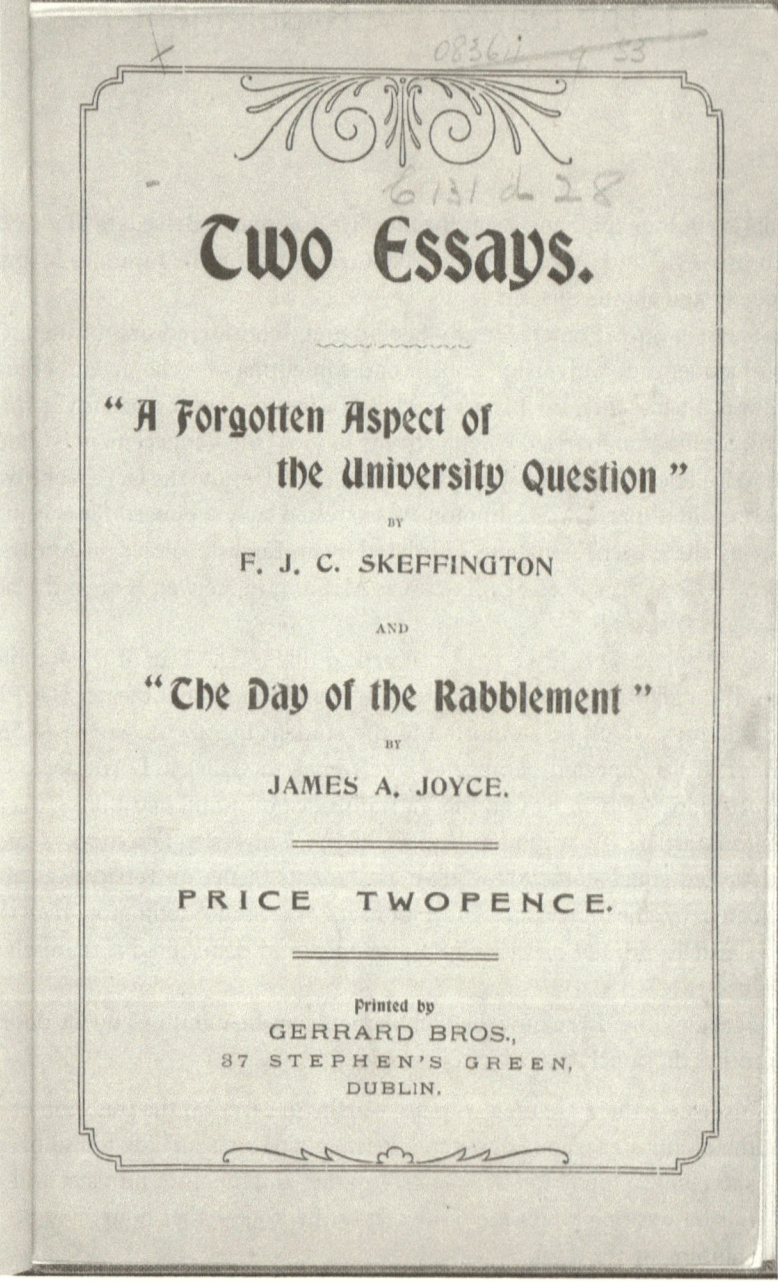

Two Essays.

"A Forgotten Aspect of the University Question"

BY

F. J. C. SKEFFINGTON

AND

"The Day of the Rabblement"

BY

JAMES A. JOYCE.

PRICE TWOPENCE.

Printed by
GERRARD BROS.,
37 STEPHEN'S GREEN,
DUBLIN.

Figure 2. Cover of "A Forgotten Aspect of the University Question" and "The Day of the Rabblement" (1901). Held by the British Library.

one day come and thunder at my door" (qtd. in *OCPW* 297n11). Joyce is obviously hinting that he will be the "third minister," ready to take the mantle
from Gerhart Hauptmann ("the writer of *Michael Kramer*"), but instead of
announcing the imminent arrival of the great artist, Maggie's parody suggests that an unruly mob is about to break in on Joyce's fantasy and bring it
rudely down to earth. The epiphany is clearly humorous, making a joke of
the hypothetical "rabblement," but Hanna's reference to an event that is sure
to draw "great crowds" may also allude to Yeats's play *The Countess Cath-
leen*, which provoked riots when it premiered at the Abbey Theatre in 1899,
and partly inspired Joyce's essay (Hayman in Joyce, *Epifanías* 35).

Skeffington's allusion to "our friend / Jocax" is explained by the fact that
the "name Joyce is derived . . . from the French *joyeux* and Latin *jocax*" (*JJII*
12). In *Stephen Hero* we are told that "Stephen had begun to regard himself
seriously as a literary artist: he professed scorn for the rabblement and contempt for authority" (*SH* 127).

Source: Buffalo 1.A.28 (*JJA* 7:21–22). Numbered 28 on the verso.

Variants: The Yale typescript adds a line break after the heading and alters the
lineation of lines 4–5 and 7–8; otherwise, it is an exact copy of Joyce's manuscript (Yale GEN MSS 108 XV.64.1503.9).

[The Stars on Joyce's Nose]

The setting, on the North Circular Road at Christmas, with the stars coming out, suggests that the speakers are going to a festive party at the Sheehys', since the North Circular Road leads to Belvedere Place, where they lived. For more on Dick Sheehy, see "Order, Order!"

Miss O'Callaghan has not been identified, though she may be related to Joyce's friend and fellow medical student Maurice O'Callaghan, "a good-natured, thick-headed fellow" Joyce stayed with on August 31, 1904 (*DD* 35, 69). Her namesake appears in "The Dead," accompanying Bartell D'Arcy on the piano before leaving with Gabriel and Gretta (*D* 166, 169). In the epiphany, Miss O'Callaghan appears to be walking to a Christmas party at the Sheehys', whereas in "The Dead" she is seen leaving the Morkans' party (often dated to January 6, the Feast of the Epiphany), which was itself based on the Flynn sisters' annual dances at 15 Usher's Island.

As Richard Brown notes, *The Escaped Nun* was "a popular one shilling novel . . . by Margaret Mary Moult published in London by Cassell & Co. It narrates the unhappy life of an English novice but its barely veiled intention is to expose the 'pettiness and worldliness' of the convent system in the manner of a number of contemporary Protestant propagandizing works. It is thus an appropriately suggestive book for the context and has a number of parallels in other books that we know Joyce used, like the better-known *Awful Disclosures of Maria Monk*" (3).

The epiphany also seems to have contributed something to César Abin's sketch of Joyce, commissioned for his fiftieth birthday, which was published in *Transition* in March 1932 (figure 3; see Beja, "Epiphany" 715–16). Both Eugène and Maria Jolas, the editors of *Transition* (and friends of Joyce), commented on the star on Joyce's nose: "For more than two weeks he kept adding new suggestions, until he was finally satisfied with it. . . . He asked that a star be put on the tip of his nose" (Jolas 7–9); "Someone had called [Joyce] 'a blue-nosed comedian,' so he insisted that a star be put on the end of his nose to illuminate it" (Maria Jolas, qtd. in *JJII* 645). Whether or not Maria Jolas is right, the epiphany is probably a source for Joyce's private joke in the caricature, particularly because the Jolases possessed their own typescript of Joyce's epiphanies (see MacDuff, "Yale").

Figure 3. César Abin, caricature of James Joyce, *Transition*, vol. 21, March 1932, p. 265. © Betsy Jolas. Reprinted with permission.

Echoes and Adaptations

The apparition of the stars in the epiphany echoes the star of the Magi in Matthew 2, the epiphanic "phenomenon" par excellence. There are several echoes of Joyce's epiphany in *Ulysses*, including Stephen's "celestial phenomenon"—a new star that rose in the W-shaped constellation of Cassiopeia to herald Shakespeare's birth in "Scylla and Charybdis" (*U* 9.939–44)—and Bloom's reflections on celestial phenomena in "Ithaca" (*U* 17.1256–58).

Source: Buffalo 1.A.30 (*JJA* 7:23–24). Numbered 30 on the verso.

Variants: The Yale typescript has a line break after the heading (line 2), four dots after "like that" (line 6), three dots after "smiles" (line 19), lineation altered (lines 5–11, 15–20) (Yale GEN MSS 108 XV.64.1503.3).

[The Hole in Georgie's Stomach]

In March 1902, Joyce's third brother, George Alfred Joyce, fell ill with typhoid at 10 Glengariff Parade. Initially he responded to treatment, but after doctors advised May Joyce that he could begin eating again in late March, Georgie declined rapidly, dying of peritonitis (*JJII* 94), specifically, "enteric fever complicated by perforation of the intestine" (Bowker, *James* 84), on March 9, 1902, at age fourteen. During his illness, Joyce was at Georgie's bedside a great deal and would play songs on the piano in the parlor for Georgie to hear.

Thus, the "hole in Georgie's stomach" must refer to his navel, from which some kind of "matter" exudes, although Mrs. Joyce's reluctance to name it creates a certain ambiguity in the text. This ambiguity is evident when Joyce asks, "What hole?"; the stage direction "stands up," immediately after Mrs. Joyce points to the spot, mischievously encourages the misunderstanding that she might be pointing at her backside. Despite her prudishness in speaking of the body, however, Mrs. Joyce's language seems to reveal the very thing she is unwilling, or unable, to describe. According to Walter Skeat's *Etymological Dictionary*, "matter" is etymologically related to "pus," which, in layman's terms, is probably what was being secreted: severe cases of peritonitis can lead to umbilical discharge.

In memory of his brother, Joyce named his own son George, and by a strange coincidence, Joyce too died of a "perforated ulcer with generalized peritonitis" (*JJII* 741).

Echoes and Adaptations

Stephen Hero

In *Stephen Hero*, the epiphany is transformed into a scene in the fatal illness of Stephen's sister Isabel:

> One evening [Stephen] sat silent at his piano while the dusk enfolded him. The dismal sunset lingered still upon the window-panes in a smoulder of rusty fires. Above him and about him hung the shadow

of decay, the decay of leaves and flowers, the decay of hope. He desist-
ed from his chords and waited, bending upon the keyboard in silence:
and his soul commingled itself with the assailing, inarticulate dusk. A
form which he knew for his mother's appeared far down in the room,
standing in the doorway. In the gloom her excited face was crimson.
A voice which he remembered as his mother's, a voice of a terrified
human being, called his name. The form at the piano answered:

—Yes?

—Do you know anything about the body? . . . .

He heard his mother's voice addressing him excitedly like the voice
of a messenger in a play:

—What ought I do? There's some matter coming away from the
hole in Isabel's . . . stomach . . . . Did you ever hear of that happening?

—I don't know, he answered trying to make sense of her words, trying to say them again to himself.

—Ought I send for the doctor . . . . Did you ever hear of that?
. . . What ought I do?

—I don't know . . . . What hole?

—The hole . . . the hole we all have . . . here.

(*SH* 162–63)

In the epiphany Stephen is "at the piano" one "evening" when his mother
"appears at the / parlour door"; Joyce's adaptation expands and embellishes
these stage directions to evoke a melancholy, twilit scene ("One evening . . .
dusk . . . dismal sunset . . . gloom"), in which Stephen feels a "shadow of
decay" hanging about him as the chords he has been playing fade into silence. In the epiphany, Mrs. Joyce appears "crimson, trembling," whereas
when Stephen's mother appears in the "gloom," she seems hectic (her "excited face was crimson," her voice "terrified"). The elaboration and transformation of the scene provide a good example of how Joyce was able to
rework a dramatic epiphany for a narrative setting (see also "Is That Mary
Ellen?").

Whereas the narrative description has been expanded, the dialogue is
repeated almost verbatim. Two narrative interpolations have been inserted,
and there are a few minor alterations, such as "Did you ever hear of that?"
for "do you / think?," but the only significant change is the removal of the
last two stage directions. Rather than spell out which hole Mrs. Daedalus
is referring to, Joyce ends the chapter with her pointing implicitly to "the
hole we all have . . . here." While readers might still wonder whether she is

pointing toward the anus, the switch from Georgie to Isabel allows for the possibility that she may be referring to some kind of vaginal discharge.

Like the epiphany, the nature of the "matter coming away from the hole in Isabel's . . . stomach" is never explained in *Stephen Hero* (indeed, the added ellipsis seems to suggest that "stomach" might be a euphemism). The next chapter begins with Isabel's death, followed by her funeral and wake, for which Joyce adapted three further epiphanies, each of which deals with his brother's death or his mother's ("Poor Little Fellow," "Two Mourners," "I Was Sorry"; *SH* 169–74). That Joyce adapted four epiphanies in seven pages to describe Isabel's death, one of the central events in *Stephen Hero*, shows the significance of Joyce's elegiac epiphanies.

Finnegans Wake

Elements of the epiphany are also alluded to in *Finnegans Wake*, book 3, chapter 3, when HCE's sexual misadventures merge with his naval ambitions as he goes "crupping into our raw lenguage navel through the lumbsmall of his hawsehole" (*FW* 323.5–6). Here the strange image of creeping/crupping/crapping into the "navel" (navy) through his "hawsehole" (a small hole on the hawse of a ship; an arsehole) mirrors the ambiguity of the epiphany (without knowing the context of Georgie's illness). In the drafts, this slippage between holes is even clearer, while the phrases Joyce adds to the typescript (marked between carats: ^ . . . ^) seem to bring out some of the linguistic implications of the epiphany: "that is crupping up into our ^+raw language+^ navel through ^+the lumbsmall of+^ his hawsehole" (*JJA* 54:122).

Source: Buffalo 1.A.42 (*JJA* 7:25–26). Lead pencil cross, upper left corner. Numbered 42 on the verso.

Variants: The Yale typescript has a line break after the heading (line 2); "Mrs. Joyce"; three dots after "body" (line 7), after "know" (lines 11 and 14), and before "here" (line 16); lineation altered in lines 6–10 and 12 (Yale GEN MSS 108 XV.64.1503.2).

[Two Mourners]

Stanislaus Joyce recollects that "Two Mourners" was written "two or three months after" May Joyce's August 13, 1903, funeral at Glasnevin Cemetery: "I remembered that I too, had noticed the pair. They were in a little group at the gate of Glasnevin Cemetery in a funeral preceding my mother's" (*MBK* 235). Stanislaus clearly thought their sorrow was insincere, writing that "the epiphany means . . . that false sentiment was [Joyce's] bugbear, all the more repugnant when he was expected to share it" (*MBK* 235). The woman's face, "small and square, the face / of a bargainer," and the girl looking up "to see if it is time / to cry," certainly fits with Stanislaus's interpretation, but the absence of a clear narrative voice or external point of view leaves the epiphany open to other readings; see "I Was Sorry" and McCann's insincerity following Isabel's death in *Stephen Hero* (169).

Echoes and Adaptations

Stephen Hero

Joyce reuses "Two Mourners" in *Stephen Hero* with minor alterations to fit the past-tense narrative. In chapter 23, when Stephen's carriage arrives at Glasnevin Cemetery for Isabel's funeral, he watches a crowd of poor mourners gathered for another funeral:

> Two of them who were late pushed their way viciously through the crowd. A girl, one hand catching the woman's skirt, ran a pace in advance. The girl's face was the face of a fish, discoloured and oblique-eyed; the woman's face was square and pinched, the face of a bargainer. The girl, her mouth distorted, looked up at the woman to see if it was time to cry: the woman, settling a flat bonnet, hurried on towards the mortuary chapel.
>
> (*SH* 167)

Besides the descriptive details added to the first sentence ("who were late," "viciously"), and the repetition of "oblique-eyed" for peasants in Mullingar

(*SH* 244), the epiphany is little changed in *Stephen Hero*. Joyce's adaptation for *Ulysses*, in contrast, is much more substantial.

Ulysses

In "Hades," "Two Mourners" is emplotted for the funeral of a child pauper. Bloom sees the destitute family from the carriage on his way to Glasnevin (*U* 6.321–25). When he arrives at the cemetery, the child's funeral has already taken place and the mourners are leaving. At this point Joyce inserts the woman and child from the epiphany, now part of a group of mourners passing through the gates of the cemetery:

> Mourners came out through the gates: woman and a girl. Leanjawed harpy, hard woman at a bargain, her bonnet awry. Girl's face stained with dirt and tears, holding the woman's arm, looking up at her for a sign to cry. Fish's face, bloodless and livid.
>
> (*U* 6.517–20)

What is most striking here is the compression. The epiphany has been reduced by about 40 percent to create Bloom's sharply focused impressions. The anaphoric structure of the original ("The girl . . . The girl's face . . . The girl") has been stripped out, with descriptions reduced to polished noun phrases (e.g., "The girl's face is the face / of a fish" becomes "Fish's face"). Specific changes and additions like "bloodless and livid" for "discoloured and oblique-eyed" or "Leanjawed harpy" help bring out the underworld themes of "Hades," as well as its symbolic focus on the heart.

There is also a fleeting echo of the epiphany in "Circe," when Mrs. Dignam and her "brood" appear in mourning: "Mrs Dignam, widow woman, her snubnose and cheeks flushed with deathtalk, tears and Tunney's tawny sherry, hurries by in her weeds, her bonnet awry," echoing the mourner in "Hades." She is followed by Patsy, Freddy, and "Susy with a crying cod's mouth" (*U* 15.3837–47), which recalls the fish-faced girl in the epiphany "look[ing] up at the woman to see if it is time / to cry."

Source: Buffalo 1.A.44 (*JJA* 7:27–28). Lead pencil cross, upper left corner. Numbered 44 on the verso.

Variants: Cornell 17.57 alters the lineation of Joyce's manuscript, but is otherwise a faithful copy (*JJA* 7:65).

[I Was Sorry]

This epiphany was written after the death of Joyce's fourteen-year-old brother Georgie on March 9, 1902. Georgie Joyce was given a public funeral at Belvedere College (*DD* 23), before being buried at Glasnevin Cemetery. Georgie's death is dealt with in "The Hole in Georgie's Stomach" and "Poor Little Fellow!"

See "The Day of the Rabblement" for notes on Skeffington.

Echoes and Adaptations

Joyce reused four epiphanies, including "I Was Sorry," for Isabel's illness and death in *Stephen Hero*. The tone of the original epiphany is hard to gauge, but its adaptation in the novel draws attention to "the network of falsities and trivialities which make up the funeral" (*SH* 168):

> —I was sorry to hear of the death of your sister . . . sorry we didn't know in time . . . to have been at the funeral.
> Stephen released his hand gradually and said:
> —O, she was very young . . . a girl.
> McCann released his hand at the same rate of release, and said:
> —Still . . . it hurts.
> The acme of unconvincingness seemed to Stephen to have been reached at that moment.
> (*SH* 169)

The dialogue here is almost identical to "I Was Sorry," but the context in *Stephen Hero* and the final line Joyce adds show how empty and unconvincing Stephen finds McCann's condolences, whereas the significance of the epiphany is open to interpretation. As though to emphasize the banality of the scene, in *Stephen Hero*, Stephen is "looking into a haberdasher's window at some ties" (*SH* 169).

Source: Buffalo 1.A.45 (*JJA* 7:29–30). Lead pencil cross, upper left corner. Numbered 45 on the verso.

Variants: The Yale typescript adds a line break after the heading, prints four dots instead of five in lines 4, 5, and 7, and alters the lineation of lines 2–5 (Yale GEN MSS 108 XV.64.1503.13).

[The Race]

The Cockney accent and slush mentioned in "The Race" might suggest a wintry event in London, but there was no racing at any of the major London racecourses during Joyce's visits in December 1902 or January 1903 (Bowker, "Joyce" 669). In "Nestor," the adaptation seemingly refers to a Dublin racetrack, implying that Cranly's real-life counterpart, J. F. Byrne, may have taken Joyce to the Leopardstown Racing Circuit in Dún Laoghaire (the only track in Dublin at the time). However, the switch to Dublin could also have been made for the sake of verisimilitude, like the real racehorses named in "Nestor" (whereas Bonny Boy appears to be Joyce's invention). The difficulty in identifying the horse and venue in "The Race," as well as its oneiric imagery, makes it possible that this was based on a dream, although other elements recall the realism of "Two Mourners."

Echoes and Adaptations

Homer's Nestor was, among other things, a "master of horsemanship" (Homer 23; Gifford and Seidman 30), and as Stephen eyes pictures of famous racehorses on the wall of Deasy's office, he recalls a visit to a racecourse:

> Where Cranly led me to get rich quick, hunting his winners among the mudsplashed brakes, amid the bawls of bookies on their pitches and reek of the canteen, over the motley slush. Fair Rebel! Fair Rebel! Even money the favourite: ten to one the field. Dicers and thimbleriggers we hurried by after the hoofs, the vying caps and jackets and past the meatfaced woman, a butcher's dame, nuzzling thirstily her clove of orange.
>
> (*U* 2.307–12)

Here the epiphany is framed as Stephen's memories of a day at the races with Cranly, which may indicate that the epiphany was, after all, based on a real event. In any case, the adaptation retains many details from the original ("bawls of bookies," "motley slush"), but particularizes them ("meatfaced woman, a butcher's dame, nuzzling thirstily her clove of orange") or adapts them to fit the narrative context ("Fair Rebel!").

Stephen recalls the same scene in "Nighttown," where his drunken hallucinations transform a fox hunt into a horse race, drawing on "The Race" for its depiction of the crowd, the shouts of bookies, and the description of the horse:

> (. . . *The crowd bawls of dicers, crown and anchor*
> *players, thimbleriggers, broadsmen. Crows*
> *and touts, hoarse bookies in high wizard hats*
> *clamour deafeningly.*)

THE CROWD

Card of the races. Racing card!
Ten to one the field!
Tommy on the clay here! Tommy on the clay!
Ten to one bar one! Ten to one bar one!
Try your luck on Spinning Jenny!
Ten to one bar one!
Sell the monkey, boys! Sell the monkey!
I'll give ten to one!
Ten to one bar one!

(A dark horse, riderless, bolts like a phantom past the winningpost, his mane moonfoaming, his eyeballs stars. The field follows, a bunch of bucking mounts. Skeleton horses, Sceptre, Maximum the Second, Zinfandel, the duke of Westminster's Shotover, Repulse, the duke of Beaufort's Ceylon, prix de Paris. Dwarfs ride them, rustyarmoured, leaping, leaping in their saddles. Last in a drizzle of rain on a brokenwinded isabelle nag, Cock of the North, the favourite, honey cap, green jacket, orange sleeves, Garrett Deasy up, gripping the reins, a hockeystick at the ready. His nag on spavined whitegaitered feet jogs along the rocky road.)
  (*U* 15.3964–85)

The sequence of perspectives in this scene is similar to the epiphany, with the description of the crowd, followed by the bookies' shouts, and then the horses running past.

Source: Buffalo 1.A.52 (*JJA* 7:31–32). Numbered 52 on the verso.

Variants: Cornell 17.49, Stanislaus Joyce's copy, omits the dash after "child" (line 12) and adds "slowly" to line 14 ("moving slowly backwards and forwards through the thick ooze"). The ellipsis in line 12 has six dots, with five in line 17. Lineation has been altered in all lines except the first (*JJA* 7:59).

[She Comes at Night]

Stanislaus Joyce provides the context for "She Comes at Night":

> Alone in Paris my brother had felt the black shadow of the priest that had fallen between him and his mother fade away into a vague, troubled memory. She had come to him in a dream confused in his sleeping brain with the image of the Virgin Mother.
>
> (*MBK* 229)

This would seem to imply that the epiphany was written during one of Joyce's sojourns to Paris (December 3–22, 1902, or January 23–April 11, 1903). However, after quoting the epiphany, probably from his own "Selections in Prose," Stanislaus comments:

> The epiphany may have been suggested by a letter of my mother. In answering one of my brother's more desperate and disheartened outpourings she had spoken comfortingly of her love for him when he was a child. The sudden summons home had come like the rude shock of reality to the softening influence of Newman's prose, revealed in the epiphany, and, weakened as he was by the manner of his life in Paris, it left indelible traces on his soul.
>
> (*MBK* 229–30)

Here, the reference to the "sudden summons" Joyce received from his father on April 10, 1903 ("MOTHER DYING COME HOME FATHER" [*JJII* 128]), suggests the epiphany was written after Joyce's return from Paris. Stanislaus is notably uncertain about the origins of the epiphany, though, speculating that "the epiphany may have been suggested by a letter" from May Joyce. If so, that letter is lost, but there is little doubt that the female figure in "She Comes at Night" is based on Mrs. Joyce.

Stanislaus provides another account of the epiphany in his *Dublin Diary*, calling it a "nocturne in prose" and relating it to poem 15 of *Chamber Music*: "Jim has written a nocturne in prose beginning 'She comes at night when the City is still,' and a matutine in verse beginning 'From dewy dreams my soul arise'" (*DD* 62). The entry, from July 31, 1904, continues "Jim's style is becoming a little congested and sententious" (62), suggesting these were recent compositions, in which case Joyce must have written the epiphany almost a year after his mother's death of August 13, 1903. This would certainly tally with the epiphany, which reads like a ghostly visitation, and the *Dublin Diary* is a more reliable guide than *My Brother's Keeper* (written in the 1950s), but it is possible that "She Comes at Night" was written earlier.

The spectral quality may partly be ascribed to "the softening influence of Newman's prose" that Stanislaus detects in the epiphany. In *Portrait*, Stephen refers to "the cloistral silver-veined prose of Newman" (*P* 5.77), and Cardinal Newman is quoted several times in the novel, including the following passage from "The Glories of Mary for the Sake of Her Son" in the 1849 volume *Discourses Addressed to Mixed Congregations*:

> He once had meant to come on earth in heavenly glory, but we sinned; and then He could not safely visit us, except with a shrouded radiance and a bedimmed majesty, for He was God. So He came Himself in weakness, not in power; and He sent thee, a creature, in His stead, with a creature's comeliness and lustre suited to our state. And now thy very face and form, dear Mother, speak to us of the Eternal; not like earthly beauty, dangerous to look upon, but like the morning star, which is thy emblem, bright and musical, breathing purity, telling of heaven, and infusing peace. O harbinger of day! O hope of the pilgrim! lead us still as thou hast led; in the dark night, across the bleak wilderness, guide us on to our Lord Jesus, guide us home.
>
> (Newman 359–60)

In light of Stanislaus's comments about May Joyce being confused with Mother Mary in Joyce's dream, and the influence of Newman, this passage offers a possible source for the epiphany, especially since Joyce quotes it almost verbatim in *Portrait* (3.1304–15), soon after Stephen's nightmarish vision of hell, which is based on another epiphany ("Half-Men, Half-Goats").

In addition to Newman, Joyce's Marian discourse draws on the Litany of Loreto for "mother most venerable" (see *P* 1.1002, 3.118) and on the writings of Saint Alphonsus Liguori. In *Portrait*, Stephen reads Liguori's *The Visits to the Most Holy Sacrament* before praying (*P* 4.177–79), leading to an adaptation of "Her Arm on My Knees." Another of Liguori's books, *The Glories of Mary*, is a likely source for "Holy Queen, Mother of Mercy," and specific phrases in "She Comes at Night"—such as the "womb" that closes the epiphany, and the "inmost heart"—are probably also drawn from *The Glories of Mary*, whose final paragraph includes "the least of thy servants" (789), echoed in Joyce's "the / least of her children."

Echoes and Adaptations

In 1912, as Joyce was struggling to find a publisher for *Dubliners*, he wrote to Nora Barnacle of "the book I have written, the child which I have carried for years and years in the womb of the imagination as you carried in your womb the children you love, and of how I had fed it day after day out of my brain and my memory" (*LII* 308–9). Like *Dubliners*, Joyce carried the epiphany "for years and years in the womb of [his] imagination," where it proved "susceptible of change" as he adapted it and transformed it in *Ulysses* and *Finnegans Wake*.

Ulysses

The clearest adaptation of "She Comes at Night" occurs in "Circe," where the ghost of May Dedalus appears to Stephen, uttering several lines that are drawn directly from the epiphany (*U* 15.4197, 15.4203–4). However, this adaptation builds on a series of echoes of the epiphany, reaching all the way back to "Telemachus," where they are introduced by another dream Joyce recorded in his Trieste notebook:

> She came to me silently in a dream after her death: and her wasted body within its loose brown habit gave out a faint odour of wax and rosewood and her breath a faint odour of wetted ashes.
>
>   (Cornell 4609 Bd Ms 1; *JJA* 7:141)

This note appears under the heading "Mother," obviously referring to May Joyce, who died of cancer on August 13, 1903, at age forty-four. With slight revision, the note is recalled in the first episode of *Ulysses*, where Stephen is in mourning for his mother:

> Silently, in a dream she had come to him after her death, her wasted body within its loose brown graveclothes giving off an odour of wax and rosewood, her breath, that had bent upon him, mute, reproachful, a faint odour of wetted ashes.
>
>   (*U* 1:102–5)

The same scene is recollected a few pages later, with the ghostly mother now "bent over [Stephen] with mute secret words" (*U* 1.270–72), suggesting a link to the unspoken knowledge of the inmost heart in "She Comes at Night" (see *U* 2.140–43). This connection is strengthened by Stephen's memories of "her glazing eyes, staring out of death, [. . .] Her hoarse loud breath rattling in horror, [. . .] Her eyes on me to strike me down," the prayer "*Liliata rutilantium*," and "Ghoul! Chewer of corpses!" in the following lines (*U* 1.274–79), all of which are recalled in quick succession when May Dedalus's ghost returns in "Circe" (*U* 15.4157–240). Initially the "Circe" apparition draws on the Trieste notebook ("her breath of wetted ashes": *U* 15.4182), but the climax of the scene is based on Joyce's epiphany, with the mother saying: "Who had pity for you when you were sad among the strangers? [. . .] Years and years I loved you, O, my son, my firstborn, when you lay in my womb" (*U* 15.4197, *U* 15.4203–4). Thus the two dreams, from the Trieste notebook and the epiphany, become fused in *Ulysses*, allowing the "silent word" uttered by the "ghoul" (*U* 15.4200) to suggest at once the "mute secret words" she breathes in "Telemachus" (*U* 1.272), the "inmost heart" of the epiphany, and the "word known to all men" (*U* 15.4192–93), which may or may not be "Love" (*U* 9.429–30).

STEPHEN

(*eagerly*) Tell me the word, mother, if you know now. The word known to all men.

THE MOTHER

Who saved you the night you jumped into the train at Dalkey with Paddy Lee? Who had pity for you when you were sad among the strangers? Prayer is allpowerful. Prayer for the suffering souls in the Ursuline manual and forty days' indulgence. Repent, Stephen.

STEPHEN

The ghoul! Hyena!

THE MOTHER

I pray for you in my other world. Get Dilly to make you that boiled rice every night after your brainwork. Years and years I loved you, O, my son, my firstborn, when you lay in my womb.
(*U* 15.4191–204)

Finnegans Wake

The significance of the epiphany is not confined to *Ulysses*; Joyce was still feeling its "imaginative influence" in the mid-1920s as he drafted the closing section of "Shem the Penman":

MERCIUS (of hisself) [. . .] Pariah, cannibal Cain, I who oathily for-
swore the womb that bore you and the paps I sometimes sucked, [. . .]
it is to you, firstborn and firstfruit of woe, to me, branded sheep, pick
of the wasterpaperbaskel, [. . .] because ye left from me, because ye
laughed on me, because, O me lonely son, ye are forgetting me!, that
our turfbrown mummy is a coming.

(*FW* 193.31–194.22)

From the first draft (January–February 1924) through to publication in
This Quarter (Autumn/Winter 1925), this section was spoken by Shaun
(*JJA* 47:380–81, 47:480; Joyce, *First-Draft* 121–22), but when Joyce revised
the chapter for *Transition* (August–September 1927), where he introduced
"Justus/Justeus" and "Museus/Mercius," he began to blend the voices (*JJA*
47:477). In the proofs for *Transition*, Justius (Shaun) speaks "to himother"
before Mercius (Shem) refers to both himself and Justius (his self) as "Pariah, cannibal Cain" (*FW* 193.31). The "womb that bore you" was present
from the first draft, accompanied by "firstborn" (cf. *U* 15.4204) in the fair
copy (*JJA* 47:428), but in the page proofs for *Transition* Joyce amplified the
echoes: "because ye left from me, because ye laughed on me, because, O me
lonly son, ye are forgetting me!" (*JJA* 47:515). Of course, the original epiphany moves from the third person ("She comes . . . She comes . . . She knows")
to the first: "I am susceptible of change." By drawing on the epiphany and
blending the twins' voices, Joyce helped smooth the flow into ALP's voice at
the end of the chapter (and into book 1, chapter 8): "our turfbrown mother
is acoming, alpilla, beltilla, ciltilla, deltilla, running with her tidings, all the
news of the great big world" (*FW* 194.22–24). The echo of "She Comes at
Night" is particularly significant at this point because book 1, chapter 7, alludes to almost all of Joyce's works before ending with the epiphany.

Among the many motifs in *Finnegans Wake*, it is interesting to note
that the who-when structure of the epiphany becomes a kind of rhythmical refrain (e.g., "who kennot tail a bomb from a painapple when he steals
one," "who cut her ribbons when nought my prowes? Who exposed that
havenlines to beachlured ankerrides when not I, freipforter?": *FW* 167.15,
548.10–12).

Source: Buffalo 1.A.56 (*JJA* 7:33). Numbered 56 on the verso.

Variants: Stanislaus Joyce made two copies of this epiphany on loose sheets
later reused for his diary (Cornell 4609 Bd Ms 3). Besides minor changes in
lineation and punctuation, both copies have "his inmost heart" for "the inmost

heart," "heart of my children" for "hearts of my children," and "alone among the strangers" for "sad among the strangers" (150v, 151v; see *JJA* 7:47, 7:49). The second copy omits "invisible, inaudible, all unsummoned" after the first line (151v; *JJA* 7:49). Further copies in the Yale typescript (GEN MSS 108 XV.64.1503.6) and Stanislaus Joyce's "Selections" (*JJA* 7:53) agree with Buffalo 1.A.56 in all respects except lineation.

[Fred Leslie's My Brother]

Kennington, the setting for the epiphany, is a residential neighborhood on the south side of the Thames, opposite Westminster; "a house" is likely a euphemism for a brothel. This is the only epiphany explicitly located in London. Joyce visited the English capital alone on his way to and from Paris in December 1902, and again in January 1903; the scene is unlikely to have occurred in April 1903, when he was rushing home to his mother's bedside.

The epiphany experiments with vernacular pronunciation and accent. With her frank reference to sex, Eva Leslie is caricatured as a prostitute, and the phonetic spelling (complete with dropped aitches) gives her a panto-mime Cockney accent, although she may have been based on a real person: Gordon Bowker points out that the 1901 census lists a twenty-four-year-old Eva Leslie living in Clerkenwell in East London ("Joyce" 679).

The dialogue in the epiphany implies that an interlocuter has queried her name, asking whether she is related to Fred Leslie, a famous burlesque co-median who performed with the D'Oyly Carte Opera Company (figure 4). The kinship she claims is highly unlikely, however, since he was not merely "awoy," but actually deceased since 1898.

Echoes and Adaptations

Joyce must have been taken with the colorful language of the epiphany, since he put the phrase "whitearsed bugger" into the mouth of Private Carr in the "Nighttown" chapter of *Ulysses*. Having fled from Bella Cohen's brothel after smashing the chandelier, Stephen is assaulted by the drunken Carr, whose parting shot as he is pulled off Stephen is: "God fuck old Ben-nett. He's a whitearsed bugger. I don't give a shit for him" (*U* 15.4795–97)

The singularly colorful "whitearsed" is also echoed repeatedly in *Finne-gans Wake*:

This is the Willingdone on his same white harse, the Cokenhape. [. . .] This is his big wide harse. [. . .] Toffeethief, that spy on the Willing-done from his big white harse [. . .]. This is the Willingdone hanking the half of the hat of lipoleums up the tail on the buckside of his big

white harse. [. . .] This is the same white harse of the Willingdone [. . .]
on the back of his big wide harse.

(*FW* 8.16–10.21)

In this tour of the "Willingdone Museyroom" (*FW* 8.9), "whitearse" is a
pun ("white horse") on the Duke of Wellington's (chestnut brown) horse
Copenhagen, but as the passage continues, Wellington and "his big wide
harse" are associated with the story of Buckley and the Russian general, a
recurrent motif that culminates in the general dropping his pants: "How
culious [arsey] an epiphany!" (*FW* 508.11).

With its depiction of prostitution in London, the epiphany might also
have contributed indirectly to a short passage on Covent Garden prostitutes
in *Portrait* (*P* 5.2092–97).

Source: Buffalo 1.A.57 (*JJA* 7:35–36). Numbered 57 on the verso.

Variants: The Yale typescript has "yer" for "yev" (line 4) and "missing" for
"musing" (lines 5 and 12). Line breaks have been added after the heading and
before "later" (line 8), with changed lineation in lines 9–13 (Yale GEN MSS 108
XV.64.1503.14).

Mr FRED LESLIE as "Rip Van Winkle."

Figure 4. Fred Leslie as Rip Van
Winkle, circa 1880s. Photograph
by Alfred Ellis and Walery.
Courtesy of the David B. Lovell
Collection of Gilbert and Sullivan
ephemera and memorabilia.
Reprinted with permission.

[The Two Sisters]

Stanislaus Joyce described "The Two Sisters" as an amusing dream-epiphany, "Another note of a dream, in which Ibsen figured and Norway is confused with Denmark in a way Norwegians do not appreciate" (*MBK* 126).

The identification of Henrik Ibsen in the epiphany is borne out by the fact that Ibsen was five foot one in height, and in his early seventies between 1900 and 1904 ("how small he is! He must / be very old"). Joyce held Ibsen in great esteem, writing a glowing review of *When We Dead Awaken* in 1900 and writing to Ibsen personally in 1901 (see "Ibsen's Age"). The reference to his "old-fashioned high hat" is explained by Stuart Gilbert: "to the Romans, Ibsen, when living in their city, was merely the Cappellone—the fellow with the big hat" (173).

Stanislaus's comment about Norway being confused with Denmark in the epiphany helps explain the dispute between the two sisters and the vexed question of "their language." Ibsen wrote his plays in Dano-Norwegian, which was "essentially a dialect of Danish" (Mamigonian and Turner 370), and he had allegiances to both countries. At the time Joyce was reading Ibsen in the late 1890s, Ibsen had returned to Norway after twenty-eight years in exile (having left in 1863 as a protest against Norway's failure to defend Denmark against the German League). During that period of exile, both Denmark and Norway claimed Ibsen as a native. In the epiphany, this dispute is represented allegorically by the two sisters who have been fighting over the playwright. The Danish sister is "churning with stout arms (their butter is / famous)," but she is "unhappy" because her Norwegian sister has "had her way," successfully claiming Ibsen for herself. This historical allegory is unusual among Joyce's dream-epiphanies, though Stanislaus comments on the allegorical significance of "An Arctic Beast" and "His Dancing."

Another distinctive feature of this epiphany is the dash after the line of dialogue: "—Are you Rina?—." Unique among the holograph epiphanies, Joyce's punctuation here may indicate that "The Sisters" was written later, although several of the epiphanies in Stanislaus's hand employ the same convention (e.g., "She Dances with Them in the Round," "Is That Mary Ellen?"), and dialogue between dashes is relatively common in Joyce's early work (see Bénéjam and Bonapfel).

Joyce did not adapt "Two Sisters" directly, but the central focus of the epiphany has echoes in the sororities of "The Sisters" and "The Dead."

Source: Buffalo 1.A.59 (*JJA* 7:37–38). Numbered 59 on the verso.

Variants: Cornell 17.50 includes numerous punctuation changes, suggesting that either Stanislaus or James Joyce revised the original. The first comma is replaced by a dash ("Yes—they are the two sisters" [line 1]), and there is a semicolon after "unhappy" (line 3). The five dots after "vain" (line 14) are replaced by a dash, with no capital for "Maybe": in Stanislaus's copy, this line reads "He must be very old and vain—maybe he isn't what I . . . . ." There are five dots in the ellipsis here, compared to three in the Buffalo manuscript (line 14), five dots instead of four after "coat" (line 12), and three after "little man" (line 16). The final ellipsis is cut from Stanislaus's "Selections," which ends "the greatest man on earth," rather than "the greatest man in the / world. . . ." (lines 16–17; *JJA* 7:60). Stanislaus's copy has been ticked in blue ink.

The Yale typescript is more accurate; besides changes to lineation and discrepancies in the length of ellipses, the only substantial changes are to "jutting" (line 12), which is misread as "putting," and "how" (line 13), which is capitalized. The typist inserted line breaks before and after the dialogue (line 7), and there is a wavy horizontal line in black ink after "I knew she was" (line 8), which seems to indicate a break before the final paragraph (Yale GEN MSS 108 XV.64.1503.19).

[I Lie along the Deck]

The crossing described in "I Lie along the Deck" took place on April 11, 1903, when Joyce traveled from Dieppe to Dublin via Newhaven, to be at his mother's bedside. Looking back at the French coast from the deck of the ferry, the speaker imagines a service in "the dark cathedral / church of Our Lady." This must be Notre-Dame in Paris, where Joyce attended Tenebrae on April 7, 8, and 9 and an Easter service on April 10 (Bowker, *James* 106), after which he returned to Hotel Corneille to find the shocking telegram: "MOTHER DYING COME HOME FATHER" (*JJII* 128).

This dating excludes it from being part of the collection of fifteen new epiphanies that Joyce refers to in a letter to his brother Stanislaus in March 1903 (*LII* 35).

Echoes and Adaptations

There are no clear adaptations of the epiphany, but David Hayman draws an interesting analogy with *Ulysses*, comparing the juxtaposition of the sea and the recollected sounds of a cathedral service in the epiphany to a similar combination in "Nausicaa," where Gerty's views across the strand and out to sea are juxtaposed with sounds of the service she hears drifting down from St. Mary's, a church in Sandymount (Joyce, *Epifanías* 56).

Source: Buffalo 1.A.65 (*JJA* 7:39–40). Numbered 65 on the verso.

Variants: Cornell 17.52–53 alters Joyce's lineation and includes a number of minor punctuation changes: the hyphen in "engine-house" (lines 1–2) is removed, the ellipses in lines 5 and 6 are extended (from two to four and five to six dots, respectively), and the commas after "walls" and "bright" (lines 7 and 8) are cut. Otherwise, Stanislaus's copy is faithful to Joyce's manuscript, making it almost certain that the word at the end of line 4 (illegible due to a hole in the page) is "coast" (*JJA* 7:62–63). In Stanislaus's copy, the epiphany has been ticked in red pencil or crayon.

[Is Mabie Your Sweetheart?]

Connaught Street is a residential street that connects with St. Peter's Terrace in Phibsborough, where the Joyces lived from October 1902 to March 1904, and where May Joyce died. "Mabie" may refer to Joyce's sister Mabel, born in 1893, although she was usually called "Baby" by the family.

Eugene Sheehy relates a comical encounter with Joyce and his brother Stanislaus on Phibsborough Road when a nurserymaid with a baby carriage bumped into Joyce and he fell into the pram (O'Connor 32–33).

Echoes and Adaptations

Ulysses

Joyce reused the epiphany in "Nausicaa," where young Tommy Caffrey is teased by Edy Boardman and his sister Cissy:

> She put an arm round the little mariner and coaxed winningly:
> —What's your name? Butter and cream?
> —Tell us who is your sweetheart, spoke Edy Boardman. Is Cissy your sweetheart?
> —Nao, tearful Tommy said.
> —Is Edy Boardman your sweetheart? Cissy queried.
> —Nao, Tommy said.
> —I know, Edy Boardman said none too amiably with an arch glance from her shortsighted eyes. I know who is Tommy's sweetheart. Gerty is Tommy's sweetheart.
> —Nao, Tommy said on the verge of tears.
> (*U* 13.64–74)

Despite a few minor alterations, the adaptation is in keeping with the original, except that in "Nausicaa" there is a more pressing reason for Tommy's discomfort: his need to urinate.

Finnegans Wake

The incestuous suggestion that Tommy might be sweet on his sister echoes into the "Games" chapter of *Finnegans Wake*, where the children play a guessing game in which Glugg (Shem) tries to guess the color of his sister's underwear:

> —Haps thee jaoneofergs?
> —Nao.
> —Haps thee mayjaunties?
> —Naohao.
> —Haps thee per causes nunsibellies?
> —Naohaohao.
> (*FW* 233.21–26)

Oddly, these guesses all shade toward a single color: "jaoneofergs" is the jaune (yoke) of eggs; "mayjaunties" suggests magenta, which may indicate jaundice; and "nunsibellies" refers to the yellowish color of a Barriga de Freira, a Portuguese pastry whose name means "nun's belly." It would be stupid to guess the same color three times, and Glugg is certainly not dim. We might think then that his yellow (cowardly?) guesses are a sign of prudishness—he is supposed to be guessing the color of his sister's underwear, after all. But Glugg's variations are slightly lurid, charged with a hint of desire, like the original epiphany and its earlier adaptation in "Nausicaa." Issy seems to be laughing at Glugg as her "Nao-hao-hao"s get longer, but her lines are obviously adapted from the epiphany, and just as the young women in "Is Mabie Your Sweetheart?" are aware of the erotic undercurrents to their questioning, so too Issy seems to understand Glugg's implications, even sharing the joke when the color is revealed. Her underwear is heliotrope, which usually refers to a purple or reddish color (as in flowers of the *Heliotropium* genus or the heliotrope gem known as bloodstone) but which literally means "sun-turning" and was originally applied to flowers that follow the sun, such as sunflowers (French *tournesol*, Italian *girasole*) and marigolds, which are bright yellow or gold.

"An Encounter"

In "An Encounter," a "queer old josser" interrogates the boy narrator and his friend Mahony about their sweethearts, giving a darker twist to the questioning in the epiphany:

Then he asked us which of us had the most sweethearts. Mahony mentioned lightly that he had three totties. The man asked me how many had I. I answered that I had none. He did not believe me and said he was sure I must have one. I was silent.

—Tell us, said Mahony pertly to the man, how many have you yourself?

The man smiled as before and said that when he was our age he had lots of sweethearts.

—Every boy, he said, has a little sweetheart.

(*D* 17)

A Portrait of the Artist as a Young Man

"Is Mabie Your Sweetheart?" is not adapted directly in *Portrait*, but when Stephen is pressured by his schoolmate Heron to admit his attraction to Emma Clery (*P* 2.595–645), the situation recalls the epiphany.

Source: Buffalo 1.A.70 (*JJA* 7:41–42). Lead pencil cross, upper left corner. Numbered 70 on the verso.

Variants: The Yale typescript changes the lineation and has "Connaught St.," with no comma following; otherwise the text is identical (Yale GEN MSS 108 XV.64.1503.11).

[The Lesson That She Reads]

"The Lesson That She Reads" has been interpreted ekphrastically as "the portrait of a woman by (or in the style of) Raffaello" (*JJA* 7:xxvii). Joyce's vignette is certainly painterly, but if he was describing an actual work of art by Raphael or anyone else, it has not been discovered. Rather, he seems to have painted from life: according to Stanislaus Joyce, the model for the woman in the epiphany was their cousin Kathleen (Katsy) Murray, daughter of Josephine and William Murray (S. Joyce, "James" 107). Richard Ellmann states that Joyce had a "transitory interest" (i.e., love interest) in Katsy (*JJII* 155), before falling for Mary Sheehy, then Nora Barnacle. This is questionable, to say the least, as Katsy was only eleven in 1900, when Joyce, then eighteen, began writing his epiphanies; if Stanislaus is right about the identification, Joyce's interest in Katsy is aesthetic and literary. The sight of Katsy reading must have been common in the household since Stanislaus recorded on April 3, 1904, that "I read, like Katsy learning her lesson, to get words" (*DD* 37). In the epiphany, Katsy is studying a particular lesson ("the lesson") in a specific book, which might suggest that the subjects mentioned are to be found in a single work, such as Richmal Mangnall's 1798 volume *Historical and Miscellaneous Questions for the Use of Young People*, which Stephen studies in the first chapter of *Portrait*. But the question in the second paragraph—"What is the lesson that she reads—of apes, / of strange inventions, or the legends of / martyrs?"—is obviously rhetorical, speculating on the kind of subjects she might be absorbed in, rather than pointing to a specific text. Nevertheless, the topics considered are significant, combining "a possible reference to Darwin and the products of modernity, with the religious literature of legends of the martyrs" (Lernout, *Help* 111).

It has been noted before that Joyce's vignette is "done in Pateresque prose" (*WD* 49), but a precise source has not been identified. One possibility is Walter Pater's extraordinary study of Leonardo da Vinci in *The Renaissance: Studies in Art and Poetry* (1873). Joyce's prose-poetic style in the lyrical epiphanies was almost certainly influenced by the lyricism of Pater's prose in *The Renaissance*, whose famous conclusion is echoed in *Stephen Hero* and *Portrait*, so it would not be surprising if Joyce returned, consciously or unconsciously, to Pater's volume, and certain phrases in the epiphany seem to echo Pater's attempt to capture "Leonardo's type of womanly beauty," as it appears across a whole series of drawings: "Daughters of Herodias, with their fantastic head-dresses knotted and folded so strangely to leave the dainty oval of the face disengaged, they are not of the Christian family, or of Raffaelle's" (74). Pater describes a marked chiaroscuro effect in Leonardo's image, the "dainty oval of the face disengaged" (drawing on a face "set in the shadow of its own hair, the cheek-line in high light against it" just before), which Joyce re-creates: "Against the dark stuff / of her dress her face, mild-featured with / downcast eyes, rises softly outlined in light." Pater's "fantastic head-dresses knotted and folded so strangely" are perhaps echoed in Joyce's description of the woman's eccentric headdress ("from a folded cap, set carelessly forward, / a tassel falls"). As a quiet, still scene of the absorption of reading, it evokes "A Story of Alsace."

Of course, the distinguishing characteristic of Leonardo's portraits ("they are not of the Christian family, or of Raffaelle's") is directly opposed to the last line of the epiphany, so one might wonder why, if Joyce was drawing on Pater's essay, he didn't write "this comeliness of Leonardo." There is a possible explanation in the fact that Pater's essay positions Leonardo explicitly in opposition to Raphael: in the "twofold" movement of the Renaissance, "Raffaelle represents the return to antiquity, and Leonardo the return to nature" (*Renaissance* 70). One would expect Joyce to side with the "modern spirit" of Leonardo, whose "finest inventions" seem to be echoed in the "strange inventions" of the epiphany, but Joyce was also aware of his literary debts. By echoing Pater but mentioning Raphael, Joyce self-reflexively draws attention to his own imaginary portrait, which takes after Pater, but is not an imitation.

Another possible source for the "comeliness of / Raffaello" is John Ruskin's *Mornings in Florence* (1875–77), a book Joyce had in his library (stamped September 1898). Ruskin's estimation of Raphael—his superlative ability to paint "draperies cast into folds" (42), for example—is perhaps echoed in the epiphany.

Echoes and Adaptations

The "brown ringletted / hair" of the woman in the epiphany can be compared to Gerty MacDowell's "wonderful hair. It was dark brown with a natural wave in it [. . .] it nestled about her pretty head in a profusion of luxuriant clusters." Similarly, Gerty's "rather sad downcast eyes" may recall the "downcast eyes" of the epiphany (*U* 13.107–27).

Source: Buffalo 1.A.71 (*JJA* 7:43–44). Numbered 71 on the verso.

Variants: Cornell 17.65 has "her ^a^ book" (line 1): Stanislaus's correction suggests that he may have copied another version of the epiphany, since "her book" is correct in the Buffalo manuscript. The change is of a different kind to the scribal error Stanislaus catches in the final sentence ("how deeply reminis meditative"). Elsewhere, there are minor lineation and punctuation changes (both commas are omitted in line 5; there are five dots at the end of the first paragraph: see *JJA* 7:69). Stanislaus's copy bears a tick in blue ink. The Yale typescript is an exact copy of the Buffalo manuscript, except for lineation and a single dot at the end of the first paragraph (Yale GEN MSS 108 XV.64.1503.8).

[Is That for Gogarty?]

This is the only surviving draft of an epiphany (figure 5), providing a unique glimpse into how Joyce composed his epiphanies. The addition to the opening stage direction specifies the location: Hamilton, Long and Company was an apothecary, perfumer, and manufacturer of mineral waters with a number of premises across Dublin, including at 5 Lower O'Connell Street, where this epiphany is set. The next two revisions ("pay" for "take it with you" and "put it on the account" for "send it on") give the exchange a pecuniary edge, bringing Gogarty's credit into focus. The change from "as" to "while" indicates the importance of aural effects, even in the dramatic epiphanies, and the phonetic extension of "Ye . . es" helps establish the tone, creating a sharp contrast between the assistant's hesitant deference and Gogarty's crisp imperatives, making Gogarty seem presumptuous.

Gogarty is a contemporary of Joyce: Oliver St. John Gogarty, a medical student at Trinity College Dublin from 1897 to 1904. Gogarty was born and brought up at 5 Rutland Square, a desirable address in what is now Parnell Square. In his autobiography, the title of Gogarty's first chapter is "5 Rutland Square. East" (the oldest and most distinguished side of the square), a sign, perhaps, of his snobbishness, which appears in the epiphany through the emphasis on "Rutland" and Gogarty's assumption that the assistant knows his address.

In the early 1900s, Gogarty was gaining a reputation as a wit and poet, with connections to W. B. Yeats and George Moore. Joyce briefly studied medicine, enrolling in the University College Medical School in October 1902, which brought him into closer contact with Gogarty; with their shared literary interests and studies, the two became friendly (*MBK* 241). However, after Gogarty returned to Dublin after two terms in Oxford, the friendship became strained. It was effectively ended by their brief shared residency in the Martello Tower in September 1904. It is likely, therefore, that this visit to a chemist took place between October 1902 and September 1904, and we can narrow the interval because Joyce was in Paris in December 1902 and January–April 1903, while Gogarty was in Oxford from January to June 1904.

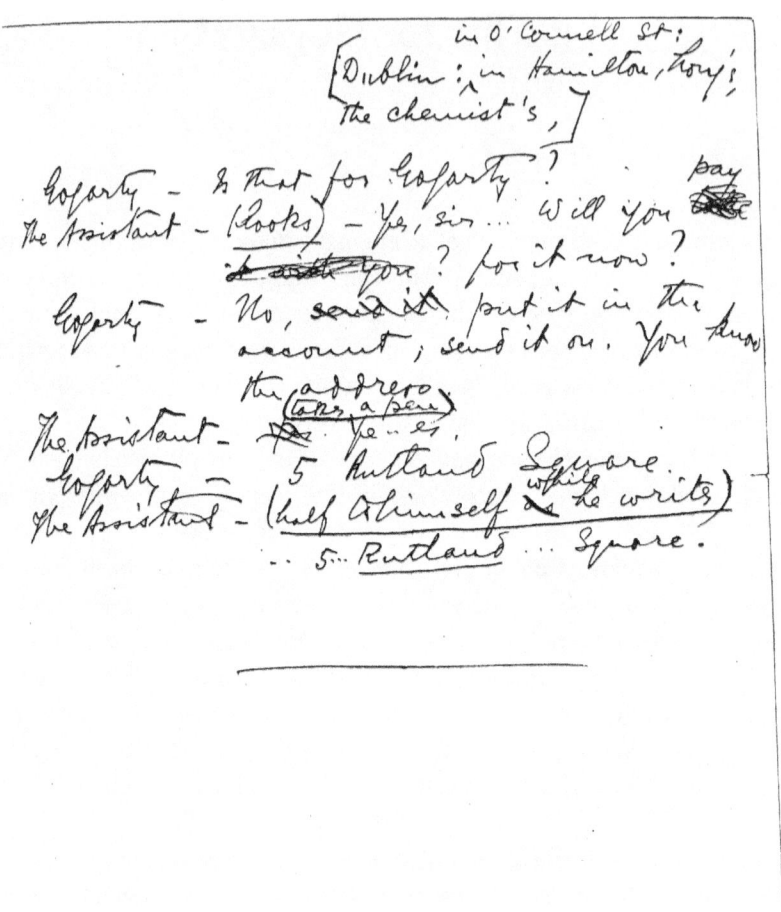

Figure 5. "Is That for Gogarty?" Cornell 18. Held by the Division of Rare and Manuscript Collections at Cornell University Library. Reprinted with the permission of the James Joyce Estate.

In his 1937 memoir *As I Was Going Down Sackville Street*, Gogarty suggests that Joyce's epiphanic note-taking was a common occurrence:

> I was trying to recall what spark had been struck or what "folk phrase" Joyce had culled from Elwood or me that sent him out to make his secret record.
>
> Secrecy of any kind corrupts sincere relations. I don't mind being reported, but to be an unwilling contributor to one of his "Epiphanies" is irritating.

Probably Father Darlington had taught him, as an aside in his Latin class—for Joyce knew no Greek—that "Epiphany" meant "a showing forth." So he recorded under "Epiphany" any showing forth of the mind by which he considered one gave oneself away.

Which of us had endowed him with an "Epiphany" and sent him to the lavatory to take it down?

(294–95)

Gogarty's *Phantasy in Fact*—the subtitle of *As I Was Going Down Sackville Street*—suggests that Joyce was in the habit of scurrying off to toilets to scribble down epiphanies, in which case one might expect more epiphanies based on Gogarty, but besides this draft, the only comparable text is the Doherty fragment, which is not usually considered an epiphany (see Crispi, "Stephen").

Stanislaus Joyce also casts doubt on Gogarty's account. Referring to "Two Mourners," written after their mother's funeral in May 1903, Stanislaus responds: "That does not mean, however, that [Joyce] was vigilant, still less that it was his habit to take notes, as Gogarty and Eglinton both assert with misleading assurance. The only note he took was the one I have quoted" (*MBK* 235). However, Joyce was in the habit of taking notes throughout his career, and many of the epiphanies are drawn from real-life events; what Stanislaus seems to object to is not the notetaking per se, but the scurrilous suggestion that Joyce's epiphanies, jotted down in privies, were invasions of privacy.

Echoes and Adaptations

There are no clear adaptations, but echoes of the epiphany may be heard in Bloom's visit to Sweny's pharmacy in "Lotus Eaters," where he thinks of "Hamilton Long's, founded in the year of the flood" (*U* 5.464–65), and again in "Wandering Rocks," where Boylan gives orders to a shop assistant with Gogarty-like assurance:

—Can you send them by tram? Now?
      A darkbacked figure under Merchants' arch scanned books on the hawker's cart.
—Certainly, sir. Is it in the city?
—O, yes, Blazes Boylan said. Ten minutes.
      The blond girl handed him a docket and pencil.
—Will you write the address, sir?

Blazes Boyan at the counter wrote and pushed the docket to her.

—Send it at once, will you? he said. It's for an invalid.

—Yes, sir. I will, sir.

(*U* 10.314–23)

Source: Cornell 18 (*JJA* 7:45). This is the only surviving draft.

[The Spell of Arms and Voices]

Joyce told his brother Stanislaus that "The Spell of Arms and Voices" was written "to mark the precise point between boyhood (*pueritia*) and adolescence (*adulescentia*)—17 years" (February 7, 1905; *LII* 79). Here, as in *Dubliners*, Joyce adopts the Roman life span, with childhood continuing until seventeen, adolescence until thirty, young manhood (*juventus*) until forty-five, and then finally old age (*senectus*) (Walzl, "Dubliners" 199–200). Joyce turned seventeen on February 2, 1899, during his matriculation year at University College Dublin, a time when he was moving away from the Jesuit curriculum to immerse himself in contemporary European literature. In the following year, while still a student, he read his first paper, "Drama and Life," to the Literary and Historical Society; published his first article, a review of Ibsen's *When We Dead Awaken* for the prestigious *Fortnightly Review* (April 1900); turned from juvenile prose and verse ("Silhouettes," *Moods*, *Shine and Dark*) to drama (*Dream Stuff*, *A Brilliant Career*); and began to compose his epiphanies.

David Weir argues that the ship imagery derives from Charles Baudelaire's 1861 poem "Le Voyage," whose voyageur imagines embarking on a grand adventure only to find the world a squalid and disappointing place. As Weir notes, both texts describe an imminent departure with "mysteriously beckoning voices and arms. In 'Le Voyage,' the voices chant, 'charmantes et funèbres,' and 'Nos Pylades là-bas tendent leurs bras vers nous'" ("Stephen" 90), echoed in the "spell of arms and voices" with "their promise of close embraces" in the epiphany and *Portrait* (*P* 5.2778–80).

The beckoning figures calling to the speaker in the second part of the epiphany also recall the mysterious robed figures who summon the narrator to join their heretical sect, the Order of the Alchemical Rose, at the climax of W. B. Yeats's 1896 story "The Tables of the Law." The language of the epiphany is Joyce's, but many of its themes and images, such as travel, voices, beckoning, wings, and transgression, are shared with Yeats's story, "whole pages of which Joyce knew by heart" (*JJII* 81). Joyce particularly praised "The Tables of the Law" and the 1897 essay "The Adoration of the Magi" when he met Yeats circa 1902 (*MBK* 180), prompting Yeats to republish them in 1904. Stephen also praises these stories in *Stephen Hero*, quoting the robed figures from "The Tables of the Law" (*SH* 176–78). Whereas Yeats's narrator flees from the heretical figures, however, Joyce's speaker is drawn to their call.

Echoes and Adaptations

Robert Scholes rightly called this a "crucial" epiphany (*WD* 40), not least because it stands at the crossroads between three texts: *Stephen Hero*, *Portrait*, and *Ulysses*.

The original draft of *Stephen Hero* included scenes of childhood like those in *Portrait* (*LII* 79), but the first 476 pages of the manuscript were lost or destroyed. The surviving pages begin midway through "The Spell of Arms and Voices," where the epiphany is transposed to fit the third-person, past-tense narrative, but otherwise little changed. This could imply that Joyce was dissatisfied with the "boyhood" sections he had written, preserving only Daedalus's adolescence in *Stephen Hero* (as defined in his letter of February 1905), or it may be explained by the revisions he made for *A Portrait of the Artist as a Young Man*.

All the material Joyce adapted from the extant portion of *Stephen Hero* appears in the last chapter of *Portrait*, culminating in Stephen's diary, which includes three epiphanies in as many pages. The last of these is "The Spell of Arms and Voices," reused with only one substantive change ("kinsmen" replaces "people"), less than ten lines from the end of the novel, as Stephen stands on the brink of departure, poised between the triumphant flight of the artist and a hubristic fall. Joyce marked "Departure for Paris" diagonally across this epiphany on the manuscript of *Stephen Hero* (*JJA* 8:1; figure 6). The note was surely made when Joyce was revising *Stephen Hero* for *Portrait*, although there is no evidence in the published novel that Stephen is destined for Paris. With the destination left vague, Joyce's lyrical prose and dreamlike associations capture a mood or "spell," rather than a specific event: "I go to encounter for the millionth time the reality of experience and to forge In the smithy of my soul the uncreated conscience of my race" (*P* 5.2788–90), Stephen declares, but in the final entry, as he calls on his namesake ("Old Father, old artificer" [*P* 5.2791]), he positions himself as both Icarus and Daedalus, "shaking the wings of their exultant and terrible youth" (*P* 5.2784).

Although "The Spell of Arms and Voices" is not reused directly in *Ulysses*, the arrival of a "threemaster, . . . a silent ship" (*U* 3.503–5) at the end of "Proteus" echoes this epiphany, as well as "The Ship."

Source: Cornell 17.40–41 (*JJA* 7:50–51). This is the only surviving copy.

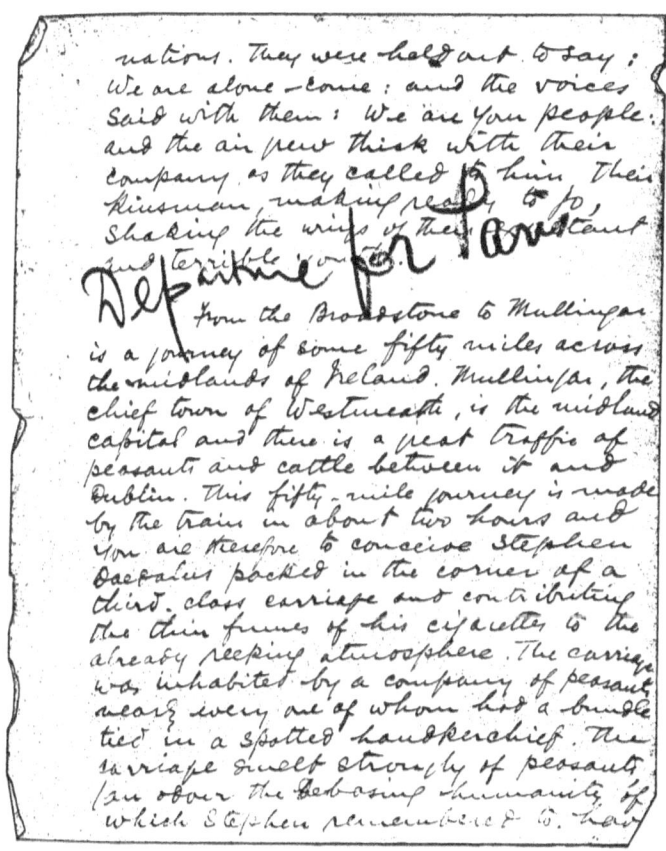

Figure 6. *Stephen Hero* 477 (the first surviving page of the manuscript). Yale 112, Series II (*JJA* 8:1). Reprinted with the permission of the James Joyce Estate.

[Her Arm on My Knees]

Stanislaus Joyce surmised that "Her Arm on My Knees" describes Hanna Sheehy, the same young woman as in "She Dances with Them in the Round" (*MBK* 257). However, there is a noticeable difference between the realism of the earlier Sheehy epiphanies, such as "Ibsen's Age," "Your Favourite Poet," and "Order, Order!" and the imagery of this epiphany, which seems to be drawn from the Song of Songs.

Joyce's image of the adored ("her eyes have revealed / her—secret, vigilant, an enclosed garden") recalls Songs 4:12: "a garden inclosed is my sister, my spouse; a spring shut up, a fountain sealed" (KJV). The "harmony of red and / white that was made for one like her" may refer to the praise of the beloved's mouth in Songs 4:2–3: "Thy teeth are like a flock of sheep that are even shorn. . . . Thy lips are like a thread of scarlet." "Telling her / names and glories" probably apostrophizes the blazon of the beloved's body in 4:1–7, importuning her to "Come with me from Lebanon, my spouse . . . : look from the top of Amana, from the top of Shenir and Hermon, from the lions' dens, from the mountains of the leopards" (4:8). The similarity with Joyce's "bidding her look / forth, a spouse, from Amana and from the / mountains of the leopards" is evident, and "bidding her arise, as for / espousal" evokes Songs 2:13 and 3:11. Clearest of all, the final line, "Inter ubera mea commorabitur," is a direct quotation from the Vulgate Song of Songs, translated in the King James Bible as "He shall lie all night betwixt my breasts" (1:13).

Echoes and Adaptations

Despite his fervent devotions, Stephen is unable to curb his emotions to achieve the perfect piety he aspires to in *Portrait* (4.1). His "soul traverse[s] a period of desolation" in which the power of the Eucharist wanes. Instead of Holy Communion, he experiences "dissolving moments of virginal self-surrender" when he is alone in church with Alphonsus Liguori's 1745 volume *The Visits to the Most Holy Sacrament and the Blessed Virgin Mary*. In these moments of private communion, images from the Song of Songs (or Canticle of Canticles, as it is known to Catholics) blend with the service:

the imagery of the canticles was interwoven with the communicant's prayers. An inaudible voice seemed to caress the soul, telling her names and glories, bidding her arise as for espousal and come away, bidding her look forth, a spouse, from Amana and from the mountains of the leopards; and the soul seemed to answer with the same inaudible voice, surrendering herself: *Inter ubera mea commorabitur*.

(*P* 4.183–88)

From "telling her names and glories," the adaptation follows the language of the epiphany closely, but there is a marked change of emphasis. In the epiphany, a mildly erotic physical experience—the young woman laying her arm on the speaker's knees—is elevated and glorified by the biblical imagery, whereas in *Portrait*, Stephen's spiritual longing is eroticized as his soul yields to the caresses of an inaudible voice. Both versions are charged by the symbolism of the Canticles, but in the epiphany it is used to spiritualize the physical, whereas the adaptation in *Portrait* associates Stephen's spiritual longing with his sexual desire.

Joyce may have culled some of the biblical quotations for the *Portrait* passage from Liguori's *Visits*, which provides prayers to Mary for each day of the month, including verses from the Canticles such as "He shall abide between my breasts" (Canticles 1:13 [Douay-Rheims]). However, other lines, such as "bidding her look forth, a spouse, from Amana and from the mountains of the leopards," appear to be adapted directly from the Song of Songs (4:8).

Source: Cornell 17.41 (*JJA* 7:51).

Variants: As well as in his "Selections in Prose from Various Authors," Stanislaus made two copies of this epiphany. Besides minor changes to lineation and punctuation, both copies have "mountain" for "mountains" (line 9) and "whereunto" for "whereto" (line 10), while Cornell 4.152v omits "her" from the phrase "bidding her arise" (line 6) (*JJA* 7:46, 7:48).

[The Big Dog]

Stanislaus Joyce attributed this epiphany to a dream of Joyce's (*MBK* 126), but in *Stephen Hero* the setting, "Where / three roads meet and before a swampy beach," is used to describe Stephen's journey home through Fairview, a coastal suburb of Dublin, "At the fork of the roads before the swampy beach" (*SH* 37). This suggests that the original epiphany may have described a dream about Fairview, or that it was transplanted onto an event there in *Stephen Hero*.

Joyce lived at a number of addresses in Fairview, including 29 Windsor Avenue, Convent Avenue, 13 Richmond Avenue, and 8 Royal Terrace, from mid-1898 to late 1901 (Igoe, *James* 71–87). From all these addresses, the route to the beach led through the reclaimed "sloblands" (*P* 5.76) that are now Fairview Park via the junction of Fairview Strand and Annesley Bridge Road to the west, or Malahide Road and Clontarf Road to the east; either of these junctions could be described as a place "where three roads meet . . . before a swampy beach."

Stanislaus explains that in this epiphany he "inhabited the body of a dog" (*MBK* 126), just as in "An Arctic Beast" he was the sluggish beast. Stanislaus was not offended by the comparisons: "When the true inwardness of the dream was explained to me, I did not object to it very much, because I like dogs anyhow, but I suggested that the lugubrious howl might have perhaps come from some secret part of his own soul" (*MBK* 126). Unlike Stanislaus, Joyce was afraid of dogs, having been "badly bitten by an excited Irish terrier" at Bray at the age of five (*MBK* 4), which left him with a scar on his chin (Sullivan 48). In the epiphany, the dog is pitiful rather than frightening, its "sorrowful howl" and "lamentation" like the unvoiced sorrow of the passersby (see also "An Arctic Beast" and "Upon Me from the Darkness").

Echoes and Adaptations

In *Stephen Hero*, this epiphany is adapted for a sequence in which Stephen decides to skip college to "follow some trivial indication of city life" (*SH* 37). "The Big Dog" describes one such "trivial indication" in his "pauses of rapture":

For not unfrequently in the pauses of rapture Dublin would lay a sudden hand upon his shoulder, and the chill of the summons would strike to his heart. One day he passed on his homeward journey through Fairview. At the fork of the roads before the swampy beach a big dog was recumbent. From time to time he lifted his muzzle in the vapourous air, uttering a prolonged sorrowful howl. People had gathered on the footpaths to hear him. [and] Stephen made one of them till he felt the first drops of rain, and then he continued his way in silence under the dull surveillance of heaven, hearing from time to time behind him the strange lamentation.

(*SH* 38)

Besides minor revisions to the tense and phrasing, there are two significant changes: first, Stephen is explicitly incorporated in the crowd in a way that the speaker of the epiphany was not; second, the comparison between the dog's cry and the voiceless cry of the spectators has been cut. Both changes accentuate the realism of the adaptation: if the original epiphany was based on a dream, here it has clearly been recast as a "real-life" event within the fictional diegesis, as a moment when the reality of Dublin breaks in on Stephen's reveries.

The crowd that has lost its voice and become a "servant" anticipates Joyce's characterization of the Irish masses' subordination to Britain as servitude (*U* 1:146, 1:312).

Source: Cornell 17.42 (*JJA* 7:52), where "voice less" appears as two words. No variants.

[Hoofs upon the Dublin Road]

With its lyrical prose and allusions to "dreams" and "dreamless sleep," "Hoofs upon the Dublin Road" is similar to Joyce's dream-epiphanies, though it was not identified as such by Stanislaus Joyce. It could have been based on a real experience—"the sound of Hoofs upon the Dublin Road" in Bray, for example—but it may also have had a literary source in W. B. Yeats's 1896 poem "The Shadowy Horses," published as "He Bids His Beloved Be at Peace" in the 1899 collection *The Wind among the Reeds*:

> I hear the Shadowy Horses, their long manes a-shake,
> Their hoofs heavy with tumult, their eyes glimmering white;
> The North unfolds above them clinging, creeping night,
> The East her hidden joy before the morning break,
> The West weeps in pale dew and sighs passing away,
> The South is pouring down roses of crimson fire:
> O vanity of Sleep, Hope, Dream, endless Desire,
> The Horses of Disaster plunge in the heavy clay:
> Beloved, let your eyes half close, and your heart beat
> Over my heart, and your hair fall over my breast,
> Drowning love's lonely hour in deep twilight of rest,
> And hiding their tossing manes and their tumultuous feet.
> (Yeats, *Poems* 79)

The language of the epiphany is not drawn directly from Yeats's poem, but in both texts the speaker lies awake hearing a horse or horses passing by and thinks of a "beloved" or a "lover" and their "heart." Yeats's description of the horses and the tired caresses is more elaborate, whereas Joyce makes the town the "weary lover," emphasizing the sound of the hoofs, and the tidings they bear, like a summons to the sleepy town, or the beating of a heart.

Yeats's *The Wind among the Reeds* "awakened [Joyce's] intense admiration when it appeared in 1899" (*JJII* 83), and this poem in particular has been read as a source of inspiration for Joyce's poem "I hear an army charging upon the land" (see Mahaffey 241–42; Pimentel 202; Wawrzycka 113–18). Joyce's poem was written in 1903, alongside Joyce's epiphanies, and has been compared to them (*WD* 5).

Echoes and Adaptations

Joyce incorporated this epiphany in Stephen's diary near the end of *A Portrait of the Artist as a Young Man*:

> 10 April: Faintly, under the heavy night, through the silence of the city which has turned from dreams to dreamless sleep as a weary lover whom no caresses move, the sound of hoofs upon the road. Not so faintly now as they come near the bridge; and in a moment as they pass the darkened windows the silence is cloven by alarm as by an arrow. They are heard now far away, hoofs that shine amid the heavy night as gems, hurrying beyond the sleeping fields to what journey's end—what heart?—bearing what tidings?
>
> (*P* 5.2728–36)

The diary adaptation is largely faithful to the original, although it has been modified to fit its new context (April in Dublin) by removing "summer," changing the "Dublin road" to "the road" and "town" to "city." Joyce's other changes may be explained by Stephen's next entry, which frames the epiphany-based passage as a self-consciously literary inscription rather than a dream: "Read what I wrote last night. Vague words for a vague emotion. Would she like it? I think so. Then I should have to like it also" (*P* 5.2738–39). Stephen's comment may be ironic, but it can also be read sincerely, with specific changes, such as "gems" for "diamonds" and "sleeping fields" for "grey, / still marshes," indicating that Joyce deliberately selected "Vague words for a vague emotion."

There is an echo of the epiphany in *Giacomo Joyce*, where the horse is ridden by Ibsen's eponymous heroine, Hedda Gabler: "Pure air and silence on the upland road: and hoofs. A girl on horseback. Hedda! Hedda Gabler!" (*PSW* 234).

Source: Cornell 17.42–43 (*JJA* 7:53).

Variants: Stanislaus made two copies of this epiphany, with a number of significant changes, on paper he later reused for his diary (Cornell 4609 Bd Ms 3 149v–52v). The first copy (149v–50v) has "passed" for "turned" (line 2), "on" for "upon" (line 4), "faint" for "faintly" (line 5), "air" for "silence" (line 7), "with" for "by" (line 8), "through" for "amid" (line 9), and "like" for "as" (line 10). There are also two changes to punctuation (a comma is placed after "bridge" in line 6 instead of a semicolon, and the final question mark is omitted), and the lineation is altered. One word is added to line 7 ("they pass *under* the dark windows" [emphasis added]), while several phrases are left out in the copy: "as a weary lover whom / no carresses [*sic*] move" (lines 3–4), "in a moment" (line 6), and "still" (line 11). The same changes appear in 151v–52v, although the second copy ends with a full stop, suggesting that the second copy was made from the first, or that both epiphanies were copied from a lost original (see *JJA* 7:46–49). The spelling mistake ("carresses" for "caresses") appears in Stanislaus's "Selections" (*JJA* 7:52).

[The Last Tram]

Judging from Joyce's adaptation in *Portrait*, "The Last Tram" seems to describe a return journey from Harold's Cross, an affluent suburb in South Dublin. Vivien Igoe dates the party to early 1893–94, when the Joyces occupied 14 Fitzgibbon Street near the North Circular Road (*James* 49). At that time, the Dublin United Transport Company ran a horse-drawn tramway from Harold's Cross to Drumcondra, which would have taken Joyce back to the vicinity of Fitzgibbon Street. The line began to be electrified in 1896, providing circumstantial evidence that the party occurred before then (Murphy). If Igoe's dating is correct, the children's party could have included Joyce's friends from Clongowes, the O'Connell Christian Brothers school (early 1894), or Belvedere College (from April 1894). Among the lists of Joyce's contemporaries at Clongowes and Belvedere, only John and Peter Verdon lived close to Harold's Cross (Bradley 19).

Echoes and Adaptations

Stephen Hero

In chapter 17 of *Stephen Hero*, Stephen meets Emma Clery at the Daniels'. Having known her as a child, he dislikes the change he sees in her, but he is nevertheless drawn to Emma, with the link between his childhood affection and teenage attraction strengthened by two scenes that recall the epiphany.

> One rainy night when the streets were too bad for walking she took the Rathmines tram at the Pillar and as she held down her hand to him from the step, thanking him for his kindness and wishing him good-night, that episode of their childhood seemed to magnetise the minds of both at the same instant. The change of circumstances had reversed their positions, giving her the upper hand. He took her hand caressingly, caressing one after another the three lines of the back of her kid glove and numbering her knuckles, caressing also his own past towards which this inconsistent hater of inheritances was always lenient. They smiled at each other; and again in the centre of her ami-

ableness he discerned a point of illwill and he suspected that by her code of honour she was obliged to insist on the forbearance of the male and to despise him for forbearing.

(*SH* 67–68)

Although the epiphany is not reused directly, the passage alludes to a prior use of "The Last Tram," presumably in the missing portion of *Stephen Hero*. The leave-taking scene at the tram at Rathmines (close to Harold's Cross) reminds Stephen of this earlier episode as he "congratulated himself that he had caught an impression of her when she was at her finest," seemingly referring to the epiphany itself or "some pages of sorry verse" inspired by it (*SH* 67). Again, in the passage quoted, "that episode of their childhood" that "seemed to magnetise the minds of both at the same instant" refers to the epiphany, with their positions now reversed (in "The Last Tram" the narrator was "on the upper step and / she on the lower"; in *Stephen Hero*, "she [holds] down her hand to him from the step"). The two moments, in childhood and adolescence, clearly echo each other, although Emma now has "the upper hand." In the epiphany, there was a strong sense of complicity between Stephen and Emma as they shared the tram ride home, whereas when the teenage Emma leaves Stephen at the tram, he seems torn between desire and affection on the one hand, and mistrust or hostility on the other. The significance of these scenes based on "The Last Tram" is underscored by their subsequent encounters: when Emma runs into Stephen outside the National Library, "the night was so fine that she thought she would not take the tram" (*SH* 152), and when they meet again on the steps of the National Library, as they walk together, they see "the tram begin to crawl off the apex of the bridge" (*SH* 188).

In chapter 25, a colloquy between an anonymous young lady and gentleman sets Stephen "composing some ardent verses which he entitled a 'Vilanelle of the Temptress'" (*SH* 211), a scene which repeats the epiphany's combination of a couple and poetic creativity.

A Portrait of the Artist as a Young Man

In *A Portrait of the Artist as a Young Man*, Joyce adapts the epiphany as part of a consciously patterned sequence—"The beautiful Mabel Hunter" (*P* 2.252–74), "Is That Mary Ellen?" (*P* 2.275–302), and "The Last Tram" (*P* 2.303–56)—each of which begins with "He was sitting":

He was sitting in the midst of a children's party at Harold's Cross. His silent watchful manner had grown upon him and he took little part in the games. The children, wearing the spoils of their crackers, danced and romped noisily and, though he tried to share their merriment, he felt himself a gloomy figure amid the gay cocked hats and sunbonnets.

But when he had sung his song and withdrawn into a snug corner of the room he began to taste the joy of his loneliness. The mirth, which in the beginning of the evening had seemed to him false and trivial, was like a soothing air to him, passing gaily by his senses, hiding from other eyes the feverish agitation of his blood while through the circling of the dancers and amid the music and laughter her glances travelled to his corner, flattering, taunting, searching, exciting his heart.

In the hall the children who had stayed latest were putting on their things: the party was over. She had thrown a shawl about her and, as they went together towards the tram, sprays of her fresh warm breath flew gaily above her cowled head and her shoes tapped blithely on the glassy road.

It was the last tram. The lank brown horses knew it and shook their bells to the clear night in admonition. The conductor talked with the driver, both nodding often in the green light of the lamp. On the empty seats of the tram were scattered a few coloured tickets. No sound of footsteps came up or down the road. No sound broke the peace of the night save when the lank brown horses rubbed their noses together and shook their bells.

They seemed to listen, he on the upper step and she on the lower. She came up to his step many times and went down to hers again between their phrases and once or twice stood close beside him for some moments on the upper step, forgetting to go down, and then went down. His heart danced upon her movements like a cork upon a tide. He heard what her eyes said to him from beneath their cowl and knew that in some dim past, whether in life or in revery, he had heard their tale before. He saw her urge her vanities, her fine dress and sash and long black stockings, and knew that he had yielded to them a thousand times. Yet a voice within him spoke above the noise of his dancing heart, asking him would he take her gift to which he had only to stretch out his hand. And he remembered the day when he and Eileen had stood looking into the hotel grounds, watching the waiters running up a trail of bunting on the flagstaff and the foxterrier scampering to and fro on the sunny lawn, and how, all of a sudden, she had broken out into a peal of laughter and had run down the sloping curve of the path. Now, as then, he stood listlessly in his place, seemingly a tranquil watcher of the scene before him.

—She too wants me to catch hold of her, he thought. That's why she came with me to the tram. I could easily catch hold of her when she comes up to my step: nobody is looking. I could hold her and kiss her.

But he did neither: and, when he was sitting alone in the deserted tram, he tore his ticket into shreds and stared gloomily at the corrugated footboard.

(*P* 2.303–56)

To introduce the scene, Joyce has added many details about the children's party and their preparations to leave, but the most significant addition to the epiphany is the increased emphasis on the children's desire. The narrator's implicit excitement as "She comes up to my step / many times and goes down again, . . . and once or twice remains / beside me, forgetting to go down" from the epiphany now figures explicitly: "His heart danced upon her movements like a cork upon a tide." Stephen's incipient attraction is romanticized in a kind of pastiche of heteronormative desire, where eternal love meets in a "tale as old as time": "He heard what her eyes said to him from beneath their cowl and knew that in some dim past, whether in life or in revery, he had heard their tale before"; "[he] knew that he had yielded to them a thousand times." This fantasy is brought down to earth by Stephen's thoughts of catching hold of Emma and kissing her. In the epiphany, the narrator's implicit desire is suppressed by the part-innocent, part-illusory "wisdom of children," which seems to hold that unfulfilled or imaginary desire is preferable to any real kiss, whereas *Portrait* shows Stephen's disappointment at failing to embrace or kiss Emma as he stares "gloomily" at the floor and tears his ticket to pieces.

In both *Stephen Hero* and *Portrait*, the young woman is named Emma Clery, and in both adaptations, she has a muse-like role, inspiring Stephen to write poetry (*SH* 67; *P* 2.612–16). As in *Stephen Hero*, the tram scene is referred to twice more in *Portrait*, and on both occasions it is linked to desire and creativity. In chapter 2, when Stephen is goaded by Heron and Wallis to admit his affection for Emma, their taunts remind Stephen of "their leavetaking on the steps of the tram at Harold's Cross, the stream of moody emotions it had made to course through him" (*P* 2.613–15). And in chapter 5, in the midst of composing his villanelle, Stephen again reaches back to the scene with Emma:

He had written verses for her again after ten years. Ten years before she had worn her shawl cowlwise about her head, sending sprays of her warm breath into the night air, tapping her foot upon the glassy road. It was the last tram; the lank brown horses knew it and shook their bells to the clear night in admonition. The conductor talked with the driver, both nodding often in the green light of the lamp. They stood on the steps of the tram, he on the upper, she on the lower. She came up to his step many times between their phrases and went down again and once or twice remained beside him forgetting to go down and then went down. Let be! Let be!

Ten years from that wisdom of children to his folly.

(*P* 5.1706–17)

Besides alterations for tense and person, this is a close adaptation of the original epiphany, including phrases such as "Let be! Let be!" and the "wisdom of children," which were excised from the earlier inscription (*P* 2.303–56). This fidelity is interesting because both adaptations are closely linked to Stephen's creativity, from his first poetic impulse (*P* 2.612–16) to the inspiration for his villanelle (*P* 5.1706–17), indicating the important role of the epiphanies in Stephen's artistic development. The scenes are also linked to a memory of dancing with Emma (*P* 5.1612–27), based on "She Dances with Them in the Round," and a series of encounters, from "Apologise" to Stephen and Eileen (*P* 1.1260–68), that bring out latent themes of sexuality and creativity.

Source: Cornell 17.44 (*JJA* 7:54). This is the only extant copy.

[She Dances with Them in the Round]

As Stanislaus Joyce recalls, Joyce was "invited to a dance at the Sheehys' to celebrate, I think an engagement. . . . To be able to go to the dance, Jim had to borrow a dress-suit from Gogarty, and although Gogarty was bulkier and there was some slight difference in height, Jim looked well in his borrowed finery. The dance was at least the occasion for an epiphany in which the girl in whose honor the dance was given figures anonymously" (*MBK* 256–57). Stanislaus was "not certain who the subject of this epiphany was" (*MBK* 257), but by narrowing down the date we can be reasonably sure that it was Hanna Sheehy. The dance must have occurred in 1902 or later, because Joyce met Gogarty that year, and the comment "You very seldom come here now" suggests that it occurred after Joyce's graduation in October 1902, when he was no longer a regular visitor at the Sheehys'. It is unlikely to have occurred in 1904, because Gogarty was in Oxford from January to June 1904, by which time Joyce had met Nora Barnacle. From late 1902 through 1903, the only Sheehy to become engaged was Hanna. Having been introduced by Joyce, she and Francis Skeffington married on June 27, 1903.

Although he didn't know her identity, Stanislaus surmised that the subject of this epiphany was the same as "Her Arm on My Knees" (*MBK* 256–57). She appears to recognize him, however; it is the only epiphany where Stanislaus is directly mentioned ("I saw your brother the other day"). Joyce's response ("Really?") suggests he does not find their likeness altogether complimentary. "She Dances" was written later, Stanislaus says, indicating some awareness of the order of composition. The dance is likely to have been traditional, like the quadrille and lancers in "The Dead."

Echoes and Adaptations

"The Dead"

The basic situation of the epiphany—a man being challenged by a woman while dancing—is echoed in "The Dead," when Gabriel's dance partner, Miss Ivors, confronts him about his writing and politics, although the tone differs greatly (*D* 147–49). Instead of his being likened to his brother, Gabriel's identity is disturbed when she whispers teasingly in his ear, "West Briton!" (*D* 149).

A Portrait of the Artist as a Young Man

As he is composing his villanelle in chapter 5 of *Portrait*, Stephen thinks of the "night at the carnival ball" when he danced with Emma:

> She passed now dancing lightly across his memory as she had been that night at the carnival ball. Her white dress a little lifted, a white spray nodding in her hair. She danced lightly in the round. She was dancing towards him and, as she came, her eyes were a little averted and a faint glow was on her cheek. At the pause in the chain of hands her hand had lain in his an instant, a soft merchandise.
> —You are a great stranger now.
> —Yes. I was born to be a monk.
> —I am afraid you are a heretic.
> —Are you much afraid?
> For answer she had danced away from him along the chain of hands, dancing lightly and discreetly, giving herself to none. The white spray nodded to her dancing and when she was in shadow the glow was deeper on her cheek.
> (*P* 5.1613–27)

The general structure of the epiphany has been retained, although Hanna's role has been transferred to Emma, and the dance is no longer for an engagement, but a carnival ball. Many of the verbal details have been preserved from the epiphany, but there are significant changes to the dialogue: "You are a great stranger now" emphasizes Stephen's separation from Emma; "born to be a monk" insists, self-defensively, on Stephen's celibacy and self-sufficiency (perhaps hinting also at the priest he believes her to be infatuated with); the heresy she charges him with may pick up on the veiled allusions to the priest, as well as Stephen's rejection of the priesthood in chapter 4 of *Portrait*; and his reply, "Are you much afraid?" can be interpreted in many ways (sad, mocking, bitter, flirtatious, challenging).

Source: Cornell 17.45 (*JJA* 7:55). It is not certain whether there is a dash after "recluse" (line 8), but an elongated dot that runs into the edge of the page indicates the same punctuation as the other lines of dialogue.

[Poor Little Fellow!]

This epiphany is one of two inspired by the death of Joyce's younger brother Georgie on March 9, 1902. See "The Hole in Georgie's Stomach" for more on Georgie.

In *My Brother's Keeper*, Stanislaus Joyce quotes "Poor Little Fellow!" to describe Joyce's response to Georgie's death, although he doesn't mention the epiphany itself: "When [Joyce] thought everybody was asleep, he went softly upstairs to see 'the poor little fellow' where he lay alone" (*MBK* 136). (See "Holy Queen, Mother of Mercy" for another example of Stanislaus appropriating material from the epiphanies.)

The speaker's admission that he cannot pray at his brother's bedside anticipates Joyce's refusal to pray at his mother's deathbed a year later, and echoes into *Ulysses*.

Echoes and Adaptations

Stephen's feelings about his sister Isabel's death in *Stephen Hero* evoke "Poor Little Fellow!":

> Stephen felt very acutely the futility of his sister's life. He would have done many things for her and, though she was almost a stranger to him, he was sorry to see her lying dead. Life seemed to him a gift; the statement "I am alive" seemed to him to contain a satisfactory certainty and many other things, held up as indubitable, seemed to him uncertain.
>
> (*SH* 165)

The scene is greatly changed from the epiphany, but the situation of watching over the body of a dead sibling remains, as does the basic response: "I am very sorry he died"—"he was sorry to see her lying dead"; and the "certainty" of being alive when "Everything else is so uncertain."

Interestingly, for Beatrice in *Exiles* it is not life, but death that is certain: "And does death not move you, Mr Rowan? It is an end. Everything else is so uncertain" (*Exiles: A Critical* 37). Likewise, Father Arnall's sermon in

Portrait underlines our inexorable fate: "It is appointed unto man to die and after death the judgment. Death is certain. The time and manner are uncertain" (*P* 3.442–43).

Source: Cornell 17.45–46 (*JJA* 7:55–56). No variants.

[Holy Queen, Mother of Mercy]

This epiphany probably describes a scene at Clongowes Wood College, which Joyce attended from 1888 to 1891. At Clongowes, the boys rose at six thirty and went to "the chapel for morning prayers and Mass," then to the "refectory for breakfast" (Bradley 33). This routine tallies with the epiphany, and the simplicity of the speaker's wishes in the epiphany seems more appropriate for a six- to nine-year-old child, as Joyce would have been at Clongowes, than for a teenager, as he was at Belvedere College.

Nevertheless, it is possible that the epiphany records an "episode in Joyce's pious phase," as Robert Scholes and Richard M. Kain contend (*WD* 17). If they are right, the scene must have taken place between 1895 and 1898 (in December 1895, at age thirteen, Joyce was received into the Sodality of the Blessed Virgin Mary; in September 1896, he was made prefect of the sodality, to which he was reelected in December 1897 [Sullivan 116–19]).

Naturally, Belvedere House on Great Denmark Street had a boys chapel (Sullivan 64), but Stanislaus Joyce implies that the scene of the epiphany may have occurred at a different chapel, accompanied by their mother. Recounting Joyce's Belvedere years, Stanislaus incorporates several phrases from the epiphany to describe "the early morning Mass which he attended with my mother after which he would stay on in the silent chapel, where Mass had come and gone so quietly, to say another prayer, while his mother whispered to him that breakfast was ready" (*MBK* 80). However, Stanislaus wrote *My Brother's Keeper* in the mid-1950s, some sixty years after the event. The fact that here and in "Poor Little Fellow!" he appropriated material from Joyce's epiphanies with no acknowledgment that he was doing so casts serious doubt on the veracity of his account.

The speaker's prayer to Mary derives from the "Salve Regina," which begins "Hail, holy Queen, Mother of mercy, hail, our life, our sweetness and our hope." A common prayer in the Catholic liturgy, it features prominently in Saint Alphonsus Liguori's *The Glories of Mary* (25–38).

Echoes and Adaptations

Although "Holy Queen, Mother of Mercy" is never directly used in Joyce's prose writings, in the third chapter of *A Portrait of the Artist as a Young Man*, Stephen becomes a prefect in the Sodality of the Blessed Virgin Mary. "On Saturday mornings when the sodality met in the chapel to recite the little office his place was a cushioned kneelingdesk at the right of the altar from which he led his wing of boys through the responses" (*P* 3.86–90). The outlines of the epiphany are recognizable, although the scene has been considerably rewritten (*P* 3.85–109).

The sense of joy and release in the epiphany is manifested in another passage in *Portrait*, where Stephen has confessed his sins, and leaves the chapel thinking of breakfast, as he does in the epiphany (*P* 3.1554–62). "It is time to go away now" is echoed again in Stephen's final departure: "Away then: it is time to go" (*P* 5.2514).

Source: Cornell 17.46–47 (*JJA* 7:56–57). No variants.

[A Story of Alsace]

Stanislaus Joyce said this epiphany was based on "a memory of [Joyce's] reading of novels by Erckmann-Chatrian—*L'Invasion* at school, *L'Ami Fritz, Le Juif Polonais*, and others for himself" (*MBK* 57). Émile Erckmann and Alexandre Chatrian wrote historical novels and plays from the 1860s through the 1880s under the joint name Erckmann-Chatrian. They "were especially noted for their descriptions of Alsatian peasant life" (*PSW* 274): *L'Invasion ou le Fou Yégof* (The invasion or the crazy Yégof, 1862) involves Alsatian villagers resisting the invasion of the Prussians after the defeat of Napoleon; *L'Ami Fritz* (Friend Fritz, 1864) is about the pastoral life of villagers in Alsace; *Le Juif polonais* (The Polish Jew, 1867) concerns a bourgeois man haunted by a rich Jewish merchant he has murdered. Since they were not translated, Joyce must have read them in French, which he began learning at Belvedere in 1894. Assuming Stanislaus is right about the epiphany, Joyce presumably read *L'Ami Fritz* and *Le Juif polonais* after *L'Invasion*, which he studied for his senior grade at Belvedere in 1898 (Bradley 139). In 1897, Joyce was living at 13 North Richmond Street. Richard Ellmann says that this address "received more attention from Joyce than any of the others" (Igoe, *James* 63). However, the epiphany also possibly describes 29 Windsor Avenue, where Joyce stayed from 1897 to May 1899.

From Joyce's description it is difficult to identify the specific "Story of Alsace" referred to in the epiphany. "Friend of my youth" may refer to Fritz Kobus, the sympathetic hero of *L'Ami Fritz*, who falls in love with a young woman named Suzel. Fritz's closest friends are Jews, especially an elderly rabbi with whom—in the words of the epiphany—"he reads the books of the philosophers." The epiphany also speaks of "the men / and women in their strange dresses": in the novel, most of a chapter is devoted to Fritz's wardrobe, as he decides what to wear at a festival at which he expects to see Suzel. But perhaps Joyce is referring to youthful reading in general, rather than *L'Ami Fritz* in particular. The work appears to have held a certain fascination for Joyce, and Pietro Mascagni's 1891 operatic version became a favorite of Joyce's sister Eileen in Trieste (Delimata 47).

Echoes and Adaptations

The description of youthful reading in the epiphany echoes into Stephen's reading of Alexandre Dumas in *Portrait* (*P* 2.90–111). As Robert Scholes and Richard M. Kain point out, the "idealistic love motif here foreshadows 'Araby' and Mercedes in *Portrait*" (*WD* 12; see also Hayman, "Purpose" 643).

Source: Cornell 17.47–48. There are no known copies of the epiphany, but Stanislaus's erasures in lines 14–15 clearly indicate that he skipped a line when copying from another version—presumably Joyce's holograph—before correcting the mistake (see *JJA* 7:57–58). Such clues, however small, to the original texts have led us to preserve Stanislaus's lineation, although in many cases it is not significant (for instance, in "Selections," Stanislaus ran out of room for the last words in lines 3, 6, 15, and 20, which run over into the following lines). The epiphany, in black ink, was later ticked in blue.

[His Dancing]

According to his brother Stanislaus, Joyce interpreted this epiphany as referring to Georgie. "He thought that by the boy in the following dream-
epiphany Georgie was intended" (*MBK* 136). Stanislaus implies that the
epiphany was written after Georgie's death in March 1902, just as "She
Comes at Night" apparently records a dream in which Joyce was visited by
the ghost of his mother.

However, the contrast between "His dancing" and "the dance of the
daughters / of Herodias" suggests that the epiphany also draws on Herodias's daughter Salome, as she was portrayed in decadent figurations such
as Gustave Flaubert's 1877 tale "Hérodias," Oscar Wilde's 1891 play *Salomé*
(translated into English as *Salome* in 1894), and perhaps especially Arthur
Symons's 1897 poem "The Dance of the Daughters of Herodias."

Like Flaubert's tale, Symons's poem describes the erotic dance of Salome,
focusing on her sensuality and femininity. Joyce's epiphany repudiates "the
dancing of harlots," celebrating instead a young male dancer. "His dancing"
is directly opposed to "the dance of the daughters / of Herodias," an exact
echo of Symons's lines "it is the dance / Of the daughters of Herodias." This
is unlikely to be a coincidence, given the many examples of Joyce echoing
Symons's language and imagery: the use of "multitude" for the audience
recalls the "multitude" of Symons's dancers; the boy is "darkly-clad," like Symons's dancers "in the cloudy darkness"; the absence of music in Symons's
poem is followed in Joyce's "There is no music / for him"; Joyce describes
the young boy's dancing as "a slow and supple movement / of the limbs,"
just as Symons emphasizes the movement of limbs. And where Salome's
dance is an awakening ("the wind of dancing in her blood / Exults, crying a
strange, awakening song"), the boy's dancing is ecstatic: "It goes up from the
midst of the / people, sudden and young and male, and / falls again to earth
in tremulous sobbing to / die upon its triumph" (recalling the link between
ejaculation and poetic creativity in Stephen's villanelle) (*P* 5.1523–767).

Symons's "The Dance of the Daughters of Herodias" was included in his
1899 volume *Images of Good and Evil*, which also contains a partial translation of Stéphane Mallarmé's 1864 poem "Herodiade," another possible
source for "His Dancing." The connection is strengthened by the fact that

Joyce met Symons with W. B. Yeats in London in December 1902. Around the same time, Joyce showed his poems to George Moore, with Moore commenting that they were "mere imitations of Arthur Symons" (*MBK* 252).

Echoes and Adaptations

David Hayman notes the similarities between this epiphany, the climactic dance of death toward the end of "Circe" (*U* 15.4139–54), and Joyce's idiosyncratic dancing (Joyce, *Epifanías* 41–42), which involved "flinging his loose limbs about in a kind of spider dance" (*JJII* 430). Phrasing reminiscent of the epiphany also occurs in "Wandering Rocks" (*U* 10.808–11, 10.822–26), while Joyce's disdain of the multitude recurs in "The Day of the Rabblement" (*OCPW* 50) and the early sketch "A Portrait of the Artist" (*PSW* 218).

Source: Cornell 17.50–51 (*JJA* 7:60–61). In the manuscript, "movement" is divided between lines 6 and 7. The epiphany has been ticked in red pencil or crayon.

[They Pass in Twos and Threes]

Stanislaus Joyce characterizes "They Pass in Twos and Threes" as a "fleeting memory of a Parisian scene" (*MBK* 254), dating it to one of Joyce's trips to Paris in December 1902 or January–April 1903. On March 9, 1903, Joyce informed Stanislaus, "I have written fifteen epiphanies—of which twelve are insertions, and three additions" (*LII* 35). This Baudelairean epiphany may well have been among them.

Equally, though, the incident may have taken place in December 1902, when Joyce seems to have visited a brothel in Paris, sending a postcard to Vincent Cosgrave describing "the *scorta* (prostitutes) of Paris in dog-Latin" (*JJII* 115). According to Richard Ellmann, the postcard (now lost) was "scatological" (*LII* 41n3). Stanislaus reads the epiphany as evidence that Joyce "disliked prostitutes though he had recourse to them—and especially disliked the more successful ones" (*MBK* 254), alluding to the judgment in the epiphany: "No man / has loved them and they have not loved / themselves: they have given nothing for all / that has been given them." This is surely a serious reflection on the cost of sex work, although Stephen's bawdy recollection of Parisian prostitutes in "Scylla and Charybdis" offers other interpretations (*U* 9.641–42).

Stephen's encounters with prostitutes in *Stephen Hero* (189–90) and *Portrait* (*P* 2.1414–58) have the same sense of guilty attraction and (self-)repulsion hinted at in the epiphany, but there is also a comic element in *Portrait* (e.g., "Good night, Willie dear!" [*P* 2.1430]), while Joyce's own comments are more studied. Remarkably, he included his epiphany in a letter to Nora Barnacle, less than two months after meeting her:

> When you went in tonight I wandered along towards Grafton St where I stood for a long time leaning against a lamp-post, smoking. The street was full of a life which I have poured a stream of my youth upon. While I stood there I thought of a few sentences I wrote some years ago when I lived in Paris—these sentences which follow—"they pass in twos and threes amid the life of the boulevard, walking like people who have leisure in a place lit up for them. They are in the pastry cook's, chattering, crushing little fabrics of pastry, or seated si-

lently at tables by the café door, or descending from carriages with a busy stir of garments soft as the voice of the adulterer. They pass in an air of perfumes. Under the perfumes their bodies have a warm humid smell"—

While I was repeating this to myself I knew that that life was still waiting for me if I chose to enter it. It could not give me perhaps the intoxication it had once given but it was still there and now that I am wiser and more controllable it was safe. It would ask no questions, expect nothing from me but a few moments of my life, leaving the rest free, and would promise me pleasure in return. I thought of all this and without regret I rejected it. It was useless for me; it could not give me what I wanted.

(*SL* 26)

Joyce must have had a copy of the epiphany at hand since he transcribed it verbatim, except for the last two lines, whose removal suspends judgment. Joyce's pose, "leaning against a lamp-post, smoking," also seems deliberately detached, as he stands on the street thinking back to "a few sentences" he had written in Paris. This self-posturing as the disinterested writer seems designed to present the epiphany as an example of Joyce's genius, emphasizing his distance from the experience (not "some years ago," but two, at most), while leaving Nora in no doubt that "that life was still waiting for me if I chose to enter it." Given the indirect allusions to "that life" in the lines he quotes, followed by the obvious allusions to prostitution in the second paragraph, Joyce's letter implies that he had already told Nora of his visits to prostitutes. While assuring Nora that he has no regrets in rejecting his former sex life, which "could not give [him] what [he] wanted," he also implies that if she does not give it to him, that "pleasure" is available elsewhere, as hinted at in the mildly titillating epiphany.

Echoes and Adaptations

"They Pass in Twos and Threes" appears in the "Proteus" draft (National Library of Ireland MS 36,639/7/A) and continues into the final version in *Ulysses*:

Paris rawly waking, crude sunlight on her lemon streets. Moist pith of farls of bread, the froggreen wormwood, her matin incense, court the air. Belluomo rises from the bed of his wife's lover's wife, the kerchiefed housewife is astir, a saucer of acetic acid in her hand.

> In Rodot's Yvonne and Madeleine newmake their tumbled beauties, shattering with gold teeth chaussons of pastry, their mouths yellowed with the pus of flan Breton. Faces of Paris men go by, their wellpleased pleasers, curled conquistadores.
>
> (*U* 3.209–15)

The first three sentences derive from *Giacomo Joyce* (*PSW* 234), but the description of Yvonne and Madeleine in Rodot's patisserie (9 Boulevard Saint-Michel) draws on the prostitutes "in / the pastry cook's" from the epiphany. The representation of the women "newmak[ing] their tumbled beauties" links them to "They Pass in Twos and Threes," although Stephen's interior monologue emphasizes their physicality and decay more vividly. The characterization of the male clients as "wellpleased pleasers" ironically condenses the last sentence of the epiphany.

There is perhaps an echo of "They Pass in Twos and Threes" in "Aeolus," as Stephen imagines rhyme words marching past, like Dante's Divine Pageant (*Purgatorio* 29.121–26): "He saw them three by three, approaching girls, in green, in rose, in russet" (*U* 7.720–21). The link to the epiphany is strengthened when the Dantean terza rima gives way to Stephen's rhymes, drawn from the vampire poem in "Proteus," which proceed in pairs ("mouth south: tomb womb" [*U* 7.723–24]), thereby linking back to the pair of prostitutes in the earlier adaptation (*U* 3:209–15).

Source: Cornell 17.51–52 (*JJA* 7:61–62). Ticked in red pencil or crayon.

[Upon Me from the Darkness]

In *My Brother's Keeper*, Stanislaus Joyce hints at the "wild life" his brother led with Oliver St. John Gogarty and John Eglinton. He then quotes this epiphany, implying that it was based on a visit to a brothel in their company in late 1903 (*MBK* 252–53).

Stanislaus thought the epiphany marked the end of Joyce's "brief appearance in the garb of a 'piping poet'" (*MBK* 253). If he was referring to Joyce's Latin Quarter hat and ashplant, he wasn't far off, but if Stanislaus thought the epiphany marked the end of a period of literary affectation, he was mistaken.

Based on fragments of Joyce's poetry from *Shine and Dark* preserved on the versos of Stanislaus's notes, Richard Ellmann states that "the idea of a supplication addressed to a woman who is both temptation and doom" had gained a powerful hold on Joyce around 1900–1901 (*JJII* 82). Of course, the femme fatale is practically a cliché in the decadent tradition, and Joyce could have found examples in many of the poets he admired, including Paul Verlaine, Charles Baudelaire, Arthur Rimbaud, Arthur Symons, and W. B. Yeats. It is difficult, therefore, to pinpoint a source, but the mating cries of "eagle to eagle / in mid air" may be indebted to Walt Whitman's 1880 poem "The Dalliance of the Eagles" (311–12). The imagery of overpowering temptation in "Upon Me from the Darkness" survives into Stephen Dedalus's poetry, such as the "Villanelle of the Temptress" in *Portrait* (*P* 5.1749–67), and the vampire poem in "Proteus" (*U* 3.397–400), and even into Joyce's mature writing, such as *Giacomo Joyce* and "A Prayer" (*PSW* 63).

Echoes and Adaptations

At the end of the second chapter of *A Portrait of the Artist as a Young Man*, Stephen is overwhelmed by his sexual desire and longs for an "iniquitous abandonment" (*P* 2.1411):

> He wanted to sin with another of his kind, to force another being to sin with him and to exult with her in sin. He felt some dark presence moving irresistibly upon him from the darkness, a presence subtle

and murmurous as a flood filling him wholly with itself. Its murmur besieged his ears like the murmur of some multitude in sleep; its subtle streams penetrated his being. His hands clenched convulsively and his teeth set together as he suffered the agony of its penetration. He stretched out his arms in the street to hold fast the frail swooning form that eluded him and incited him: and the cry that he had strangled for so long in his throat issued from his lips. It broke from him like a wail of despair from a hell of sufferers and died in a wail of furious entreaty, a cry for an iniquitous abandonment, a cry which was but the echo of an obscene scrawl which he had read on the oozing wall of a urinal.

(P 2.1392–413)

There are substantial alterations to the original epiphany, but the repetition of a "dark presence moving irresistibly," a "presence subtle and murmurous as a flood," and the "cry for an iniquitous abandonment" (now negatively troped) shows clearly how Joyce adapted "Upon Me from the Darkness" to serve as the prelude to Stephen's climactic encounter with a prostitute at the end of this chapter of *Portrait*.

Source: Cornell 17.53 (*JJA* 7:63). In Stanislaus's "Selections," "darkness" is divided between lines 5 and 6. The epiphany has been ticked in red pencil or crayon.

[Is That Mary Ellen?]

Richard Ellmann notes that the scene described in "Is That Mary Ellen?" "presumably took place in Joyce's great-aunts' house on Usher's Island" (*PSW* 274; see also *JJII* 84). Joyce's mother, Mary (May) Murray, was educated at her aunts' finishing school for young ladies at 15 Usher's Island on the south bank of the Liffey. As Joyce was growing up, he visited his maternal great-aunts, Julia Clare Lyons, Ellen Callanan, Elizabeth "Eliza" Josephine Flynn, and Anne "Nannie" Flynn. Eliza in the epiphany is Aunt Eliza, who died on July 31, 1900, at age seventy.

Eliza's demise was the first of several in the family during the period Joyce was writing epiphanies: his brother Georgie died in March 1902 (see "The Hole in Georgie's Stomach," "I Was Sorry," "Poor Little Fellow!," "His Dancing"), his mother died in August 1903 (see "Two Mourners" and "She Comes at Night"), Aunt Ellen died in December 1904, and Aunt Julia died in the middle of 1905.

Also present at the finishing school at Usher's Island was Ellen's daughter, Mary Ellen Callanan. She was Joyce's cousin, once removed, and the model for Mary Ellen in the epiphany, although Ellmann was mistaken in assuming that the scene occurred after her death (*PSW* 274); Mary Ellen Callanan died on March 10, 1909, at age thirty-eight (Simpson, "Flynnlandia").

The identity of the unnamed woman bustling about is unclear. She may be Aunt Ellen or Aunt Julia. Nannie Flynn is less likely, because she died in 1895.

Joyce's interest in the Flynn sisters led to the representation of Nannie and Eliza Flynn in "The Sisters," which shares the funereal tone of the epiphany. John Simpson identifies Julia and Kate Morkan from "The Dead" with Eliza and Nannie Flynn, strengthening the connection noted by Robert Scholes and Richard M. Kain: "In this [epiphany's] association of ghostly atmosphere and the house of Usher's Island we have one of the earliest seeds of mood and idea that ultimately flowered in 'The Dead'" (*WD* 15).

Echoes and Adaptations

A Portrait of the Artist as a Young Man

In *Portrait*, the epiphany is incorporated into a series of passages beginning "He was sitting"—the Mabel Hunter passage (*P* 2.252–74), which may be based on a lost epiphany, "Is That Mary Ellen?" (*P* 2.275–302), and "The Last Tram" (*P* 2.303–56). In this adaptation, Stephen is approached by Ellen, who, due to the darkness, mistakes him for Josephine:

> He was sitting in the narrow breakfast room high up in the old dark-windowed house. The firelight flickered on the wall and beyond the window a spectral dusk was gathering upon the river. Before the fire an old woman was busy making tea and, as she bustled at her task, she told in a low voice of what the priest and the doctor had said. She told too of certain changes that she had seen in her of late and of her odd ways and sayings. He sat listening to the words and following the ways of adventure that lay open in the coals, arches and vaults and winding galleries and jagged caverns.
>
> Suddenly he became aware of something in the doorway. A skull appeared suspended in the gloom of the doorway. A feeble creature like a monkey was there, drawn thither by the sound of voices at the fire. A whining voice came from the door, asking:
> —Is that Josephine?
> The old bustling woman answered cheerily from the fireplace:
> —No, Ellen. It's Stephen.
> —O . . . . O, good evening, Stephen.
> He answered the greeting and saw a silly smile break out over the face in the doorway.
> —Do you want anything, Ellen? asked the old woman at the fire.
> But she did not answer the question and said:
> —I thought it was Josephine. I thought you were Josephine, Stephen.
> And, repeating this several times, she fell to laughing feebly.
> (*P* 2.275–302)

Many of the descriptive details from the epiphany have been elaborated, with brief notes like "dusk outside" expanded into sentences: "beyond the window a spectral dusk was gathering upon the river." The gothic effect of the original remains, but the context is much clearer in *Portrait*: Stephen is now sitting in a "narrow breakfast room," and the adaptation makes it clearer that Stephen's imagination wanders among the intricate "arches and vaults and winding galleries and jagged caverns" of the coals in the fire as he listens to the old woman bustling about. She remains difficult to identify, as in the epiphany, but in *Portrait*, the old woman is clearly one of the interlocutors, responding cheerily to Ellen, before asking her if she wants anything, whereas the speakers in the epiphany are obscure. These dialogue revisions remove any doubts about the "creature" in the epiphany, who is now clearly Ellen. From a biographical point of view, this seems to transfer Eliza's role in the epiphany to Joyce's great-aunt Ellen Callanan, who ran the finishing school at Usher's Island. Joyce wrote of her to Nora Barnacle in September 1904, "You will be sorry to hear that my great-aunt is dying of stupidity" (*LII* 51), which may explain why Stephen sees "a silly smile break out over the face in the doorway" and Ellen falls "to laughing feebly." Ellen Callanan died on December 4, 1904, at 41 Aughrim Street, at the age of seventy-two, four years after Eliza Flynn. The change from Mary Ellen to Josephine in Ellen's misidentification of Stephen is perhaps a subtle reference back to Aunt Eliza, whose full name was Elizabeth Josephine; alternatively, it may be a nod to Joyce's maternal aunt, Josephine Murray (née Giltrap).

"Ithaca"

In *Portrait*, the bustling old woman is unnamed, as in the epiphany, but in "Ithaca," a list of people who have lit fires for Stephen includes "his godmother Miss Kate Morkan in the house of her dying sister Miss Julia Morkan at 15 Usher's Island" (*U* 17.139–41). The reference to fires, the house, and the two sisters, one dying, evokes the circumstances of the original epiphany. Here, however, Joyce refers back to the fictional versions of the two Flynn sisters, Nannie and Eliza, who appeared in "The Dead" as Kate and Julia Morkan.

"Counterparts" and "Proteus"

Two further scenes of mistaken identity, one in *Dubliners* and one in *Ulysses*, seem to echo the epiphany. At the end of "Counterparts," Farrington returns home, drunk and embittered:

A little boy came running down the stairs.
—Who is that? said the man, peering through the darkness.

—Me, pa.
—Who are you? Charlie?
—No, pa. Tom.
  (*D* 74)

The misidentifications in the epiphany are understandable, given the lack of light, but Farrington's failure to recognize his own son's voice is a damning indictment of his paternal role. Whereas the coals flickering in the darkness create a gothic effect in the epiphany, Tom's helpless pleas for mercy in a dark kitchen with an unlit fire create the blackest of comedies in "Counterparts."

The situation and dialogue of the epiphany are also echoed in "Proteus" as Stephen passes close by the home of his uncle, Richie Goulding (based on William Murray, Joyce's maternal uncle), and imagines the scene if he were to drop in unannounced:

I pull the wheezy bell of their shuttered cottage: and wait. They take
me for a dun, peer out from a coign of vantage.
—It's Stephen, sir.
—Let him in. Let Stephen in.
  A bolt drawn back and Walter welcomes me.
—We thought you were someone else.
  (*U* 3.70–76)

Source: Cornell 17.56 (*JJA* 7:64). At the end of the first line, "firelight" is divided by a hyphen.

[Images of Fabulous Kings]

This is probably another of Joyce's dream-epiphanies, this time with shades of the Celtic Twilight. In the titular poem of W. B. Yeats's 1897 volume *The Secret Rose*, a list of fabulous kings includes Conchubar, king of Ulster,

> whose eyes
> Saw the Pierced Hands and Rood of Elder rise
> In Druid vapour and make the torches dim;
> Till vain frenzy awoke and he died.
>   (*Major* 33)

According to Yeats, Conchubar "was converted to Christianity at the end of his life, and felt such a furious desire to kill the Jews who had crucified Christ that his brains spilt out of his head, and he died" (*Poems* 469). Joyce's association of the "pillars / of dark vapours" with the "errors of men" may recall Conchubar's fury and the "Druid vapour" in Yeats's poem, as well as the "pillar of cloud by day" and the "pillar of fire by night" that guide Moses in Exodus 13:22. The "weariness" of kings is a recurring motif in Joyce's early writing (e.g., *P* 2.1269, 4.592–605, 5.1702).

Echoes and Adaptations

A Portrait of the Artist as a Young Man

In Stephen's diary, an entry dated "*25 March, morning*" (*P* 5.2671) records a dream based on "Images of Fabulous Kings":

> A troubled night of dreams. Want to get them off my chest.
> A long curving gallery. From the floor ascend pillars of dark va-pours. It is peopled by the images of fabulous kings, set in stone. Their hands are folded upon their knees in token of weariness and their eyes are darkened for the errors of men go up before them for ever as dark vapours.
> Strange figures advance from a cave. They are not as tall as men. One does not seem to stand quite apart from another. Their faces are

phosphorescent, with darker streaks. They peer at me and their eyes
seem to ask me something. They do not speak.

    (*P* 5.2674–83)

Besides minor changes in punctuation, the first paragraph is virtually identical to the original epiphany. The fact that it is quoted almost verbatim
raises the question of whether the second paragraph is also based on a lost
epiphany, or whether Joyce added it as another example of Stephen's dreams.
In either case, the adaptation shows how seamlessly Joyce incorporates his
epiphanies into Stephen's diary—and elsewhere in *Portrait*.

    Richard Ellmann associates this passage with "the saint-studded gal-
lery at Clongowes," a gallery containing framed portraits of distinguished
alumni (*Ulysses* 71).

Ulysses

There is another echo of the epiphany in "Nestor." As Stephen sits beside
Sargent, helping him with his sums, Stephen identifies with the boy, even as
he contemplates the separation between them:

> Secrets, silent, stony sit in the dark palaces of both our hearts: secrets
> weary of their tyranny: tyrants, willing to be dethroned.
>
>   (*U* 2.170–72)

Here the "Secrets" appear to be private moments of pain, humiliation, tenderness, and intimacy that Stephen identifies with, but Stephen's images
("stony sit in the dark palaces," "weary of their tyranny: tyrants, willing to
be dethroned") recall the stone effigies of weary kings sitting in the dark,
palatial gallery of the epiphany. Stanislaus Joyce quotes these lines from
"Nestor" in *My Brother's Keeper* (93) in the context of Joyce's resistance to
the idols of Ireland.

Source: Cornell 17.56–57 (*JJA* 7:64–65).

[The Ship]

"The Ship" appears to be another of Joyce's dream-epiphanies. It is not possible to locate the boat or the harbor in the original manuscript, whose imagery recalls Arthur Rimbaud's 1871 poem "Le Bateau Ivre" (The drunken boat) and Charles Baudelaire's 1861 poem "Le Voyage," but the adaptation in *Portrait* suggests that Joyce identified the scene with the return of Charles Stewart Parnell's body to Ireland after his death on October 6, 1891.

Echoes and Adaptations

A Portrait of the Artist as a Young Man

Having been pushed into the square ditch at Clongowes, Stephen becomes feverish and is sent to the infirmary, where he thinks of "a book in the library about Holland. There were lovely foreign names in it and pictures of strangelooking cities and ships" (*P* 1.692–93). These images merge with the wavy light from the fire, and the voices of the brothers rising and falling, as Stephen's febrile imagination flits between sleeping and waking:

> He saw the sea of waves, long dark waves rising and falling, dark under the moonless night. A tiny light twinkled at the pierhead where the ship was entering: and he saw a multitude of people gathered by the waters' edge to see the ship that was entering their harbour. A tall man stood on the deck, looking out towards the flat dark land: and by the light at the pierhead he saw his face, the sorrowful face of Brother Michael.
> He saw him lift his hand towards the people and heard him say in a loud voice of sorrow over the waters:
> —He is dead. We saw him lying upon the catafalque.
> A wail of sorrow went up from the people.
> —Parnell! Parnell! He is dead!
> They fell upon their knees, moaning in sorrow.
> (*P* 1.700–712)

Stephen's vision is clearly drawn from "The Ship," although the context in *Portrait* gives it a new significance. Having been asked by an older boy in the infirmary to "tell him all the news in the paper" (*P* 1.625–26), Brother Michael informs Stephen of Parnell's death. This sets the scene on or close to October 6, 1891, the day Parnell died. However, in Stephen's feverish imagination Parnell's death becomes confused with images from the book about Holland and the death of Little, a fellow student at Clongowes, who was also borne on a "catafalque" (*P* 1.598–99, and see 2.1166). Now it is Parnell "lying upon the catafalque" before a "multitude of people" wailing in sorrow, an allusion to the vast crowd who followed the funeral cortege to Glasnevin Cemetery, where Parnell was buried on October 11, 1891 (Lyons 556).

Counting back from the calendar in Stephen's desk, Hans Walter Gabler calculates that Stephen's first day at Clongowes was October 6, 1891. The passage of time in chapter 1, section 2, is not always clear, but Gabler makes a strong case that the scene based on the epiphany takes place at dawn on October 11, just as Parnell's body was being returned to Ireland (106–7).

Stephen recalls this moment on several occasions: "he remembered the evening in the infirmary in Clongowes, the dark waters, the light at the pierhead and the moan of sorrow from the people when they had heard" (*P* 1.1005–7), but "he had not died then. Parnell had died" (*P* 2.1167–68). Each time the scene is recollected, Joyce strengthens the connection between Stephen's recovery from illness and the death of Parnell, as though to imply that Parnell's spirit lives on, at least in Stephen's imagination.

Ulysses

A trace of the epiphany also survives into *Ulysses*, as Stephen looks back to see a ship entering a harbor at the end of "Proteus":

> Moving through the air high spars of a threemaster, her sails brailed up on the crosstrees, homing, upstream, silently moving, a silent ship.
>
> (*U* 3.503–5)

Source: Cornell 17.57 (*JJA* 7:65).

[Half-Men, Half-Goats]

The epiphany's reference to "half-men, half-goats" suggests mythical satyrs, originally men with horse's tails, ears, and sometimes legs, but later associated with goats. In classical mythology, they were typically portrayed with long beards and erect phalli. Among the sources familiar to Joyce was Friedrich Nietzsche's description of "the bearded satyr, who borrowed his name and attributes from the goat," a figure of "extravagant sexual licentiousness" that unleashes a "horrible mixture of sensuality and cruelty" (6).

The "confused / forms" of the satyrs in Joyce's dream-epiphany seem to displace the erect phalli of classical satyrs onto their "great / tails" and "stiff / weeds" in the field, although representations on Greek vases typically feature long tails and beards. In Christian iconography, satyrs were often seen as figures of the devil, an interpretation hinted at in the "secret personal sin," "old sin," and "malevolence" of Joyce's creatures.

Robert Scholes and Richard M. Kain characterize "Half-Men, Half-Goats" as a "dream-epiphany of hell" (*WD* 16), assuming that it is the "Epiphany of Hell" referred to in Joyce's notes at the back of his sister Mabel's copybook (*JJA* 7:70–94; *WD* 68–74). These notes were written in January 1904 and sketch out the plan for chapters 8–11 of *Stephen Hero* (now lost). Page 16 of the copybook summarizes a chapter dealing with the retreat for the feast of Saint Francis Xavier (chapter 3 in *Portrait*), listing two epiphanies in parentheses:

August 1893 to December 1893

1) ~~Sensations coming home.—~~
2) Gradual irreligiousness ~~(Epiphany of Thornton)~~
3) Return to Belvedere: in second class: prefect
    at sodality: Fr MacNally.
4) Retreat before feast of S Francis Xavier.
    Six lectures

(Epiphany of Hell)

1)	Introductory,	evening before 1st Day
2)	Death		2nd Day
3)	Judgement	
4)	Hell		3rd Day
5)	Hell	
6)	Heaven	morning after 4th Day

(*JJA* 7:86; see figure 1)

If we read back from Stephen's vision of hell in *Portrait*, the "Epiphany of Hell" can be identified with "Half-Men, Half-Goats" (*P* 3.1285). Without this narrative context, the original phrase, written diagonally across the six lectures, might be interpreted as a reference to the entire experience of the hellfire sermon, rather than to "Half-Men, Half-Goats" in particular, but this is inconsistent with the brevity of Joyce's epiphanies, and the statement in *Stephen Hero* that epiphanies record a "*sudden* spiritual manifestation" (*SH* 211, emphasis added). For this reason, it is more likely that the parentheses indicate that the epiphany is to be inserted as an exemplum of hell, somewhere among the fourth and fifth sermons, in the same way that the "Epiphany of Thornton" presumably exemplifies "Gradual irreligiousness."

Bonnie Kime Scott provides an alternative explanation, suggesting that this epiphany derives from a scene in George Moore's 1895 volume *Celibates*, in which "Kitty Hare, a young victim of rape in the *Celibates* story, 'John Norton,' has a nightmare." She quotes Moore: "The claws of the hyena are heard upon the crumbling tombs, and the suffocating girl strives with her last strength to free herself from the thrall of giant lianas. But there comes a hirsute smell; she turns with terrified eyes to plead but meets only dull, liquorish eyes, and the breath of the obscene animal upon her face" (45–46).

Curiously, in summer 1904, as he lay ill and alone, Stanislaus Joyce recorded a dreamlike passage that reads like a half-remembered imitation of "Half-Men, Half-Goats":

A long string of faces pass slantwise up before my eyes, so quickly that I can hardly distinguish them, but they are grotesque, unhuman, like the faces you see in hucksters' windows painted in cheap yellow paint on cardboard and they are hitched one under the other. I cannot prevent myself seeing them as they fly up noiselessly with interminable length, before my eyes. My palate is quite hard and stiff; everything I touch is stiff and rough.

(*DD* 75)

Echoes and Adaptations

A Portrait of the Artist as a Young Man

Terrified by Father Arnall's fire-and-brimstone sermon in chapter 3 of *Portrait*, Stephen crawls into bed, where he sees a terrible vision:

> A field of stiff weeds and thistles and tufted nettlebunches. Thick among the tufts of rank stiff growth lay battered canisters and clots and coils of solid excrement. A faint marshlight struggled upwards from all the ordure through the bristling greygreen weeds. An evil smell, faint and foul as the light, curled upwards sluggishly out of the canisters and from the stale crusted dung.
>
> Creatures were in the field; one, three, six: creatures were moving in the field, hither and thither. Goatish creatures with human faces, hornybrowed, lightly bearded and grey as india rubber. The malice of evil glittered in their hard eyes, as they moved hither and thither, trailing their long tails behind them. A rictus of cruel malignity lit up greyly their old bony faces. One was clasping about his ribs a torn flannel waistcoat, another complained monotonously as his beard stuck in the tufted weeds. Soft language issued from their spittleless lips as they swished in slow circles round and round the field, winding hither and thither through the weeds, dragging their long tails amid the rattling canisters. They moved in slow circles, circling closer and closer, to enclose, to enclose, soft language issuing from their lips, their long swishing tails besmeared with stale shite, thrusting upwards their terrific faces . . . . .
>
> Help!
>
> He flung the blankets from him madly to free his face and neck. That was his hell. God had allowed him to see the hell reserved for his sins: stinking, bestial, malignant, a hell of lecherous goatish fiends. For him! For him!
>
> (*P* 3.1261–87)

Stephen's vision elaborates on the original epiphany with "tufted nettle-bunches," evil-smelling "canisters," and ordure ("clots and coils of solid excrement," "stale crusted dung," "tails besmeared with stale shite"), emphasizing Stephen's fear and disgust. The devilishness of the creatures is also accentuated by their "hornybrowed" "bony faces" etched with "a rictus of cruel malignity." However, Joyce's adaptation replaces the reference to their "secret personal sin" with the "soft language issuing from their lips," perhaps because in *Portrait* the vision stands for Stephen's personal vision of hell, "the hell reserved for his sins." Whereas "hither and thither" occurs once in the epiphany, it becomes a minor motif in *Portrait*, where it is repeated ten times, and later echoes into *Finnegans Wake* (e.g., "hitherand-thithering" [*FW* 216.04], "Hitherzither!" [*FW* 360.01], "Hinther and thon-ther" [*FW* 365.22]).

Finnegans Wake

There is also an echo of "Half-Men, Half-Goats" in Taff's exclamation at Butt's tale of shooting HCE in *Finnegans Wake*, book 3, chapter 3:

> TAFF (*who, asbestas can, wiz the healps of gosh and his bluzzid maikar, has been sulphuring to himsalves all the pungataries of sin practice in failing to furrow theogonies of the dommed*). Trisseme, the mangoat! And the name of the Most Marsiful, the Aweghost, the Gragious One! In sobber sooth and in souber civiles? And to the dirtiment of the curtailment of his all of man? Notshoh?
>
> (*FW* 352.37–353.05)

The manifest content of the passage is a description of how Taff has been suffering all the purgatories of Saint Patrick and following the agonies of the damned, but Joyce's Wakese language recalls the epiphany in its references to a "mangoat," "sulphuring," and the "pungataries of sin practice," while the "dirtiment of the curtailment" suggests the great "tails" and "dirtiness" of the version in *Portrait*.

Source: Cornell 17.57–58 (*JJA* 7:65–66). In the manuscript, "confused," "india-rubber," "clasping," and "complains" are divided by line breaks (lines 1–2, 4–5, 6–8); we have left the hyphen in "india-rubber."

[The Girls, the Boys]

"The Girls, the Boys" probably describes an experience during Joyce's student years at University College Dublin (1898–1902). Adaptations of the epiphany in *Stephen Hero* and *Portrait* make it likely that the scene occurred on the steps of the National Library of Ireland.

Evidently a group of girls or young women have been sheltering from an April shower. It is not certain which convent they are returning to, but one possibility, based on Joyce's adaptation, is Loreto College, on St. Stephen's Green, which both Mary Sheehy, Joyce's onetime sweetheart, and Mary Elizabeth Cleary, the inspiration for Emma Clery in *Stephen Hero* and *Portrait*, attended between 1899 and 1901. Both Sheehy and Cleary would then have been students, like the young women in the analogous scene in *Stephen Hero* (see below). At that time, Loreto College was the principal Catholic women's college in Dublin, having opened a university department in 1893 (the establishment of the Royal University of Ireland in 1879 allowed Irish women to obtain a degree, but they were not admitted to Trinity College Dublin until 1904, or to other institutions until the Irish Universities Act of 1908 [Raftery, Harford, and Parkes]).

The second section of the epiphany juxtaposes the well-bred girls with a group of "noisy and hungry" boys in a refectory. The "high plain / building" in "a flat rain-swept country" may be based on Clonliffe College, the principal seminary for Catholic priests in Dublin, which Stephen Daedalus visits in *Stephen Hero*.

Echoes and Adaptations

Stephen Hero

In chapter 24 of *Stephen Hero*, McCann (modeled on Francis Skeffington) publishes a sensational review: "In the porch of the Library were a little knot of young men and a little knot of young women, all provided with copies of the new review. All were laughing and talking, making the rain an excuse for lingering under shelter" (*SH* 183). The group includes Emma Clery, who attracts Stephen's gaze:

Stephen leaned against one of the stone pillars and regarded the farther group. She stood in a ring of her companions, laughing and talking with them. The anger with which the new review had filled him gradually ebbed away and he chose to contemplate the spectacle which she and her companions offered him. As on his entrance into the grounds of Clonliffe College a sudden sympathy arose out of a sudden reminiscence, a reminiscent sympathy toward a protected seminarist life the very virtues of which seemed to be set provokingly before the wild gaze of the world, so provokingly that only the strength of walls and watchdogs held them in a little circle of modish and timid ways. Though their affections often lacked grace and their vulgarity wanted only lungs to be strident the rain brought him charity. The babble of the young students reached him as if from a distance, in broken pulsations, and lifting his eyes he saw the high rain-clouds retreating across the rain-swept country. The quick light shower was over, tarrying, a cluster of diamonds, among the shrubs of the quadrangle where an exhalation ascended from the blackened earth. The company in the colonnade was leaving shelter, with many a doubting glance, with a prattle of trim boots, a pretty rescue of petticoats, under umbrellas, a light armoury, upheld at cunning angles. He saw them returning to the convent—demure corridors and simple dormitories, a quiet rosary of hours—while the rain-clouds retreated towards the west and the babble of the young men reached him in regular pulsations. He saw far away amid a flat rain-swept country a high plain building with windows that filtered the obscure daylight. Three hundred boys, noisy and hungry, sat at long tables eating beef fringed with green fat like blubber and junks of white damp bread, and one young boy, leaning upon his elbows, opened and closed the flaps of his ears while the noise of the diners reached him rhythmically as the wild gabble of animals.

(*SH* 183–84)

As Stephen's anger and jealousy at McCann's review subside, he turns his attention to Emma and her companions, a group of female students. The "sudden sympathy" he feels for them arises from a "sudden reminiscence" of the sympathy he felt "toward a protected seminarist life," when, in an earlier chapter, he contemplated joining the priesthood himself and visited Clonliffe College. In other words, the fellow-feeling Stephen once felt for the boys in the seminary—his "reminiscent sympathy"—allows him to sympathize with the young women, who are probably students at Loreto College, a convent school and women's college on St. Stephen's Green. The "sudden reminiscence" introduces a passage based on "The Girls, the Boys," showing how, in *Stephen Hero* at least, the epiphany moves from the narrative present, under the colonnade of the National Library, to an earlier memory of Clonliffe. The rain helps smooth this transition: like the "reminiscent sympathy," it softens Stephen's hostility; it brings the groups of young men and women together in search of shelter; and the "babble" of their voices reaches Stephen in rain-like "pulsations." It was also raining in the earlier scene at the seminary, so when Stephen looks up and sees "the high rain-clouds retreating across the rain-swept country," he seems to be carried back to the "flat rain-swept country" of Clonliffe. There is a subtle shift in vision here, from immediate perception ("he saw the high rain-clouds retreating") to a scene Stephen imagines as the girls leave the colonnade ("He saw them returning to the convent") to a distant memory ("He saw far away amid a flat rain-swept country a high plain building"). Again, the rain helps connect these scenes, because in the original epiphany, the first paragraph ends with the girls returning to the convent, "having heard the fair promises of Spring, that well-graced / ambassador . . . . ," whereas the version in *Stephen Hero* substitutes "while the rain-clouds retreated towards the west and the babble of the young men reached him in regular pulsations," using the conjunction and repetition as a bridge to the boys eating in the refectory. As with the description of the girls returning to the convent, this scene is closely based on the epiphany, although the end of the passage replaces earthy vegetables with blubbery meat, soggy bread, and the animal noises of the diners.

Besides emphasizing the contrast with the "demure" girls, the "wild gabble of animals" links back to Clonliffe, where Stephen and Wells first see the seminary building, "a big square block of masonry looming before them through the faint daylight," surrounded by cattle grazing in the rain (*SH* 72–73):

The mist of the evening had begun to thicken into slow fine rain and Stephen halted at the end of a narrow path beside a few laurel bushes, watching at the end of a leaf a tiny point of rain form and twinkle and hesitate and finally take the plunge into the sodden clay beneath. He wondered was it raining in Westmeath, [were the cattle standing together patiently in the shelter of the hedges]. He remembered seeing the cattle standing together patiently in the hedges and reeking in the rain. A little band of students passed at the other side of the laurel bushes: they were talking among themselves:

—But did you see Mrs Bergin?

—O, I saw her . . . with a black and white boa.

—And the two Miss Kennedys were there.

—Where?

—Right behind the Archbishop's Throne.

—O, I saw her—one of them. Hadn't she a grey hat with a bird in it?

—That was her! She's very lady-like, isn't she.

(*SH* 74)

There are several similarities between the epiphany and this scene. In place of a "quick light shower," there is "slow fine rain," yet the "tiny point of rain" Stephen sees "form and twinkle" is not unlike the "cluster of diamonds" in the epiphany. There the rain "tarries . . . / among the shrubs" and vapor rises from "the black earth," whereas Stephen halts "beside a few laurel bushes," watching a raindrop "plunge into the sodden clay." It is also interesting to note the contrast between "the cattle standing together patiently . . . in the rain" and the "little band of students . . . talking among themselves." These details, together with Wells's description of the food ("not so bad, but so dull" [*SH* 72]) a few pages earlier, and the explicit connection between this moment at Clonliffe and the epiphany-based passage later in *Stephen Hero*, suggest that Joyce had "The Girls, the Boys" in mind for the description of Clonliffe. Given that the manuscript bears few signs of revision or correction, Joyce does not seem to have revised this passage to fit the adaptation in chapter 24, which makes it likely that the description of the boys in the epiphany was originally based on Clonliffe College Seminary.

A Portrait of the Artist as a Young Man

"The Girls, the Boys" is also adapted in chapter 5 of *A Portrait of the Artist as a Young Man*. In the midst of a long conversation on aesthetics, among other things, Lynch and Stephen encounter Cranly on the steps of the National Library, where Stephen sees Emma Clery sheltering from the rain:

Their voices reached his ears as if from a distance in interrupted pulsation. She was preparing to go away with her companions.

The quick light shower had drawn off, tarrying in clusters of diamonds among the shrubs of the quadrangle where an exhalation was breathed forth by the blackened earth. Their trim boots prattled as they stood on the steps of the colonnade, talking quietly and gaily, glancing at the clouds, holding their umbrellas at cunning angles against the few last raindrops, closing them again, holding their skirts demurely.

And if he had judged her harshly? If her life were a simple rosary of hours, her life simple and strange as a bird's life, gay in the morning, restless all day, tired at sundown? Her heart simple and wilful as a bird's heart?

(*P* 5.1509–22)

Besides minor revision to the tense and punctuation, the central paragraph closely mirrors the opening of the epiphany, but the sentence describing the girls returning to the convent is omitted in *Portrait*, as is the entire paragraph about the boys in the refectory. These cuts, removing any reference to the convent or the seminary, suggest that by this point in *Portrait*, Stephen has moved on from his religious phase, and is no longer drawn back to thoughts of joining a seminary; instead, the epiphany provides a glimpse of demure young women, like Emma Clery, whom he both judges and desires.

The final version of the scene also references Gerhart Hauptmann's 1903 play *Rosa Bernd*: "the rainladen trees of the avenue evoked in [Stephen], as always, memories of the girls and women in the plays of Gerhart Hauptmann; and the memory of their pale sorrows and the fragrance falling from the wet branches mingled in a mood of quiet joy" (*P* 5.71–75).

Source: Cornell 17.57–58 (*JJA* 7:67–68).

Works Cited and Further Reading

Abrams, M. H. *A Glossary of Literary Terms*. 7th ed., Heinle and Heinle, 1999.

———. *Natural Supernaturalism: Tradition and Revolution in Romantic Literature*. W. W. Norton, 1971.

Alexandrov, Vladimir. *Nabokov's Otherworld*. Princeton UP, 1991.

Aubert, Jacques. *The Aesthetics of James Joyce*. Johns Hopkins UP, 1992.

———. "Joyce's Romantic Propositions and Position." *Romantic Joyce: Papers from the Meeting on Romantic Joyce*, edited by Franca Ruggieri, Bulzoni Editore, 2003, pp. 13–24.

———. "L'Épiphanie selon James Joyce: Effet de sens ou significance." *Bulletin du Centre de recherches sémiologiques et linguistiques*, vol. 6, 1978, pp. 189–95.

———. "Of Heroes, Monsters and the Prudent Grammartist." *A Collideorscape of Joyce: Festschrift for Fritz Senn*, edited by Ruth Frehner and Ursula Zeller, Lilliput Press, 1998, pp. 83–90.

Azérad, Hugues. *L'univers constellé de Proust, Joyce et Faulkner: Le concept d'épiphanie dans l'esthétique du modernisme*. Peter Lang, 2002.

Balinisteanu, Tudor. *Religion and Aesthetic Experience in Joyce and Yeats*. Palgrave Macmillan, 2015.

Barthes, Roland. *The Preparation of the Novel. Lecture Courses and Seminars at the Collège de France (1978–1979 and 1979–1980)*. Translated by Kate Briggs, Columbia UP, 2011.

Baudelaire, Charles. *Paris Blues: The Poems in Prose*. Translated by Francis Scarfe, Anvil Press Poetry, 2012.

Baxter, Charles. "Against Epiphanies." *Burning Down the House: Essays on Fiction*. By Charles Baxter, expanded ed., Graywolf Press, 2008, pp. 41–62.

Bazargan, Susan. "Epiphany as Scene of Performance." *A New and Complex Sensation: Essays on Joyce's "Dubliners,"* edited by Oona Frawley, Lilliput Press, 2004, pp. 44–54.

Beck, Harald. "The Short but Remarkable Life of John O'Mahony." *James Joyce Online Notes*, http://www.jjon.org/jioyce-s-people/o-mahony. Accessed 1 July 2023.

Beebe, Maurice. "Joyce and Aquinas: The Theory of Aesthetics." *Philological Quarterly*, vol. 36, Jan. 1957, pp. 30–34.

Beja, Morris. "Epiphany and the Epiphanies." *A Companion to Joyce Studies*, edited by Zack Bowen and James F. Carens, Greenwood Press, 1984, pp. 707–25.

———. *Epiphany in the Modern Novel*. Peter Owen, 1971.

———. "The Incertitude of the Void: Epiphany and Indeterminacy." *Joyce, the Artist Manqué, and Indeterminacy*, by Morris Beja, Colin Smyth, 1989, pp. 27–32.

———. "James Joyce and the Taxonomy of Modernism." *A Collideorscape of Joyce: Festschrift for Fritz Senn*, edited by Ruth Frehner and Ursula Zeller, Lilliput Press, 1998, pp. 353–67.

———. "Mau-Mauing the Epiphany Catchers." *PMLA*, vol. 87, no. 5, 1972, pp. 1131–32.

———. "One Good Look at Themselves: Epiphany in *Dubliners*." *Work in Progress: Joyce Centenary Essays*, edited by Richard F. Peterson, Alan M. Cohn, and Edmund L. Epstein, Southern Illinois UP, 1983, pp. 3–14.

———. "The Wooden Sword: Threatener and Threatened in the Fiction of James Joyce." *James Joyce Quarterly*, vol. 2, no. 1, 1964, pp. 33–41. Revised for *James Joyce, "Dubliners" and "A Portrait of the Artist as a Young Man": A Selection of Critical Essays*, edited by Morris Beja, Macmillan, 1973, pp. 208–23.

Bénéjam, Valérie. "A Writer 'dans le temps': Dramatic Time and Timing in Joyce's Aesthetics." *Reading Joycean Temporalities*, edited by Jolanta Wawrzycka, Brill Rodopi, pp. 13–30.

Bénéjam, Valérie, and Elizabeth M. Bonapfel. "Dialogue between Dashes: A Reconstructed Edition of *Dubliners*." *James Joyce Quarterly*, vol. 57, nos. 1–2, 2019–20, pp. 30–51.

Bidney, Martin. *Patterns of Epiphany: From Wordsworth to Tolstoy, Pater, and Barrett Browning*. Southern Illinois UP, 1997.

Bloom, Harold. *The Visionary Company: A Reading of English Romantic Poetry*. Rev. ed. Cornell UP, 1971.

Boheemen-Saaf, Christine van. "Epiphany and Postcolonial Affect." *Moments of Moment: Aspects of the Literary Epiphany*, edited by Wim Tigges, Brill Rodopi, 1999, pp. 195–205.

Bohrer, Karl-Heinz. *Suddenness: On the Moment of Aesthetic Appearance*. 1981. Columbia UP, 1994.

Bowen, Zack. "'Circe' and the Epiphany Concept." *Joyce and Paris: 1902 . . . . . 1920–1940 . . . . . 1975: Papers from the Fifth International James Joyce Symposium*, edited by Jacques Aubert and Maria Jolas, Éditions du CNRS, 1979, pp. 11–14.

———. "Epiphanies, Stephen's Diary, and the Narrative Perspective of *A Portrait of the Artist as a Young Man*." *James Joyce Quarterly*, vol. 16, no. 4, 1979, pp. 485–88.

———. "Joyce and the Epiphany Concept: A New Approach." *Journal of Modern Literature*, vol. 9, no. 1, 1981–82, pp. 103–14.

Bowen, Zack, and Paul Butera. "The New Bloomusalem: Transformations in Epiphany Land." *Modern British Literature*, vol. 3, no. 1, 1978, pp. 48–55.

Bowen, Zack, and James F. Carens, editors. *A Companion to Joyce Studies*. Greenwood Press, 1984.

Bowker, Gordon. *James Joyce: A Biography*. Weidenfeld and Nicolson, 2010.

———. "Joyce in England." *James Joyce Quarterly*, vol. 48, no. 4, 2011, pp. 667–81.

Bradley, Bruce. *James Joyce's Schooldays*. Gill and Macmillan, 1982.

Brown, Richard. "The Escaped Nun." *James Joyce Broadsheet*, no. 2, May 1980, p. 3.

Budgen, Frank. *James Joyce and the Making of "Ulysses."* 1934. Indiana UP, 1960.

Chappell, Sophie Grace. *Epiphanies: An Ethics of Experience*. Oxford UP, 2022.

Chayes, Irene Hendry. "Joyce's Epiphanies." 1946. *James Joyce: Two Decades of Criticism*, edited by Seon Givens, Vanguard Press, 1963, pp. 27–46.

Cixous, Hélène. "Ensemble Joyce." *Prénoms de personne*, by Hélène Cixous, Éditions du Seuil, 1974, pp. 233–331.

———. *The Exile of James Joyce*. Translated by Sally A. J. Purcell, David Lewis, 1972.

———. "Joyce: The (R)Use of Writing." *Post-Structuralist Joyce: Essays from the French*, edited by Derek Attridge and Daniel Ferrer, Cambridge UP, 1984, pp. 15–30.

———. "Reaching the Point of Wheat, or A Portrait of the Artist as a Maturing Woman." *New Literary History*, vol. 19, no. 1, 1987, pp. 1–21.

———. "Writing and the Law: Blanchot, Joyce, Kafka, and Lispector." *Readings: The Poetics of Blanchot, Joyce, Kafka, Kleist, Lispector, and Tsvetayeva*, edited by Verena Andermatt Conley, Harvester Wheatsheaf, 1992, pp. 3–9.

Connolly, Thomas E., editor. *James Joyce's Scribbledehobble: The Ur-Workbook for "Finnegans Wake."* Northwestern UP, 1961.

———. "Joyce's Aesthetic Theory." *Joyce's Portrait: Criticisms and Critiques*, edited by Thomas E. Connolly, Peter Owen, 1964, pp. 266–71.

Cooper, David E. "In Praise of Epiphanies." *Los Angeles Review of Books*, 6 Jan. 2014.

Crangle, Sara. *Prosaic Desires: Modernist Knowledge, Boredom, Laughter, and Anticipation*. Edinburgh UP, 2010.

Crispi, Luca. "Epiphanies I." James Joyce Catalog, *University at Buffalo: James Joyce Collection*, https://library.buffalo.edu/jamesjoyce/catalog/i-epiphanies/. Accessed 1 July 2023.

———. "Stephen Dedalus from *A Portrait of the Artist as a Young Man* to *Ulysses*." *James Joyce Quarterly*, vol. 57, nos. 1–2, 2019–20, pp. 67–79.

Crowley, Ronan. "Things Actually Said: On Some Versions of Joyce's and Yeats's First Meeting." *Joyce, Yeats and the Revival*, edited by John McCourt, Edizioni, 2015, pp. 31–54.

Culler, Jonathan. *Structuralist Poetics: Structuralism, Linguistics and the Study of Literature*. 1975. Routledge, 2002.

Curran, C. P. *James Joyce Remembered*. Oxford UP, 1968.

Daly, Leo. *James Joyce and the Mullingar Connection*. Dolmen Press, 1975.

D'Annunzio, Gabriele. *The Flame of Life*. Translated by Kassandra Vivaria, L. C. Page, 1909.

———. *The Triumph of Death*. Translated by Georgina Harding, William Heinemann, 1898.

Dante Alighieri. *The Divine Comedy*. Translated by C. H. Sisson, Oxford UP, 1998.

Davison, Neil R. "Joyce's Matriculation Examination." *James Joyce Quarterly*, vol. 30, no. 3, 1993, pp. 393–407.

Day, Robert Adams. "Dante, Ibsen, Joyce, Epiphanies, and the Art of Memory." *James Joyce Quarterly*, vol. 25, no. 3, 1988, pp. 357–62.

Delimata, Bozena Berta. "Reminiscences of a Joyce Niece." Edited by Virginia Moseley. *James Joyce Quarterly*, vol. 19, no. 1, 1981, pp. 45–62.

Delville, Michel. "'At the Center, What?': *Giacomo Joyce*, Roland Barthes, and the Novelistic Fragment." *James Joyce Quarterly*, vol. 36, no. 4, 1999, pp. 765–80.

———. "Epiphanies and Prose Fragments: James Joyce and the Poetics of the Fragment." *Giacomo Joyce: Envoys of the Other*, edited by Louis Armand and Clare Wallace, 2nd ed., Litteraria Pragensia, 2006, pp. 100–130.

De Man, Paul. *The Rhetoric of Romanticism*. Columbia UP, 1984.

Dettmar, Kevin J. H. *The Illicit Joyce of Postmodernism: Reading against the Grain*. U of Wisconsin P, 1996.

Ebury, Katherine. "Becoming Animal in the Epiphanies: Joyce between Fiction and Non-Fiction." *Joyce's Non-Fiction Writings: "Outside His Jurisfiction,"* edited by Katherine Ebury and James Alexander Fraser, Palgrave Macmillan, 2018, pp. 175–94.

Eco, Umberto. *The Aesthetics of Chaosmos: The Middle Ages of James Joyce*. Translated by Ellen Esrock, Harvard UP, 1989.

———. "Joyce et d'Annunzio: Les sources de la notion d'Epiphanie." Translated by Elisabeth Hollier. *L'Arc*, vol. 36, 1968, pp. 29–38.

Ellmann, Richard. *The Consciousness of Joyce*. Oxford UP, 1977.

———. *The Identity of Yeats*. Oxford UP, 1954.

———. *James Joyce*. 1959. Oxford UP, 1982.

———. *Ulysses on the Liffey*. Oxford UP, 1972.

Erckmann, Émile, and Alexandre Chatrian. *L'Ami Fritz*. Hachette, 1864.

———. *Le Juif polonais*. J. Hetzel, 1867.

———. *L'Invasion ou le Fou Yégof*. J. Hetzel, 1862.

Faucheux, Pierre, André Noël, and Johnny Friedlaender. *James Joyce: Sa vie, son œuvre, son rayonnement*. La Hune, 1949.

Ferrer, Daniel, and Claude Jacquet, editors. *Writing Its Own Wrunes for Ever: Essais de génétique joycienne*. Éditions du Lérot, 1998.

Feshbach, Sidney. "Hunting Epiphany-Hunters." *PMLA*, vol. 87, no. 2, 1972, pp. 304–6.

Fitch, Noel Riley. *Sylvia Beach and the Lost Generation: A History of Literary Paris in the Twenties and Thirties*. W. W. Norton, 1985.

Fordham, Finn. "The Anatomy of Moments." *Modernist Cultures*, vol. 13, no. 2, 2018, pp. 165–86.

Frank, Joseph. "Spatial Form: An Answer to Critics." *Critical Inquiry*, vol. 4, no. 2, 1977, pp. 231–52.

———. "Spatial Form in Modern Literature." *The Widening Gyre: Crisis and Mastery in Modern Literature*, by Joseph Frank, Rutgers UP, 1963, pp. 3–62.

———. "Spatial Form in Modern Literature: An Essay in Three Parts." *Sewanee Review*, vol. 53, nos. 1–3, 1945, pp. 221–40, 433–56, 643–53.

———. "Spatial Form: Some Further Reflections." *Critical Inquiry*, vol. 5, no. 3, 1978, pp. 275–90.

French, Marilyn. *The Book as World: James Joyce's "Ulysses."* Harvard UP, 1976.

Frye, Northrop. *The Anatomy of Criticism: Four Essays*. 1957. Princeton UP, 1973.

———. "Quest and Cycle in *Finnegans Wake*." 1955. *Northrop Frye on Twentieth-Century Literature*, edited by Glen Robert Gill, U of Toronto P, 2010, pp. 105–13.

Gabler, Hans Walter. "The Genesis of *A Portrait of the Artist as a Young Man*." *Critical Essays on James Joyce's "A Portrait of the Artist as a Young Man,"* edited by Philip Brady and James F. Carens, G. K. Hall, 1998, pp. 83–114.

Garrett, Peter K. *Scene and Symbol from George Eliot to James Joyce*. Yale UP, 1969.

Gifford, Don, and Robert J. Seidman. *"Ulysses" Annotated: Notes for James Joyce's "Ulysses."* 2nd ed., U of California P, 1988.

Gilbert, Stuart. *James Joyce's "Ulysses": A Study*. Rev. ed., Vintage Books, 1955.

Gillespie, Gerald. *Proust, Mann, Joyce in the Modernist Context*. 2nd ed., Catholic U of America P, 2010.

Gingrich, Brian. "Pace and Epiphany." *New Literary History*, vol. 49, no. 3, 2018, pp. 361–82.

———. *The Pace of Fiction: Narrative Movement and the Novel*. Oxford UP, 2021.

Gogarty, Oliver St. John. *As I Was Going Down Sackville Street: A Phantasy in Fact*. 1937. Sphere Books, 1968.

Goldberg, S. L. *The Classical Temper: A Study of James Joyce's "Ulysses."* Chatto and Windus, 1961.

———. *Joyce*. Oliver and Boyd, 1962.

Gorman, Herbert. *James Joyce: A Definitive Biography*. Bodley Head, 1941.

Gornat, Tomasz. *"A Chemistry of Stars": Epiphany, Openness and Ambiguity in the Works of James Joyce*. Wydawnictwo Uniwersytetu Opolskiego, 2006.

Groden, Michael. *"Ulysses" in Progress*. Princeton UP, 1977.

Gumbrecht, Hans Ulrich. *Production of Presence: What Meaning Cannot Convey*. Stanford UP, 2004.

Hallett, Cynthia Whitney. *Minimalism and the Short Story: Raymond Carver, Amy Hempel, and Mary Robison*. Edwin Mellen Press, 1999.

Harrison, Kate. "The Portrait Epiphany." *James Joyce Quarterly*, vol. 8, no. 2, 1971, pp. 142–50.

Hart, Clive. *Structure and Motif in "Finnegans Wake."* Faber and Faber, 1962.

Hartman, Geoffrey. "Poem and Ideology: A Study of Keats's 'To Autumn.'" *The Fate of Reading and Other Essays*, U of Chicago P, 1975, pp. 124–46.

Hayman, David. "Attitudinal Dynamics in Narrative: Flaubert, Lawrence, Joyce." *Journal of Modern Literature*, vol. 19, 1995, pp. 207–14.

———. "Epiphanoiding." *Genitricksling Joyce*, edited by Sam Slote and Wim van Mierlo, Brill Rodopi, 1999, pp. 27–42.

———. "The Joycean Inset." *James Joyce Quarterly*, vol. 23, no. 2, 1986, pp. 137–55.

———. "*A Portrait of the Artist as a Young Man* and *L'Education Sentimentale*: The Structural Affinities." *Orbis Litterarum*, vol. 19, 1964, pp. 162–75. Reprinted as "Joyce's *Portrait* and Flaubert's *L'Education Sentimentale*," *Critical Essays on James Joyce's "A Portrait of the Artist as a Young Man,"* edited by Philip Brady and James F. Carens, G. K. Hall, 1998, pp. 115–29.

———. "The Purpose and Permanence of the Joycean Epiphany." *James Joyce Quarterly*, vols. 35–36, nos. 4 and 1, 1998, pp. 633–55.

Heller, Vivian. *Joyce, Decadence, and Emancipation*. U of Illinois P, 1995.

Höllerer, Walter. "Die Epiphanie als Held des Romans." *James Joyce's "Portrait": Das Jugendbildnis im Lichte neurer deutscher Forschung*, edited by Wilhelm Füger, Wilhelm Goldmann, 1972, pp. 65–74.

Homer. *The Odyssey*. Translated by Walter Shewring. 1980. Oxford UP, 1998.

Hong, Dauk-Suhn. "Epiphany in Modernist Literature: The Sacred and the Secular." *James Joyce Journal*, vol. 12, no. 1, 2006, pp. 5–22.

Igoe, Vivien. *James Joyce's Dublin Houses and Nora Barnacle's Galway*. Lilliput Press, 2007.

———. *The Real People of Joyce's "Ulysses": A Biographical Guide*. U College Dublin P, 2016.

Iser, Wolfgang. *Walter Pater: The Aesthetic Moment*. 1960. Translated by David Henry Wilson, Cambridge UP, 1987.

Jacobs, Joshua. "Joyce's Epiphanic Mode: Material Language and the Representation of Sexuality in *Stephen Hero* and *Portrait*." *Twentieth-Century Literature*, vol. 46, no. 1, 2000, pp. 20–33.

Jacquet, Claude, editor. *Genèse de Babel: Joyce et la création*. Éditions du CNRS, 1985.

———, editor. *Genèse et métamorphoses du texte joycien*. Publications de la Sorbonne, 1985.

———. "James Joyce: Les 'Épiphanies' et le *Portrait*." *Gaéliana*, vol. 3, 1981, pp. 129–47.

———. "James Joyce: Quelques épiphanies du monde extérieur." *Cahiers Victoriens et Édouardiens*, no. 14, 1981, pp. 71–87.

———, editor. *Scribble 1: Genèse des textes*. Lettres Modernes, 1988.

Jacquet, Claude, and Jean-Michel Rabaté, editors. *Scribble 3: Joyce et l'Italie*. Lettres Modernes, 1994.

Jacquet, Claude, and André Topia, editors. *Scribble 2: Joyce et Flaubert*. Lettres Modernes, 1990.

Jolas, Eugène. "My Friend James Joyce." *James Joyce: Two Decades of Criticism*, edited by Seon Givens, Vanguard Press, 1963, pp. 3–18.

Joyce, James. *Anna Livia Plurabelle: The Making of a Chapter*. Edited by Fred H. Higginson, U of Minnesota P, 1960.

———. *The Critical Writings of James Joyce*. Edited by Ellsworth Mason and Richard Ellmann, Viking, 1959.

———. *Digte og epifanier*. Translated by Arne Herløv Petersen, Brøndums Forlag, 1991.

———. *Dubliners*. Penguin, 2000.

———. *Epifanías*. Translated by Isabel Galdámez, edited by David Hayman, Montesinos, 1996.

———. *Epifanias*. Translated by Tomaz Tadeu, Autêntica Editora, 2018.

———. *Epifanie*. Translated by Adam Poprawa, Biuro Literackie, 2016.

———. *Epifanie (1900–1904)*. Edited by Giorgio Melchiori, Mondadori, 1982.

———. *Epiphanien*. Translated by Klaus Reichert, Suhrkamp, 1968.

———. *Épiphanies*. Translated by Jacques Aubert. *Œuvres complètes*, by James Joyce, edited by Jacques Aubert, vol. 1, Gallimard, 1982, pp. 85–105. Reprinted as solo volume, Trente-trois morceaux, 2016.

———. *Epiphanies*. Edited by Oscar A. Silverman, U of Buffalo, 1956.

———. *Epiphanies-Epifanie*. Edited by Carlo Avolio, Editrice Clinamen, 2014.

———. *Exiles: A Critical Edition*. Edited by A. Nicholas Fargnoli and Michael Gillespie, UP of Florida, 2016.

———. *Exiles: A Play in Three Acts*. J. Cape, 1972.

——. *Faneroseis*. Translated by Dimitris Chouliarakis, To Rodakio, 1994.

——. *Finnegans Wake*. Penguin, 1992.

——. *A First-Draft Version of "Finnegans Wake."* Edited by David Hayman, Faber and Faber, 1963.

——. *The James Joyce Archive*. Edited by Michael Groden, Hans Walter Gabler, David Hayman, A. Walton Litz, and Danis Rose, 63 vols., Garland, 1977–79.

——. "La teoria della epifanie." Translated by Luigi Berti. *Inventario*, vol. 1, no. 2, 1946, pp. 54–56.

——. *Letters of James Joyce*. Edited by Stuart Gilbert and Richard Ellmann, 3 vols., Viking, 1957–66.

——. *Occasional, Critical, and Political Writing*. Edited by Kevin Parry, Oxford UP, 2000.

——. *Poems and Shorter Writings*. Edited by Richard Ellmann, A. Walton Litz, and John Whittier-Ferguson, Faber and Faber, 1991.

——. *A Portrait of the Artist as a Young Man: Authoritative Text, Backgrounds and Contexts, Criticism*. Edited by John Paul Riquelme, Hans Walter Gabler, and Walter Hettche, W. W. Norton, 2007.

——. *Selected Letters of James Joyce*. Edited by Richard Ellmann, Viking, 1966.

——. *Steban el héroe*. Translated by Roberto Bixio, Editorial Sur, 1960.

——. *Stephen der Held: Ein Porträt des Künstlers als junger Mann*. Translated by Klaus Reichert, edited by Klaus Reichert and Fritz Senn, Suhrkamp, 1972.

——. *Stephen Hero*. Edited by Theodore Spencer, revised ed. by John J. Slocum and Herbert Cahoon, New Directions, 1963.

——. *Stephen le Héros: fragment de la première partie de Dedalus*. Translated by Ludmila Savitsky, Gallimard, 1948.

——. *Ulysses: The Corrected Text*. Edited by Hans Walter Gabler, Penguin, 1986.

Joyce, Stanislaus. *The Dublin Diary of Stanislaus Joyce*. Edited by George Harris Healey, Faber and Faber, 1962.

——. "James Joyce's Dublin." *Partisan Review*, vol. 19, no. 1, 1952, pp. 103–9.

——. *My Brother's Keeper: James Joyce's Early Years*. Edited by Richard Ellmann, 1958. Da Capo Press, 2003.

Kain, Richard M. "Epiphanies of Dublin." *Approaches to Joyce's Portrait: Ten Essays*, edited by Thomas F. Staley and Bernard Benstock, U of Pittsburgh P, 1976, pp. 91–112.

Kearney, Richard. "Epiphanies in Joyce." *Voices on Joyce*, edited by Anne Fogarty and Fran O'Rourke, U College Dublin P, 2015, pp. 239–59.

Kenner, Hugh. *Dublin's Joyce*. Chatto and Windus, 1955.

Kermode, Frank. "A Reply to Joseph Frank." *Critical Inquiry*, vol. 4, no. 3, 1978, pp. 579–88.

——. *Romantic Image*. 1957. 2nd ed., Routledge, 2002.

——. *The Sense of an Ending*. 1967. Oxford UP, 2000.

Kim, Sharon. *Literary Epiphany in the Novel, 1850–1950: Constellations of the Soul*. Palgrave Macmillan, 2012.

Kumar, Shiv K. "Joyce's Epiphany and Bergson's 'L'intuition Philosophique.'" *Modern Language Quarterly*, vol. 20, no. 1, 1959, pp. 27–30.

Kurnick, David. *Empty Houses: Theatrical Failure and the Novel*. Princeton UP, 2012.

Lacan, Jacques. *The Sinthome*. Edited by Jacques-Alain Miller, Polity Press, 2016.

Langbaum, Robert. "The Epiphanic Mode in Wordsworth and Modern Literature." *New Literary History*, vol. 14, 1983, pp. 335–58.

———. *The Poetry of Experience: The Dramatic Monologue in Modern Literary Tradition*. W. W. Norton, 1957.

Lernout, Geert. "The *Finnegans Wake* Notebooks and Radical Philology." *European Joyce Studies*, vol. 5, 1995, pp. 19–48.

———. *Help My Unbelief: James Joyce and Religion*. Continuum, 2010.

Levin, Harry. *James Joyce: A Critical Introduction*. Faber and Faber, 1944.

Levina, Jūratė. "The Aesthetics of Phenomena: Joyce's Epiphanies." *Joyce Studies Annual*, 2017, pp. 185–219.

Leypoldt, Günter. "Raymond Carver's 'Epiphanic Moments.'" *Style*, vol. 35, no. 3, 2001, pp. 531–46.

Liguori, Alphonsus. *The Glories of Mary*. 1852. P. J. Kenedy and Sons, 1888.

———. *The Visits to the Most Holy Sacrament and the Blessed Virgin Mary*. 1745. Burns and Lambert, 1855.

Litz, A. Walton. *The Art of James Joyce: Method and Design in "Ulysses" and "Finnegans Wake."* Oxford UP, 1961.

Losey, Jay B. "Epiphany in Pater's Portraits." *English Literature in Transition, 1880–1920*, vol. 29, no. 3, 1986, pp. 297–308.

———. *Modern Epiphany from Wordsworth to Joyce*. 1986. U of Virginia, PhD dissertation.

———. "Pater's Epiphanies and the Open Form." *South Central Review*, vol. 6, no. 4, 1989, pp. 30–50.

Lucente, Gregory L. "D'Annunzio's *Il fuoco* and Joyce's *Portrait of the Artist*: From Allegory to Irony." *Italica*, vol. 57, no. 1, 1980, pp. 19–33.

Lyons, F. S. L. *Charles Stewart Parnell: A Biography*. Oxford UP, 1977.

MacDuff, Sangam. "Death and the Limits of Epiphany: Wordsworth's 'Spots of Time' and Joyce's Epiphanies of Death." *James Joyce Quarterly*, vol. 53, nos. 1–2, 2015–16, pp. 61–74.

———. *Panepiphanal World: James Joyce's Epiphanies*. UP of Florida, 2020.

———. "The Yale Epiphanies: A New Typescript." *Genetic Joyce Studies*, no. 17, 2017, https://www.geneticjoycestudies.org/articles/GJS17/GJS17_Macduff.

MacGregor, Geddes. "Artistic Theory in James Joyce." 1947. *Joyce's Portrait: Criticisms and Critiques*, edited by Thomas E. Connolly, Appleton-Century-Crofts, 1962, pp. 221–30.

Mahaffey, Vicki. *States of Desire: Wilde, Yeats, Joyce and the Irish Experiment*. Oxford UP, 1998.

Maltby, Paul. *The Visionary Moment: A Postmodern Critique*. State U of New York P, 2002.

Mamigonian, Marc A., and John Noel Turner. "Annotations for *Stephen Hero*." *James Joyce Quarterly*, vol. 40, no. 3, 2003, pp. 347–518.

Mangnall, Richmal. *Historical and Miscellaneous Questions for the Use of Young People.* 1798. Longman, Brown, Green, Longmans and Roberts, 1859.

Marangopoulos, Aris. "Epifaneia, faneroseis kai 'spitika glyka.'" *Poiisi,* vol. 4, 1994, 227–30.

Marcus, Phillip L. "George Moore's Dublin 'Epiphanies' and Joyce." *James Joyce Quarterly,* vol. 5, no. 2, 1968, pp. 157–61.

McCourt, John. "Epiphanies of Language, Longing, Liminality in *Giacomo Joyce.*" *Giacomo Joyce: Envoys of the Other,* edited by Louis Armand and Clare Wallace, 2nd ed., Litteraria Pragensia, 2006, pp. 228–48.

McFadzean, Angus. "The Aesthetic of Transgression: Love and Limits in the Early Work of James Joyce." *James Joyce Quarterly,* vol. 60, nos. 1–2, 2022–23, pp. 17–38.

———. *Epiphany and Transgression: From Aesthetics to Narrative in the Novels of James Joyce.* 2012. U of Oxford, PhD dissertation.

McGowan, John. "From Pater to Wilde to Joyce: Modernist Epiphany and the Soulful Self." *Texas Studies in Literature and Language,* vol. 32, no. 3, 1990, pp. 417–45.

McGurl, Mark. *The Program Era: Postwar Fiction and the Rise of Creative Writing.* Harvard UP, 2009.

Melchior, Claus. *Stephen Hero: Textentstehung und Text. Eine Untersuchung der Kompositions—und Arbeitsweise des frühen James Joyce.* 1988. Ludwig-Maximilians-Universität München, PhD dissertation.

Miller, J. Hillis. *The Linguistic Moment: From Wordsworth to Stevens.* Princeton UP, 1985.

Millot, Catherine. "Épiphanies." *Joyce Avec Lacan,* edited by Jacques Aubert, Navarin Editeur, 1987, pp. 87–95.

———. "On Epiphanies." *James Joyce: The Augmented Ninth,* edited by Bernard Benstock, Syracuse UP, 1988, pp. 207–9.

Moliterno, Frank. *The Dialectics of Sense and Spirit in Pater and Joyce.* ELT Press, 1998.

Moore, George. *Celibates.* Walter Scott, 1895.

Müller, Klaus Peter. *Epiphanie: Begriff und Gestaltungsprinzip im Frühwerk von James Joyce.* Peter Lang, 1984.

Murphy, Francis J. "Dublin Trams 1872–1959." *Dublin Historical Record,* vol. 33, no. 1, 1979, pp. 2–9.

Nabokov, Vladimir. *Lectures on Literature.* Edited by Fredson Bowers, Harcourt, 1980.

Natali, Ilaria. "A Portrait of James Joyce's *Epiphanies* as a Source Material." *Humanicus,* no. 6, 2011.

———. "Questioning Genetic Criticism: The Dossier of *A Portrait of the Artist as a Young Man.*" *Joyce in Progress: Proceedings of the 2008 James Joyce Graduate Conference in Rome,* edited by Franca Ruggieri, John McCourt, and Enrico Terrinoni, Cambridge Scholars, 2009, pp. 35–48.

———. "'This Diverting Chase of the Presumable': Procedures of Rewriting in the Dossier of *A Portrait of the Artist as a Young Man.*" *Genetic Joyce Studies,* no. 8, 2008, https://www.geneticjoycestudies.org/articles/GJS8/GJS8_Natali.

———. *The Ur-Portrait: Stephen Hero ed il processo di creazione artistica in "A Portrait of the Artist as a Young Man."* Firenze UP, 2008.

Neuhold, Birgit. *Measuring the Sadness: Conrad, Joyce, Woolf and the European Epiphany*. Peter Lang, 2009.

Newman, John Henry. *Discourses Addressed to Mixed Congregations*. 6th ed., Burns and Oates, 1881.

Nichols, Ashton. *The Poetics of Epiphany: Nineteenth-Century Origins of the Modern Literary Moment*. U of Alabama P, 1987.

Nietzsche, Fredrich. *The Birth of Tragedy*. Translated by Clifton P. Fadiman, Dover, 1995.

Noel, Jean C. "De quelques épiphanies de James Joyce dans le contexte du manuscrit 'Cornell 17.'" *Genèse et métamorphoses du texte joycien*, edited by Claude Jacquet, Publications de la Sorbonne, 1985, pp. 3–24.

Noon, William T. *Joyce and Aquinas*. Oxford UP, 1957.

Norris, Andrew. "Joyce and the Post-Epiphanic." *Hypermedia Joyce Studies*, vol. 5, no. 2, 2005, http://hjs.ff.cuni.cz/archives/v3/contents.html.

O'Connor, Ulick, ed. *The Joyce We Knew: Memoirs of Joyce*. Brandon, 2004.

O'Keefe, Declan. "A Beacon in the Twilight: Matthew Russell, S.J. and the *Irish Monthly*." *Studies: An Irish Quarterly Review*, vol. 99, no. 394, 2010, pp. 169–79.

Olson, Liesl. *Modernism and the Ordinary*. Oxford UP, 2009.

Pater, Walter. *Imaginary Portraits and Gaston de Latour: An Unfinished Romance*. Cambridge UP, 2011.

———. *Marius the Epicurean: His Sensations and Ideas*. 1885. 2 vols., Cambridge UP, 2011.

———. *The Renaissance: Studies in Art and Poetry*. 1873. Edited by Adam Phillips, Oxford UP, 1998.

Peake, C. H. *James Joyce: The Citizen and the Artist*. E. Arnold, 1977.

Pelaschiar, Laura. "Of Brother, Diaries, and Umbrellas: News from Stanislaus Joyce." *Fin de Siècle and Italy*, edited by Franca Ruggieri, Bulzoni, 1998, pp. 213–23.

———. "Stanislaus Joyce's 'Book of Days': The Triestine Diary." *James Joyce Quarterly*, vol. 36, no. 2, 1999, pp. 61–71.

Perlis, Alan D. "Beyond Epiphany: Pater's Aesthetic Hero in the Works of Joyce." *James Joyce Quarterly*, vol. 17, no. 3, 1980, pp. 272–79.

Pimentel, Luz Aurora. "The Precise Music of the Imprecise: Joyce's Poetry and the Influence of Verlaine." *Anuario de Letra Modernas*, 1984, pp. 189–205.

Prescott, Joseph. "James Joyce's Epiphanies." *Modern Language Notes*, vol. 64, no. 5, 1949, p. 346.

Rabaté, Jean-Michel. "Alimentaire et vestimentaire dans *Finnegans Wake*." *Études Anglaises*, vol. 35, no. 3, 1982, pp. 268–79.

———. *The Future of Theory*. Blackwell, 2002.

Raftery, Deirdre, Judith Harford, and Susan M. Parkes. "Mapping the Terrain of Female Education in Ireland, 1830–1910." *Gender and Education*, vol. 22, no. 5, 2010, pp. 565–78.

Ricca, Giulia. "Like an Alchemist: The Artist between D'Annunzio and Joyce." *MLN*, vol. 132, no. 1, 2017, pp. 121–62.

Robbe-Grillet, Alain. *Instantanés*. Les Éditions de Minuit, 1962.

Ruskin, John. *Mornings in Florence: Being Simple Studies of Christian Art, for English Travellers*. 1875–77. Lovell Brothers, 1899.

Russell, Matthew. *Erin: Verses Irish and Catholic*. M. H. Gill, 1881.

Saltzman, Arthur M. "Epiphany and Its Discontents: Coover, Gangemi, Sorrentino, and Postmodern Revelation." *Journal of Modern Literature*, vol. 15, no. 4, 1989, pp. 497–518.

Săndulescu, C. G. "Epifanie și structură la Joyce." *Secolul*, vol. 20, no. 6, 1968, pp. 20–27.

Sarraute, Nathalie. *Tropismes*. Éditions Denoël, 1939.

Sartre, Jean-Paul. *La Nausée*. Éditions Gallimard, 1938. Published in English translation as *Nausea*, New Directions, 1949.

Sayeau, Michael. *Against the Event: The Everyday and Evolution of Modernist Narrative*. Oxford UP, 2013.

Scholes, Robert. "Joyce and the Epiphany: The Key to the Labyrinth?" *Sewanee Review*, vol. 72, no. 1, 1964, pp. 65–77.

———. *Structuralism in Literature: An Introduction*. Yale UP, 1974.

———. "*Ulysses*: A Structuralist Perspective." *James Joyce Quarterly*, vol. 10, no. 1, 1972, pp. 161–71.

Scholes, Robert, and Marlena G. Corcoran. "The Aesthetic Theory and the Critical Writings." *A Companion to Joyce Studies*, edited by Zack Bowen and James F. Carens, Greenwood Press, 1984, pp. 689–705.

Scholes, Robert, and Richard M. Kain, editors. *The Workshop of Daedalus: James Joyce and the Raw Materials for "A Portrait of the Artist as a Young Man."* Northwestern UP, 1965.

Scholes, Robert, and Florence L. Walzl. "The Epiphanies of Joyce." *PMLA*, vol. 82, no. 1, 1967, pp. 152–54.

Scott, Bonnie Kime. *Joyce and Feminism*. Indiana University Press, 1984.

Scotto, Robert M. "'Visions' and 'Epiphanies': Fictional Technique in Pater's *Marius* and Joyce's *Portrait*." *James Joyce Quarterly*, vol. 11, no. 1, 1973, pp. 41–50.

Simpson, John. "Flynnlandia, or the Rise (and Fall) of the House of Usher" *James Joyce Online Notes*, https://www.jjon.org/jioyce-s-people/flynn1. Accessed 1 July 2023.

———. "They Simply Fade Away: News on the Life and Death of an Old Soldier—Joseph Casey." *James Joyce Online Notes*, https://www.jjon.org/jioyce-s-people/joseph-casey. Accessed 1 July 2023.

Skeat, Walter. *An Etymological Dictionary of the English Language*. Oxford UP, 1910.

Slote, Sam. "Epiphanic 'Proteus.'" *Genetic Joyce Studies*, no. 5, 2005, https://www.geneticjoycestudies.org/articles/GJS5/GJS5lote.

———. "Protean Phenomenology and Genealogy." *Dublin James Joyce Journal*, no. 2, 2009, pp. 128–42.

Spencer, Theodore. "A Succession of Epiphanies." *James Joyce's "Dubliners": A Critical Handbook*, edited by J. R. Baker and T. F. Staley, Wadsworth, 1969, pp. 10–11.

Spielberg, Peter, compiler. *James Joyce's Manuscripts and Letters at the University of Buffalo: A Catalogue*. U of Buffalo, 1962.

Steppe, Wolfhard. "The Merry Greeks (with a Farewell to *epicleti*)." *James Joyce Quarterly*, vol. 32, nos. 3–4, 1995, pp. 597–617.

Stern, Jerome. *Making Shapely Fiction*. 1991. W. W. Norton, 2001.

Sullivan, Kevin. *Joyce among the Jesuits*. Columbia UP, 1957.

Symons, Arthur. "The Dance of the Daughters of Herodias." *Images of Good and Evil*, by Arthur Symons, W. Heinemann, 1899, pp. 42–48.

——. *The Symbolist Movement in Literature*. 1900. Edited by Matthew Creasy, Carcanet Press, 2014.

Tigges, Wim, editor. *Moments of Moment: Aspects of the Literary Epiphany*. Brill Rodopi, 1999.

——. "The Significance of Trivial Things: Towards a Typology of Literary Epiphanies." *Moments of Moment: Aspects of the Literary Epiphany*, edited by Wim Tigges, Brill Rodopi, 1999, pp. 11–36.

Tindall, William York. *James Joyce: His Way of Interpreting the Modern World*. Scribner's, 1950.

——. *A Reader's Guide to James Joyce*. Farrar, Straus and Cudahy, 1951.

Tynan, Katharine. *A Little Book for John O'Mahony's Friends*. Pear Tree Press, 1906.

Van Ghent, Dorothy. *The English Novel: Form and Function*. Rinehart, 1953.

Walzl, Florence L. "Dubliners." *A Companion to Joyce Studies*, edited by Zack Bowen and James F. Carens, Greenwood Press, 1984, pp. 157–228.

——. "The Liturgy of the Epiphany Season and the Epiphanies of Joyce." *PMLA*, vol. 80, no. 4, 1965, pp. 436–50.

Ward, Margaret. *Fearless Woman: Hanna Sheehy-Skeffington, Feminism and the Irish Revolution*. U College Dublin P, 2019.

——, editor. *Hanna Sheehy-Skeffington: Suffragette and Sinn Féiner; Her Memoirs and Political Writings*. U College Dublin P, 2017.

Warner, Susan [Elizabeth Wetherell, pseud.]. *The Wide, Wide World*. G. P. Putnam, 1850.

Watts, Isaac. *Divine and Moral Songs for Children*. Religious Tract Society, 1715.

Wawrzycka, Jolanta. "'Ghosting Hour': Young Joyce Channelling Early Yeats." *Joyce, Yeats, and the Revival*, edited by John McCourt, Edizioni, 2015, pp. 103–18.

Weir, David. "Epiphanoumenon." *James Joyce Quarterly*, vol. 31, no. 2, 1994, pp. 55–64.

——. "Stephen Dedalus: Rimbaud or Baudelaire?" *James Joyce Quarterly*, vol. 18, no. 1, 1980, pp. 87–91.

Weiskel, Thomas. *The Romantic Sublime: Studies in the Structure and Psychology of Transcendence*. Johns Hopkins UP, 1976.

Weninger, Robert K. *The German Joyce*. UP of Florida, 2012.

Whitman, Walt. *Leaves of Grass*. 1855–92. Modern Library, 1944.

Yeats, W. B. *The Major Works: Including Poems, Plays, and Critical Prose*. Edited by Edward Larrissy, Oxford World Classics, 2008.

——. *The Poems*. Edited by Daniel Albright, Everyman, 1999.

——. *The Secret Rose, Stories by W. B. Yeats: A Variorum Edition*. Edited by Warwick Gould, Phillip L. Marcus, and Michael J. Sidnell, 2nd ed., Palgrave Macmillan, 1992.

Zaniello, Thomas. "The Epiphany and the Object-Image Distinction." *James Joyce Quarterly*, vol. 4, no. 4, 1967, pp. 286–88.

Ziolkowski, Theodore. "James Joyces Epiphanie und die Überwindung der empirischen Welt in der modernen deutschen Prosa." *Deutsche Vierteljahresschrift für Literaturwissenschaft und Geistesgeschichte*, vol. 35, no. 2, 1961, pp. 594–616.

Index of Epiphanies

Index

Page references in *italics* refer to figures.

Sangam MacDuff is a research fellow at the University of Lausanne, where his research, funded by the Swiss National Science Foundation, focuses on logic and modern literature from 1850 to the present. He has published a monograph, *Panepiphanal World: James Joyce's Epiphanies*, as well as a dozen articles on Joyce and modernism in the *James Joyce Quarterly*, *James Joyce Broadsheet*, *Swiss Papers in English Language and Literature*, *Genetic Joyce Studies*, and *European Joyce Studies*.

Angus McFadzean is the program director of the Oxford University Summer School for Adults and teaches on international programs for the Department of Continuing Education. He completed his doctorate at Wadham College, Oxford, with the thesis "Epiphany and Transgression: From Aesthetics to Narrative in the Novels of James Joyce." He has published with the *James Joyce Quarterly* and is the author of *Suburban Fantastic Cinema: Growing Up in the Late Twentieth Century* as well as articles on Thomas Pynchon and Hollywood cinema.

Morris Beja is Academy Professor emeritus, and was chair of the English Department, at Ohio State University. He has been visiting professor in Greece, Ireland, and China, as well as at Northwestern University, and has received a Guggenheim Fellowship and two Fulbright Lectureships. His books include *Epiphany in the Modern Novel, Film and Literature, James Joyce: A Literary Life*, and edited volumes on film, Joyce, Virginia Woolf, Samuel Beckett, and Orson Welles. He is past president and honorary trustee for life of the International James Joyce Foundation.

The Florida James Joyce Series

Edited by Sam Slote

Cannibal Joyce, by Thomas Jackson Rice (2008)

Manuscript Genetics, Joyce's Know-How, Beckett's Nohow, by Dirk Van Hulle (2008)

Catholic Nostalgia in Joyce and Company, by Mary Lowe-Evans (2008)

A Guide through "Finnegans Wake," by Edmund Lloyd Epstein (2009)

Bloomsday 100: Essays on "Ulysses," edited by Morris Beja and Anne Fogarty (2009)

Joyce, Medicine, and Modernity, by Vike Martina Plock (2010; first paperback edition, 2012)

Who's Afraid of James Joyce?, by Karen R. Lawrence (2010; first paperback edition, 2012)

"Ulysses" in Focus: Genetic, Textual, and Personal Views, by Michael Groden (2010; first paperback edition, 2012)

Foundational Essays in James Joyce Studies, edited by Michael Patrick Gillespie (2011; first paperback edition, 2017)

Empire and Pilgrimage in Conrad and Joyce, by Agata Szczeszak-Brewer (2011; first paperback edition, 2017)

The Poetry of James Joyce Reconsidered, edited by Marc C. Conner (2012; first paperback edition, 2015)

The German Joyce, by Robert K. Weninger (2012; first paperback edition, 2016)

Joyce and Militarism, by Greg Winston (2012; first paperback edition, 2015)

Renascent Joyce, edited by Daniel Ferrer, Sam Slote, and André Topia (2013; first paperback edition, 2014)

Before Daybreak: "After the Race" and the Origins of Joyce's Art, by Cóilín Owens (2013; first paperback edition, 2015)

Modernists at Odds: Reconsidering Joyce and Lawrence, edited by Matthew J. Kochis and Heather L. Lusty (2015; first paperback edition, 2020)

James Joyce and the Exilic Imagination, by Michael Patrick Gillespie (2015)

The Ecology of "Finnegans Wake," by Alison Lacivita (2015; first paperback edition, 2021)

Joyce's Allmaziful Pluralities: Polyvocal Explorations of "Finnegans Wake," edited by Kimberly J. Devlin and Christine Smedley (2015; first paperback edition, 2018)

Exiles: A Critical Edition, by James Joyce, edited by A. Nicholas Fargnoli and Michael Patrick Gillespie (2016; first paperback edition, 2019)

Up to Maughty London: Joyce's Cultural Capital in the Imperial Metropolis, by Eleni Loukopoulou (2017)

Joyce and the Law, edited by Jonathan Goldman (2017; first paperback edition, 2020)

At Fault: Joyce and the Crisis of the Modern University, by Sebastian D. G. Knowles (2018; first paperback edition, 2021)

"Ulysses" Unbound: A Reader's Companion to James Joyce's "Ulysses," Third Edition, by Terence Killeen (2018)

Joyce and Geometry, by Ciaran McMorran (2020)

Panepiphanal World: James Joyce's Epiphanies, by Sangam MacDuff (2020)

Language as Prayer in "Finnegans Wake," by Colleen Jaurretche (2020)

Rewriting Joyce's Europe: The Politics of Language and Visual Design, by Tekla Mecsnóber (2021)

Joyce Writing Disability, edited by Jeremy Colangelo (2022)

Joyce, Aristotle, and Aquinas, by Fran O'Rourke (2022)

Time and Identity in "Ulysses" and the "Odyssey," by Stephanie Nelson (2022)

Joyce without Borders: Circulations, Sciences, Media, and Mortal Flesh, edited by James Ramey and Norman Cheadle (2022)

An Irish-Jewish Politician, Joyce's Dublin, and "Ulysses": The Life and Times of Albert L. Altman, by Neil R. Davison (2022)

Beating the Bounds: Excess and Restraint in Joyce's Later Works, by Roy Benjamin (2023)

Genetic Joyce: Manuscripts and the Dynamics of Creation, by Daniel Ferrer (2023)

Collected Epiphanies of James Joyce: A Critical Edition, edited by Sangam MacDuff, Angus McFadzean, and Morris Beja (2024)